Colonial Childhoods

Anthem South Asian Studies
Series Editor: Crispin Bates

Other titles in the series:

Brosius, Christiane *Empowering Visions* (2005)
Mills, Jim (ed) *Subaltern Sports* (2005)
Joshi, Chitra *Lost Worlds: Indian Labour and its Forgotten Histories* (2005)
Dasgupta, Biplab, *European Trade and Colonial Conquest* (2005)
Kaur, Raminder *Performative Politics and the Cultures of Hinduism* (2005)
Rosenstein, Lucy *New Poetry in Hindi* (2004)
Shah, Ghanshyam, *Caste and Democratic Politics in India* (2004)
Van Schendel, Willem *The Bengal Borderland: Beyond State and Nation in South Asia* (2004)

Colonial Childhoods

The Juvenile Periphery
of India, 1850–1945

SATADRU SEN

Anthem Press

Anthem Press
An imprint of Wimbledon Publishing Company
75-76 Blackfriars Road, London SE1 8HA
or
PO Box 9779, London SW19 7ZG
www.anthempress.com

This edition first published by Anthem Press 2005
Copyright © Satadru Sen 2005

The moral right of the author has been asserted

All rights reserved. Without limiting the rights under copyright reserved above, no part of this publication may be reproduced, stored or introduced into a retrieval system, or transmitted, in any form or by any means (electronic, mechanical, photocopying, recording or otherwise), without the prior written permission of both the copyright owner and the above publisher of this book.

British Library Cataloguing in Publication Data
A catalogue record for this book is available from the British Library.

Library of Congress Cataloging in Publication Data
A catalog record for this book has been requested.

1 3 5 7 9 10 8 6 4 2

ISBN 1 84331 177 1 (Hbk)
ISBN 1 84331 178 X (Pbk)

Cover photograph: Boys drilling at the Matunga Reformatory, Circa 1908, courtesy of the British Library.

Typeset by Footprint Labs Ltd, London
www.footprintlabs.com

Printed in the United Kingdom

TABLE OF CONTENTS

Acknowledgements	vii
Introduction	1
1. State of the Experiment: Experts, Parents and the Reformatory	9
2. The Nature of the Beast: The Content of Institutionalized Childhood	51
3. Experimental Childhoods: Pain and the Reformatory	89
4. Gendering the Reformatory	115
5. Masters and Servants: School, Home and Aristocratic Childhood	143
6. The Politics of Deracination	187
Conclusion	211
Notes	215
Bibliography	241
Index	249

To Carolyn Ruth Keller, 1937–2001

ACKNOWLEDGMENTS

While I am indebted to numerous colleagues, friends, editors and archivists for their help with researching and writing this book, I am particularly grateful to Crispin Bates, who organized the seminars at the University of Edinburgh where this project took shape; to Radhika Singha, George Behlmer, Swapna Banerjee, Harald Fischer-Tiné and Ian Duffield; and as always, to Jim Mills and Elizabeth Kolsky. My student Lindsay Nencheck deprived me of the joy of preparing the index, and did so with diligence and care.

INTRODUCTION

In India in 1876, the colonial government passed the Reformatory Schools Act, providing a common structure of guidelines and rules to a mechanism of juvenile delinquency that had been taking shape in the provinces since mid-century. In the same decade, British educators and administrators in the princely states established the institutions that became known as the Chiefs' Colleges. Linking these apparently disparate episodes is the child: the criminalized child from the margins of native society, the effete child of the decadent aristocracy, and always, in the shadows, the European child that might serve as model, measure and foil. These childhoods emerged at a particular moment in the encounter between a western-European metropole, its imperial agents and people who would be described by Kipling as 'half devil and half child'. Reformatories and boarding schools enabled experiments with the relationship between the devil and the child, and raised questions about whether devilry and childhood could co-exist. From the outset, as such, colonial child-saving developed as an 'investigative modality'.[1]

In the mid-nineteenth century, the dominant metropolitan assumptions about childhood were its plasticity and its innocence.[2] These assumptions were hardly uniform, being contingent upon the location of the child on the metropolitan map of class, gender, race and urban/rural geography.[3] Some children — the poor, the delinquent, the Irish, the gypsy, the girl, the homosexual, the 'precocious', the adolescent — were either more plastic and innocent, or less so, than others; germs of instability were ingrained in the Victorian child. When the normative model of childhood was taken into the colony, it was destabilized further. There, the nature of the child and that of the native not only reinforced each other, they also undermined each other in extraordinarily productive ways. Even as some colonial observers 'discovered' the native child, the sites of discovery produced a widespread conviction that 'native childhood' was an oxymoron. Reformatories, boarding schools and authoritative texts were energized by the putative plasticity of the child, but they were also paralyzed by an articulation of difference that implied that native children were essentially small, perverse adults. The juvenile was thus produced as a deviant and the children's institution as a failure.

The children of the colony were conceived and raised by adults engaged in a series of political clashes; between the 1850s and the 1940s, they were valuable to colonial as well as national projects. Indians who sought to decolonize the institutions of childhood had to reclaim the native child from institutional and disciplinary spaces in which the lines between child and adult had been obfuscated, by appropriating the modern molds within which the recovered child might be placed. They carried on not only 'direct' conversations with their white counterparts and each other, but also 'indirect' conversations with children, and through the mechanism as well as the content of the conversations, bestowed and claimed some attributes of nationhood and modernity. Childhood was thus an important ingredient in the making of empire, race and nationhood at a time when new meanings were attached to perceived distinctions between white and black children, girl and boy children, aristocratic and middle class children, 'westernized' and 'authentic' children, and between the offspring of the elite and those of the poor and provincial. One set was central (as future adults) to the colony and the emerging nation, while the other was relegated to the fringes. Both were located in what I have called the juvenile periphery.[4]

The periphery, in this formulation, is a shifting and productive zone at the edge of the modern — the colonial horizon of the metropolitan, the universal, the national, the middle class and the authoritative. It is informed by the modern but not bound to replicate the modern, because it sustains (and is sustained by) a pervasive skepticism about the compatibility between natives and modernity.[5] It facilitates the generation, the containment and the investigation of specimen populations; it generates authority and political imperatives that are substantially autonomous of the metropolitan and the national. Its products, such as expertise, deviance, childhood, adulthood, etc. are highly unstable and subject to contestation, not least because the periphery does not bestow its rewards equally. While peripheral status is a source of power to some (for instance, the colonial child correction administrator who seeks to create his own authoritative space), it is galling to others (who resent their location in second tier institutions, or in suspect childhoods that lead to second-rate adulthoods).

Childhood itself might be regarded as a periphery in a cultural environment in which adulthood enjoyed unprecedented and distinctive privileges. To be a child, in Britain and its colonies in the nineteenth century, was to be excluded from various forms of political, economic, social and sexual privilege, and consigned to innocence and dependency.[6] Within this, native childhood was a further marginality, deriving not only from notions of adulthood but also from assumptions about race, moral content and political status, and serving as a model for the marginality of various segments of the colonized.[7] At the same time, to be stripped of the status of a child constituted a more severe marginality, since a native who was not a child to begin with would never outgrow the periphery.

British experts engaged in the juvenile periphery of India generally saw native children as distorted mirror images of the children they imagined at 'home'. Certain categories of native youth appeared to have their counterparts in the Dickensian world of the English slum, and were recognizable and even normal within a deviant social context. Elite children, on the other hand, seemed curiously alien — overly dependent, sexually knowing, insufficiently heterosexual, politically wayward and averse to discipline, although here too, there were uncomfortable glimpses of what was familiar but disavowed in upper-class Britain. Eager to ascertain peculiarity or universality, British observers of Indian schools, prisons and homes conducted experiments in which social influences were radically altered, and children removed from the immediate supervision of their biological parents. The experiments were utilized to speculate upon the relative impact of nature (biological formulations of race, and childhood itself) or nurture (adult influence and other alterable circumstances) upon the development of children. The production of the native child under these circumstances was also the simultaneous production and evaluation of the native parent and the native itself, as entities that were both biologically and culturally implicated in the native-juvenile condition.

There is now a large body of literature that explores the history of childhood in the metropole. In most such studies, modern childhood has been constructed as a European archipelago, isolated from and innocence of the native child in the colony.[8] Scholars of Victorian and Edwardian 'boy culture' have been more attentive to empire, and Dawson is outstanding in his implication of colonial warfare in the construction of English boyhood, but the attention has generally not gone beyond noting the influence of the Boer War and the 'Sepoy Mutiny' in the production of particular trends.[9] Springhall, for instance, is not unaware of certain ideological links between the empire and the metropole in this context — he notes, in passing, the American Social Darwinist G Stanley Hall's insistence that adolescents 'recapitulated' the various stages of human/racial development as they matured.[10] He does not go further, and the 'empire' in the title of his work remains an unfulfilled promise. What is missing from these analyses is the recognition that British adults did not simply encounter other adults in the colonies. They also encountered Other children, and the judgments they passed upon these children both drew from and shaped the norms of British society. There is a mutual implication between what might be considered the 'overflow' of metropolitan childhoods (Tom Brown, Alice, Mary Carpenter, Baden Powell) and the 'backwash' (Kim, the street Arab, Ranjitsinhji, Baden Powell) — an interplay between unstable norms and the imperial context of their destabilization.[11]

This interplay has largely escaped the attention of historians of India too. Most scholars who have approached the Indian juvenile have focused on children rather than childhood. The psychoanalytical studies by Nandy and Kakar are exceptions, but their evidentiary bases in mythology and anthropology render Indian childhood as a conglomerate of stable essences, rather than shifting clusters of historically shaped ideas.[12] This reifies concepts like 'the Hindu mind' — a problem that Kakar acknowledges.[13] Gautam Chatterjee's work on juvenile delinquency, like the scholarship on colonial education, is interested in the institutional sites of utilitarian intervention in the lives of native children, but does not problematize childhood itself.[14] The child drops fully formed into the institution. Viswanathan notes the colonizing power of the English curriculum that is brought to bear on native youth,[15] Lelyveld is aware of the struggle over 'parental' influence at Aligarh,[16] and Maskiell implies a relationship between the peripherality of mid-nineteenth-century Punjab and experiments with children's education,[17] but none asks whether the child that is subjected to these power relationships might be an unstable element produced by a wider set of colonial conversations. Yet the children's institution can only be very incompletely understood, and a range of anxieties and contests in colonial society can be missed entirely, if the nature of the child is not politicized. Dirks has pointed out that colonialism in India generated an 'institutional self-mimesis…that was completely at odds with its own self-representation and rhetoric'.[18] Such misalignments rarely go unchallenged. The British construction of the native child as the anti-child and nationalist recuperations of Indian childhood both reflect the politics of constructing, recognizing and subverting the colony.

A second field of scholarship that my study intersects is the work on Indian domesticity.[19] Feminist historians in the vanguard of this scholarship have overwhelmingly privileged the conjugal relationship; the child has appeared primarily in the context of the age of consent.[20] Yet childhood deserves more attention in the history of gender and colonial families. It is, after all, a heavily gendered concept. The opposite of masculinity, Nandy observes, is not only femininity or effeminacy, but also childishness.[21] Children, no less than women, inhabited the space that has hitherto been subsumed within the 'women's question'.[22] British interventions in native childhood were both complicated and encouraged by the accompanying process of intervention in families and homes — the criminalizing family of the juvenile delinquent, the effeminizing *zenana* of the decadent aristocrat, the murderous home of the 'infanticidal' Rajput, the spurious home of the middle-class mimic of English respectability.[23] Childhood functioned as a point of obstruction, negotiation and facilitation in these colonizing manoeuvres. While it was, in some contexts, shielded by the domestic nationhood that Partha Chatterjee has outlined,[24] it was at other times laid bare to the colonial state by national elites eager to claim the modern ground of parenting.

That the family and the nation are both 'imagined communities' is not a new insight.[25] More interesting is the interpenetrating nature of the two acts of imagination in a setting where 'surrogate' families were imagined into existence to serve the ideological and political needs of aspiring hegemons. In her study of class formation and family politics in Victorian America, Nicola Beisel has argued that constructions of 'our children' involve exclusions that generate politically useful communities — the white/Protestant/native-born imagination of 'American' childhood facilitated the formation of a 'middle' class through the production of civil society organizations that transmitted the advantages of privileged parents.[26] In India, the comparable manoeuvre of the imagination was less straightforwardly exclusive. Elite Indians who were deeply ambivalent about the institutionalization of their 'own' children frequently assisted in the colonization of other, inferior natives. Simultaneously, however, they 'adopted' these latter children and invested them with their own desires and resentments. Exclusion and inclusion, 'colonization' and 'liberation' become almost hopelessly entangled when the colonial institution is also the instrument for producing national children and modern adults.

The negotiations within the tangle are especially revealing when the children in question are female. We find, for instance, much caution on the part of British administrators when it came to removing girls from their families; yet the corresponding anxiety in the nation of parents is remarkably inconsistent. When the fragmented nature of the 'Indian parent' is taken into consideration, it becomes necessary to examine Indian childhood not only as a colonialist or nationalist project of modernity but also as a fault-line within Indian society. Across this line, some Indian elites confronted other elites and various groups of non-elites and women and men confronted each other. The bodies of children could be inscribed with knowledge about these others, and deployed as vehicles of competition, mobility and resistance.

A third broad area of historiographical overlap is the scholarship on the princely states.[27] Recent forays into the history of educational regimes for a privileged class of 'endangered' colonial youth have not attempted to relate the 'danger' to 'youth' itself.[28] Nor have they asked how the childhood of the decadent native aristocracy might represent a window of opportunity for investigators of similarity and difference at a time when the princes were regarded by the British with a sympathy rooted in Tod-inspired romanticism and Curzonian calculations of expediency, and a contempt generated by their apparent unfitness for anything that might be construed as useful. Little effort has been made to inquire into the perception of failure that plagued these experiments in transformation.

Failed institutions are in some ways more revealing than 'successful' ones. The consensus between white teachers and brown parents about the 'failure' of the Chiefs' Colleges barely disguises an ideological misalignment between collaborators engaged in the simultaneous construction of a colonial childhood and a colonial polity. For British educators, the institutionalization of princely children produced natural shortcomings that qualified the adulthood of a native elite. Princely parents were interested in the institutional tools that produced disciplined subjects, but uninterested in the production of colonial curiosities, and unwilling to cede their parental prerogatives. Not surprisingly, they subverted the child/family models that the educators encouraged. Ramya Sreenivasan and Sumit Guha have shown that Rajput and Maratha familialities were highly responsive to the political needs of the moment and constructed interactively with pre-colonial states.[29] Such fluidity in the normative relationships between children and adults did not cease when the princes were reduced to the status of subdued allies of the British. Indeed, it became a central concern of parents as they struggled to respond to the new experts on child rearing.

Since this expertise was identified with the modern and the colonial regime, it was endowed with an authority that elite Indians could not ignore. They could, however, influence its deployment as they sought to position themselves as being both like and unlike modern 'westerners'. Once again, the agenda of middle-class, nationalist, Indian delineators of childhood is comparable with that of American child-savers in the early twentieth century — each was driven by a desire for, as well as fear of, a measure of egalitarianism in society and politics.[30] Confronted with the demands of modernity and British critiques of native degeneracy, elite parents, writers and educators in India sought to reconstruct the child not only as the repository of imperilled, pre-modern and essential Indian pasts that might be regenerated within the colonial present, but also as the embodiment of a universal individuality.[31] Going well beyond the search for indigenous scientific traditions that Gyan Prakash has described, they affiliated themselves with metropolitan traditions and rejected the translated, tropicalized science of colonial child correction.[32] By the 1880s and 1890s, Indian professionals had emerged as occasionally dissenting voices within the colonial reformatory, and in the years after the Great War they moved aggressively to decolonize the periphery by questioning its ambiguous modernity. However 'fractured' their own modernity may have been,[33] they were not inclined to tolerate fractures that signified their inferiority.

While these clashes are inseparable from simultaneous conflicts over the home, family, education, sex and work, there is no doubt that childhood itself was being redefined — not only as a state of preparation for the battles of adulthood, but also as a set of moral meanings and normative (and abnormal) behaviours that might be mapped onto colonizers and the colonized, and onto various related oppositions. The contradictory discourses of conflict and accommodation that constitute Indian articulations of how children should be treated by adults, 'outsiders' and the state might be understood as attempts to ignore (in some contexts) and control (in other contexts) the discursive, institutional and human resources of an emergent modernity. It was when the Indian elite were uncertain of this control, and unable to ignore the pressures of colonial intervention in the theatres of adulthood, that they became critics of 'foreign' models of childhood and institutions of child management. Childhood became a window through which the native elite imagined the impact of colonialism upon the Indian self, derived their reformulations of the self, and engaged in a variation of the 'passive revolution' that Partha Chatterjee has ascribed to bourgeois nationalism in the colonized world.[34] In limited, often disingenuous but powerfully subversive ways, the child and the adult came to stand for each other.

The flowering of interest in the Indian child in the second half of the nineteenth century need not be interpreted, as Elias and Aries have done in the European case, as an invention of childhood itself.[35] Elias' emphasis on 'manners' and shame responses that served to modulate a distance from adulthood[36] cannot easily be transferred to India. Normative adulthood in the colony was constituted by variables with their own histories imbedded in the colonial experience. Aries' well-known assertion that childhood was invented in Europe in the sixteenth and seventeenth centuries has been justifiably criticized as overly simplistic,[37] and refuted through even more simplistic models such as DeMause's six-stage conceptualization of the adult-child relationship, each stage progressively enlightened and less insistent upon differentiating the child from the adult.[38] Cunningham has attempted to reconcile Aries with DeMause by pointing out that while there has been a growing insistence since the eighteenth century upon seeing childhood as a 'special' time and state, there has been a simultaneous conviction that childhood is an antidote to adulthood, and adults must keep alive their 'inner child' and move closer to a childlike mode of being.[39] Each movement is informed by romanticism.[40] The romantic was not, however, embraced without ambivalence, and Sandner has argued that the late-Victorian English home was as much a shelter from the emotional excesses of romanticism as a sanctuary of pre-adult innocence.[41] Not surprisingly, while romantic notions of childhood surface in the most utilitarian of colonial projects, the child and the home fashioned in Indian reformatories and dormitories are also sites of savagery and sexual/emotional indiscipline.

I am not interested in replaying the Aries-DeMause quarrel in an Indian setting. Whether 'childhood' existed in India prior to the colonial interventions of the nineteenth century is beyond the scope of this book. What is more pertinent is that administrators who intervened in the juvenile periphery of the colony were frequently unable to find recognizable models of childhood in the natives who became inmates in their institutions. It is, moreover, clear that specific models of juvenile existence emerged from these interventions, and it is with these models, and with the processes of their emergence, that I am concerned.

Experiments with children overlapped other Liberal-Utilitarian projects,[42] such as the creation and supervision of colonial prisons, hospitals, lunatic asylums and other institutional spaces for the incarceration of deviants. Building explicitly and implicitly on the work of Foucault,[43] the scholarship on these 'enclaves' of disciplinary power has broadly emphasized the utility of deviance in the extension of the state into the uncolonized spaces of native society,[44] the creation of knowledge through observation and classification, and in some cases, the attempt to correct flawed political relationships between the deviant subject and the normative authority.[45] Each of these functions can readily be discerned in the British encounter with the colonized child. Perhaps obviously, caution must be exercised in reading this encounter through a Foucauldian lens. Scholars who have taken that approach to the history of modern childhood and the family have, on occasion, seriously overestimated the unified and crushing nature of the normalizing forces directed at parents and children.[46] In India, it is now established, not even colonial enclaves were immune to resistance and the need for compromise.[47] Authority in the juvenile enclaves was perpetually 'frustrated', but I argue that frustration was a critical ingredient of expertise in the periphery — a productive weakness that could be grounded in the natures of natives. A Foucauldian vision of power is not without utility if the blind spots are recognized and put to analytical use.

This book is not a history of Indian children. It is not my objective to narrate what they did or what was done to them, although such narratives can hardly be excluded from work of this nature. This is primarily a study of how the condition of childhood was identified and imagined by adults, and very secondarily a study of how the children themselves influenced the processes of identification and imagination. It is not meant to be a comprehensive study of colonial childhood in all conceivable contexts. It is intended to relocate children to the centre of academic investigations of colonial society and politics, to propose an analytical strategy that might be applied fruitfully to other areas of the history of childhood (such as child labour), and to posit the juvenile periphery as a politically significant zone that is worthy of examination precisely because it is a periphery. In other words, a modern periphery matters because it invites intervention, experimentation, colonization and reclamation.

1

STATE OF THE EXPERIMENT: EXPERTS, PARENTS AND THE REFORMATORY

> At present it must only be regarded as an experiment, though an experiment with a very fair chance of success, and one in which a little success will counterbalance many failures.
>
> Bengal committee on reformatory schools, 1874[1]

Expertise and experiments, rather than reformed children, were the prized products of the colonial reformatory. Not long after the initiation of the reformatory project in India, a curious assortment of career jailors, modernizing bureaucrats, native authority figures, women social workers, capitalists and religious colonizers had gathered under the umbrella of juvenile reform. As a group, they were similar to the 'voluntary empire' that Patricia Barton has identified in early twentieth-century entrepreneurial oversight, but not identical or coterminous, being much more closely affiliated with the state.[2] Simultaneously, the increasing significance and authority of the 'professional' had expanded and complicated the qualifications that were required of the supervisors of institutionalized children. Under the circumstances, expertise and authority were not stable in their disciplinary, racial, geographical and gendered locations. They were contested continuously between 'qualified' professional and 'unqualified' worker, expert and expert, scientist and bureaucrat, birth parent and surrogate parent, European and native, metropolitan specialist and colonial improviser, institutional patriarch and female interloper.

This instability increased in the closing years of the nineteenth century as middle-class Indians became more assertive in the reformatory, because these men (and eventually women) brought with them their peculiar political imperatives. The criminality that European observers might locate in the nature of the native, middle-class Indians tended to locate in the nature of the child, or in the nature of the marginal. By the 1920s, this contest had undermined — but not fully transformed or destroyed — the nature of expertise itself, as correction overflowed the reformatory into legislative chambers, courts and mechanisms of parole and extra-institutional monitoring that were largely in the hands of Indians. The child in a racially charged colonial society thus provided a specific site where the substantive content and the political significance of expertise could be articulated and evolved.

The colonial reformatory was a legal experiment: a series of investigations of the legislative expertise of the state, and of the extent to which the Macaulayan legal project might anticipate and encompass native society.[3] Extrapolating from Peter Fitzpatrick's analysis of the writings of Francisco Vitoria in the early Spanish empire, it might be posited that while the Indian reformatory was undergirded by a legal universalism, the experiment itself constantly produced peculiarity (savagery), undermining the universal nature of humanity and justifying the denial or postponement of the sovereignty of colonized populations. The fitness of colonial law could ultimately be investigated only through the resistance of those subjected to the law, but resistance also proved the unfitness of the native for universalistic institutions of law, correction and government.[4] These investigations show a pervasive pessimism on the part of colonial administrators, with few exceptions. Pessimism may appear to be at odds with a project driven by expertise. Nevertheless, it is consonant with the nature of expertise in a colonial environment, because the pessimism of the expert is itself rhetoric of discovery — the discovery, for instance, of racial difference that is beyond the transforming power of colonial law, and that must be allowed to persist if colonialism is to continue as an encounter with inferiority. When the law and the reformatory were perceived as having failed, a greater failure was typically identified in the native child and its parents. Thus, like colonialism itself, the reformatory and its legal structure were self-limiting experiments, in which 'success' — the wholesale expansion of the experiment beyond the institutional enclave — was not seriously imagined, and in which the discourse of 'failure' was actually a validation and a valid product.

The experiments and arguments of the juvenile periphery were enabled by the peripheral nature of the colony: the child, the punisher and the reformer in India existed at a productive distance from the discourses and procedures that surrounded the 'known' metropolitan child. The periphery is not, however, an empty space inhabited only by experts and their subjects. It is politically meaningful and productive because even on the margins of the metropole, the performer of expertise could imagine an audience that might praise or criticize, restrain or facilitate. This audience was sometimes imagined as a generic metropolitan 'public', or the same repository of opinion that sustained various other kinds of political discourse in nineteenth-century

India. At other times, and especially in the eyes of Indian child correction professionals, the public that might judge the experiment became unstable and potentially national/Indian, claiming the child and the experiment even as it was claimed by the expert.

The audience thus signified the professional, national, racial and gendered locations of the expert. Experiments in the juvenile periphery were typically conducted with one eye on metropolitan discourses of delinquency and punishment, and Marriott (following Cohn's lead) has described the racialization of delinquency in the colony and metropole as simultaneous developments in a 'unitary field' of power-knowledge.[5] The unitary field, however, was not without its fissures. Colonial experts did not seek simply to imitate the metropole, or to close the gap that they perceived between colonial practice and metropolitan recommendation. The discrepancies were worthy of preservation and even exaggeration, because articulating them allowed jailors, administrators, educators and doctors to insert themselves into the desirable cores of professionalism and, of course, race. While universalistic rhetoric closed the civilizational gap between the Indians and the whites, the colonial and the metropolitan, and so on, particularistic discourses such as race and 'orthodoxy' could be deployed strategically to widen the gaps, including those between competing groups in Indian society. For Indian experts, in general, explicit comparisons between metropolitan and colonial reformatories carried the implicit accusation that the hegemonic universality of the European model was actually fraudulent and that white administrators were making illegitimate distinctions between institutionalized English children (that were plastic and in school) and native juveniles (hardened, quasi-adult and in jail). The space between the center and the periphery produced the peculiarities of native children that validated the peculiar expertise of colonial experts, white as well as native, and provided a forum upon which Indians could address wider issues of injustice in colonial society.

The expert, the experiment and the experimental child in the juvenile periphery were thus simultaneously particular and universal. The tension between particularity and universality, and the frequent attempts by colonial professionals to cross-reference Indian practice against metropolitan precedents and models, stemmed from the reality that whereas English mechanisms for identifying and punishing juvenile delinquents had moved progressively away from mechanisms for adults, India had witnessed a convergence between models of adult and juvenile punishment, even as the child was increasingly recognized as a separate entity. This was due, in part, to a generalized inclination towards institutional architectural modernization that affected children and adult offenders in ways that were more similar than different. It was due also to the peculiarities of the colonial vision of adult delinquency, which was based on conceptions of 'native nature'. Differentiating between juveniles and adults, and between the parent and the child, thus presented greater challenges in India than it did in the metropole.

Native parents and families, in fact, occupied ambiguous positions in the colonial reformatory, not least because it remained uncertain whether they were 'in' the reformatory (defined as the broad project of professional child correction) or beyond its limits. Colonial administrators of juvenile punishment saw native families as a moral and political challenge to their authority and their vision of correction, and as factors in the criminality of Indian children. They were, however, far from being uniformly hostile to native parents. Motivated by sentimental Victorian formulations of familiality, they hesitated to disrupt irreversibly the 'natural' relationship between parent and child, or to endorse their own colleagues' speculation that the reformatory was better equipped than the family when it came to preserving the malleable, innocent period in the life of the individual native. The parent-child bond was, in fact, seen by many colonial experts as being more vital to the nature of the native child than of the European, and the increasingly medicalized expert in child correction was impelled to attach to it a positive, if qualified, evaluation.

In the new century, additional factors reinforced the native parent as a tangible presence at the edge of the reformatory. Negotiating the rights, responsibilities and limits of the parent became inevitable when the child was redefined as having rights, which flowed not only from an old presumption of dependence but also from a new assumption of autonomous claims upon the state.[6] This was not a recession of the parent before the expanding construct of the child. The parent, too, had expanded as a discursive and legal entity, acquiring a measure of individuality, new responsibilities and duties, and new areas of specialized authority and expertise.

The idea of the native parent should not be taken literally. Indian adults who participated in conversations about juvenile reform spoke not only from assumptions of expertise but also from their adoption of the role of national parents. The juvenile offender was thus contested by more than one set of surrogate parents. For Indian surrogate parents, the institutionalized juvenile from the margins of colonial society was hardly a child that could be embraced without reservations. Also, middle-class children were generally not a part of the debate, protected as they were by an extension of the domestic walls that Chatterjee has noted in his well-known formulation of nationalism and Indian women.[7] In the limited context of the reformatory that had been constructed with explicit reference to race, however, the abstracted and incarcerated native child could and did represent a politically useful alternative self for middle-class Indians, and the reformatory itself came to represent a tool of colonial oppression.

Expertise in the Periphery

The men who supervised Indian juvenile wards and reformatories in the nineteenth century were overwhelmingly 'amateurs'. They were not specialists in the sense in which Walter Crofton in Ireland, Frederic-Auguste Demetz in France, or even Mary Carpenter 'specialized' in the new field of child-correction, and few were securely rooted in the disciplinary soil that Garland has described.[8] Early Indian reformatories, like large prisons and lunatic asylums, were headed by military doctors who had no particular training in the treatment of children, but who might be broadly knowledgeable about the subjection of bodies to what, Ignatieff reminds us, was intended to be a 'just measure of pain'.[9] Beyond this limited expertise, superintendents of juvenile wards were career jailors who had hitherto managed adult convicts, and had then been put in charge of children and told to do their best.[10] Their own superiors were usually bureaucrats with even less experience in the 'science' of juvenile delinquency and its treatment. Well into the interwar years, the colonial reformatory was run by makeshift personnel, with uneven levels of commitment to modern ideas of punishment and rehabilitation.

There can be little doubt that amateur status on the margins of metropolitan expertise gave administrators of juvenile punishment a discursive space within which they could construct their credentials as men who were both colonial pioneers and members of a disciplinary field centred on the metropole. As Governor of Madras in the late 1860s, Lord Napier best exemplified this type of amateur expert, using his privileged positions in the colonial administration and white society as launching pads for forays into experiments with the modern possibilities of empire, from architecture to child correction.[11] He maintained a keen interest in the Sassoon Reformatory in Bombay, was a vocal partisan of building a wider network of reformatories in India, and was one of the first officials to use the expression 'juvenile delinquency' in the Indian context.[12] While he cannot be seen as the originator of a discourse of delinquency and correction in colonial India, he was very much in the vanguard of a movement that constructed the incarceration of native children as a self-conscious exercise in the ordering of knowledge, authority and institutional space.

In 1867, Napier and his allies in Bombay launched a powerful governmental and rhetorical initiative aimed at persuading the Government of India to create what eventually became the Reformatory Schools Bill (henceforth, RS

Bill or Act). In the process, he collected and forwarded a substantial body of statistical information about criminal convictions involving juveniles in British India (especially Madras), and the incarceration of children. While the exercise in colonial record-keeping established the reality of the juvenile delinquent, Napier's own role as the collector of records and assessor of their significance established his expertise, no less than the pointed references that he made to his sponsorship of a new reformatory in Madras.

Napier made no bones about the experimental character of the juvenile archipelago that he envisioned in 1867. Aware that his opponents in Lord Lawrence's administration saw reformatories as an extravagant solution to a relatively small penological problem, he told the Viceroy that the limited numbers of children ought to be regarded as a fortuitously limited opportunity:

> The experiment can now be made on a small scale on parties carefully selected, with a view to their character and position. The Magistrates would for the most part continue their present practice, only sentencing to confinement in the Reformatory the offenders who may appear peculiarly susceptible to improvement, or peculiarly devoid of all protection or control in regard to their family relations. I have not yet contemplated more than an experimental institution of the simplest kind as an accessory to the Madras Penitentiary and the nearest Jails of the Tamil country, adapted for thirty or forty inmates. The subsequent course of Government would be regulated by the success or failure of the first Establishment. If it succeeded, it would be expanded, and three or four others, answering to the geographical and ethnological divisions of the Presidency, would be founded. If it failed, the scheme would be abandoned without any discredit.[13]

By implying that all the empire was a laboratory, Napier located the experimental reformatory within the ethnographic state.[14] He did not neglect to add some pragmatic points of consideration — reformatories would eventually prove themselves 'profitable to society' by reducing property crimes and eliminate the need to modify existing prisons 'for the discipline and training of juvenile offenders'.[15] The competitive civilizational urgency of the project remained in focus: 'it is an expenditure which every civilized Government in the world, except that of British India, is undergoing for the benefit of its subjects,' Napier wrote, adding, 'I include the Government of Pondicherry.'[16]

The new expert in child correction, situated at the leading edge of this civilized and civilizing enterprise, remained in focus as well. Napier did not call for professionals in the specialized sense of the word. Nor did he call for a supervisory corps that was exclusively or even substantially white.

Europeans and Eurasians who might be available to direct colonial juvenile wards and reformatories were 'altogether unfitted for such a task,' he wrote, urging that it would be better to 'associate Native intelligence and Native sympathies with the exertions of Government in initiating a social amelioration so interesting and important'. The correction of female children might be entrusted to 'some Christian lady – a Missionary's widow, or a member of some Roman Catholic Order of Mercy – who, in some place apart, would undertake the duties of restraint, reformation, and education for the love of God'.[17] Napier's vision of expertise thus had considerable space for the experienced amateur, and for evangelical women like Mary Carpenter. The preference for native officers was both ideological and practical: Indian adults of the right sort might be better suited as role models for native children, they would not come burdened with the moral-racial baggage of Eurasian identity,[18] and they would be cheaper than whites of a comparable level of respectability. Napier's vision represents an emergent discipline in search of a well-equipped laboratory, enthusiastic researchers and political-bureaucratic blessing. Not surprisingly, his 1867 missive to Lawrence has the flavor of an application for a research grant.

The language of the memo is very much that of the scientist, analyzing geographic and climatic factors, and correlating those with architectural possibilities and physiological necessities. Napier is ethnologist, criminologist, geneticist and anatomist in turns, insisting that 'crime is hereditary, it goes down from generation to generation, and the reformatory is the beneficial power that breaks the chain of transmitted guilt', and urging the central government towards 'a mature reflection…of the physiognomy and history of crime in India'.[19] In 'the country of Thugs, Maravers, Dundassies, Pullers and Kullers,' he writes, 'a hereditary character must be more deeply stamped on crime than in England.' Napier was not arguing that Indian child offenders were the same as their English counterparts and he was rebutting the viewpoint (put forward by bureaucrats such as E C Bayley) that colonial child-saving experts were weak imitations of metropolitan models. By constructing a problem that was different from metropolitan delinquency but equally vital and challenging, Napier sought to legitimize the colonial experiment as an exploration of difference, and the colonial expert as somebody who was peculiarly qualified to test and compensate for such differences.

A critically important aspect of Napier's construction of expertise was the language of experience, or the frequently articulated reminder that the colonial child-saver spoke from a record of past encounters with children in the laboratory. In a context that privileged the amateur over the formally qualified specialist, the ability to refer to such encounters was an essential source of discursive authority, not only for Napier and his contemporaries, but also, to a great extent, their successors. S Lynch, the prison administrator who supported Napier's demand for a network of juvenile reformatories, based his recommendations on his sense of himself as an innovator who had already moved to separate children from adults in Calcutta's Presidency Jail, and reinforced this identity by referring to 'my own experience' with the juvenile experiment.[20] Near the end of the century, the Deputy Commissioner of Sialkot urged his superior to see the institutionalization of unconvicted children as an ideal solution to the problem of the Criminal Tribes (hereafter, CT), modestly adding:

> The question raised…is a very large and important one, and one which must be dealt with by officers of much greater experience than myself. I have, however, had some years' experience of Criminal Tribes in Ludhiana and in this district. There are many officers in the Commission of experience who are interested in the Criminal Tribes and who would agree with my views.[21]

Produced by colonial experience, the expert on the colonial child was himself a creature of the periphery. There is no doubt that this marginal location generated certain anxieties. When Lynch made his remarks to the government, he was supported by F J Mouat, a long term member of the penal establishment in Bengal (first as a jailor, then as Inspector General of Prisons, and also as an articulate advocate of specialized reformatories). Mouat wrote:

> An impression has been created in England that no attention has been paid to the [juvenile reformatory] in India, and that we are ignorant of, or undervalue it. [But] the experiment [in India] has undoubtedly been successful, and the management of the juvenile delinquent ward is most creditable to the care, constant attention and humanity of Dr. Lynch.[22]

The experimental character of colonial child-saving could thus function in a compensatory capacity, redeeming the expert who was located far from Europe. Mouat was not antagonistic to the 'true' experts in the metropole. He saw himself as their extension, and to some extent, as their pupil. Nevertheless, he was eager to claim the colony as a peculiar area of expertise, where the white observer of the native child might be substantially free from rules generated by metropolitan norms. 'We have not at present sufficient experience of the subject as applied to Natives of India,' he wrote, calling for a reformatory where power would be generated by the panoptic 'eye of the Superintendent and of the European Jailor' rather than a rigid code of regulations.[23]

Imbedded in Mouat's comments is a tension between two notions of expertise — one that derived from colonial experience and another that was transmitted by metropolitan authority. When European jailors and child-savers travelled to India, their interactions with their colonial counterparts was marked by this tension, because colonial experts had constructed a peculiar relationship with the observer that might recognize, reward, critique, or alter the performance of expertise. Men who asserted expertise in the colony, especially in the early years of the reformatory, imagined a 'public' that was both specifically metropolitan and so general that it was practically ethereal. J G Kirschner, the superintendent of the Alipore reformatory, could thus express a kind of performance anxiety before an audience of ghosts — 'If [habitually idle] boys should relapse into their old habit, either from want of means of support, or from other causes, the public, who do not know the real cause, will lay the blame at the door of those who have been immediately in charge of the boys during their stay at the school.'[24]

For Napier, who wanted colonial reformatories to be 'subjected to public view', the public in question was similarly insubstantial.[25] Subjection to public view meant a certain openness before Indians, including, presumably, the Indians whose children might become inmates. Such natives could be allowed to see the reformatory at work, but not the workings of the reformatory. To a greater extent, it meant exposure to English-educated Indians; in the 1860s, however, these could provide opinion, support and even criticism, but not direction or authoritative censure. It meant transparency before the 'home' press, metropolitan experts and ultimately the India Office and Parliament, but these were so far removed that their oversight could only be sporadic, superficial and of dubious authority.

The 'audience' was thus highly uneven, and the only section of it to which Napier would grant meaningful authority was a small circle of white officials and experts in the colony, or an intimate group of his own peers. It did not mean shutting out metropolitan experts — Mouat and Alfred Lyall (who, like Napier, opposed the skeptical Bayley on the issue of reformatories in India) both admired Demetz, and Lyall supported his case against Bayley by referring the latter to 'the ablest and most philanthropic men in Europe and America [who] have devoted themselves to devising systems which are intended [to] exercise a reformatory influence.'[26] Nevertheless, this admiration came attached to an implication that the 'true' expert in the metropole would undoubtedly (and tautologically) support the work of his colonial counterparts.

The tension between colonial experience and metropolitan authority can be detected two generations after Napier, Mouat and Lyall, when the government of British Burma invited A Paterson, the Commissioner of Prisons for England and Wales and 'an acknowledged expert in all matters relating to the treatment of the juvenile criminals', to advise the education ministry on the finer points of reformatory management.[27] In spite of the different political circumstances of Burma in 1928, peripherality of expertise imposed a measure of continuity with the 1870s. Paterson reported to a committee on juvenile delinquency made up largely of colonial jailors, educators and reformatory administrators. They were not uniformly hostile, but they were consistent in resisting his efforts to introduce 'European' innovations such as 'farm schools' and 'camp schools', and to place the Burmese reformatory in the hands of officials trained along metropolitan lines. Paterson, as the metropolitan expert, imagined a universality of crime, punishment and institutional management that only metropolitan experts such as he could properly supervise. His colonial counterparts, being more invested in a fundamental difference that their experience qualified them to interpret, preferred white men who 'know the Burman intimately', i.e. white men who recognized racial difference.[28] Both perspectives are racially informed, but Paterson assumed that universal expertise (itself focused within a racial identity) transcended the racial content of the native child.

In Mouat's own time, this tension was highlighted in the encounter between colonial child-savers and the formidable Mary Carpenter. Carpenter belongs to a genre of social workers that includes Florence Nightingale, Elizabeth Fry, Emily Hobhouse and Jane Addams — women driven by middle-class anxieties about urbanity and colonialism. Armed with great religious and cultural confidence, an expansive notion of 'women's work' and a willingness to take on entrenched bastions of male authority in assorted bureaucracies, they were at the forefront of a wave of legal and institutional reform that began in England the 1830s and lasted into the Progressive era in America. They were, as such, both reactionary in their attitudes towards the poor, the foreign, the heathen and the non-white, and subversive in their willingness to critique the institutions and practices of their own social milieus: a combination that made them uneasy allies and frequent antagonists of colonial penal scientists like Mouat and Lynch.[29]

Carpenter's reforming zeal was based more in religious faith than a sense of her place in an experimental vanguard. The daughter of a Unitarian minister, she maintained a catholic interest in other faiths; this reflected not only a vexed curiosity about why their adherents refused to convert, but also her fascination with Ram Mohun Roy, whom she had known in Bristol in 1830.[30] This childhood encounter (Roy had died in the care of her father) led her, as an adult, to befriend elite Indians, especially Brahmos, who travelled to England, and to assert a privileged status as a living connection to Roy. Contact with Indians intensified her anxiety about their moral condition and she sailed to India in 1867 with a well-defined agenda of reform. Her primary mission was to solicit support from elite Indians, Anglo Indians and ultimately, the colonial government for a school, headed by European women, that would train Indian women as teachers.[31]

At the time, Carpenter was established as an authority on child criminals and their reforming institutions, having worked extensively with the children of the English and Irish poor. In India, she hoped to persuade the colonial government to fund the building of reformatories where convicted children as well as non-convicted delinquents could be held for extended periods of time instead of being sent to ordinary jails. Her two favourite projects — the normal school and the reformatory — were closely related. They both aimed to expose the elusive, uncolonized areas of the native family to the moral searchlight of middle-class colonialism. Carpenter's evangelicalism should not obscure the fact that she was a firm believer in modern punitive strategies. An opponent of corporal punishment, she admired Crofton's 'Irish system', which required incarcerated children to progress through several grades of rehabilitation by demonstrating their acceptance of the discipline of the reformatory.[32]

Carpenter discovered that reformatories in India were a far cry from the ideal she had in mind, and she made sure that her findings were reported sensationally in the British press.[33] She discovered, also, the frustrations of lobbying the colonial government to build a more satisfactory set of juvenile institutions. Prison administrators and government officials were hostile to Carpenter, not only because they resented her interference in their male professional domain,[34] but also because they believed that she had no understanding of the peculiarities of Indian criminals and criminalized children, especially their immunity to shame and lack of a reformable plasticity.[35] Bayley declared that Carpenter had failed to grasp how 'ancestral pursuit' — by which he meant caste — erased the imprints of punishment upon the released child offender.[36]

The skeptical reception reflected a resistance to schemes that relied upon an expanded carceral gaze, which Bayley and many penal administrators of his time saw as a problem rather than a solution. Placing large numbers of juvenile offenders under the surveillance of the state, Bayley wrote, would be 'a very mischievous and impolitic' measure that would only guarantee the criminalization of children.[37] Such caution marked a schism between 'conservative' administrators in the central government and their more 'progressive' counterparts in the provinces. The latter, who included Napier, Mouat and F Brand (Inspector General of Prisons in Madras) were no less frustrated than was Carpenter by Bayley's reluctance to sanction a network of centrally funded reformatories.[38] Yet Bayley was quite interested in the punishment of native children, and, we shall see, had given much thought to the subject. He was hostile to particular experimental strategies, but not to the experiment itself.

The hostility that Carpenter encountered was thus not a uniform response. She shared much ground with 'progressives' like Napier and Mouat, who agreed with her demand that corporal punishment of children be discontinued in favour of a graded system of confinement, deprivation and reward.[39] It is evident that her tour pushed the colonial government into initiating the interprovincial dialogue that led, after many hiccups, to the RS Act of 1876.[40] Nevertheless, even her allies felt threatened by her intervention in the periphery. Mouat, for instance, remarked defensively that 'the ignorance and indifference alleged [by Carpenter] to exist in [Indian prison regimes]…is simply untrue'. He added:

> The juvenile ward of the Presidency Jail fulfils most of the objects that a reformatory for criminal children is intended to fulfil. I am surprised that Miss Carpenter should apparently have overlooked this ward in her visit to the Presidency Jail.[41]

The encounter between Carpenter and the British Indian penal establishment highlights the instability as well as the value of expertise in the colonial reformatory as it emerged from the Mutiny. It is convenient, at best, to use the expression 'British Indian penal establishment' or to refer to a common body of expert knowledge; these were contested categories even before Indians entered the field of contestation. Nevertheless, it is also remarkable that Carpenter earned the ire of practically every section of the penal bureaucracy in India, including men whose ideas were not fundamentally incompatible with hers. By the mid-1860s, the colonial child-correction expert had developed as an entity with a claim on a distinct field of expertise, entrenched within the government bureaucracy and with political boundaries to defend from natives, missionary freelancers, women and metropolitan visitors. Not until the 1920s would Indians, private experts and women gain anything resembling a secure foothold in this field.[42]

The Reformatory and Indian Opinion

Adding to the discomfiture of government officials who followed her tour of India, Carpenter engaged in a lively conversation about reformatories with elite Indians in Bombay, Ahmedabad and Calcutta, and attempted to enlist their 'authentic' voices in support for her plans. The fact that she had chosen to bring natives into the discussion was not the problem, since the colonial regime itself maintained open channels of communication with the 'right sort' of Indians on the issue of juvenile institutions. Carpenter, however, bypassed the filters, the selectivity and the bureaucratic controls that the government usually insisted upon. Parsis, Brahmos, 'native Christians' and Jews demonstrated a particular eagerness to participate in this conversation. Each group agreed with Carpenter that sophisticated reformatory regimes were urgently needed in India. In the process, they competed for the badges of expertise, civilization and modernity — with each other, with British critics of Indian civilization, with the negligent colonial state and with the 'unenlightened mass' of natives.

Carpenter's encounter with Bombay's Jewish community is especially revealing of the contentious heart of the colonial reformatory. Like Parsis, Indian Jews were able to use the delinquency of other Indians as an opportunity to underline their own 'foreign' origin, and articulate a moral outlook that was aligned with that of the colonizer. In concrete terms, the Jewish community could show Carpenter something that the Parsis, Brahmos and native Christians could not: a reformatory of their own. The David Sassoon reformatory had been founded in 1857. It was not an entirely new institution, but rather the adoption by the Sassoons of the Bombay School of Industry, which had been set up seven years earlier by the provincial government to deal with arrested children, and to facilitate the 'apprenticeship' of poor children to local employers.[43] When the institution ran into financial difficulties, the Sassoons provided the money and the new name, and were given a measure of control over the administration.[44] The move was part of a wider engagement by the Sassoons with colonial disciplining institutions — in 1863, David Sassoon offered Rs. 60,000 towards a 'mechanic's institute' in Bombay, on condition that the colonial government match the offer. The government was pleased to agree.[45] In 1867, the board of the reformatory included Parsis and Englishmen as well as members of the Sassoon family. Juvenile delinquency was not only a forum of elite competition, but also one of strategic alliances.

Perhaps obviously, the inmates of the Sassoon Reformatory were not themselves Jewish or Parsi. Juvenile delinquency in the colonial context was always a moral flaw in the other and a civilizational boundary between the expert observer and the observed specimen. Broken down by religion — which they inevitably were in British records and eyes — the children in Sassoon represented roughly equal numbers of Hindus and Muslims, with a sprinkling of Christians.[46] They came from all over the Bombay Presidency. In this sense, the institution functioned much like the reformatories that were run directly by the governments of Punjab, Madras and Bengal in the period before the legislative effort of 1876 — it concentrated the refuse of a wider criminal/juvenile geography.

There were, however, significant differences between Sassoon and those other institutions. Sassoon was, in many ways, a more developed experiment. It was not attached to a prison as a semi-disguised youth wing and it sought to retain its children beyond the terms of their sentences. It was during this period, when the reformatory had no legal authority to compel inmates to stay, that the children were apprenticed, i.e. put to work within and without the institution as carpenters, metal workers, cooks and gardeners. Delinquency, understood as the possibility of relapse, was thus extended into the boundaries of reform. The more 'reformed' boys were recruited as teachers of the other children. Sassoon inmates were regularly apprenticed to the locomotive workshops of the Great Indian Peninsula Railway; others worked in privately owned cotton mills.[47] They were paid small stipends for their work, and fed and clothed at the expense of the reformatory. It seems clear that some children and parents saw this as an economic arrangement that suited their needs.[48] As Mills has pointed out, Indians confronted with incarceration often coopted colonial institutions for their own purposes.[49]

While the Indians who introduced Carpenter to the Sassoon regime were understandably proud of this evidence of their own expertise, the apparent consensus is misleading. When apprenticeship was introduced in other reformatories, Indians were openly skeptical about its benefits and drew disagreeable parallels between its exploitative ramifications and their own subordinate status in colonial professions and institutions. Omrita Nath Mitter, one of four Indian members of the Alipore Board of Management in the 1890s, usurped the language of institutional reform — which, Foucault reminds us (albeit not without contest), is built into the modern prison[50] — as he warned his colleagues:

> The system of licensing, instead of benefiting the youthful offenders, may become an engine of oppression at the hand of unkind employers. Moreover…it will be contrary to, and frustrate the primary objects of, the Reformatory Act, to send away youthful offenders for employment by outsiders, who certainly cannot be expected to take so much care of the boys as in a reformatory school, which the Government, in its philanthropy, has decided to reform.[51]

Mitter's fears were perhaps unfounded, but they are nevertheless significant. After the passage of the RS Act, the Alipore Reformatory in Calcutta had sought to place its children with 'trustworthy and respectable' employers and guardians. In 1896, it came to light that in the nearly two decades of the scheme, not a single child had actually been apprenticed. In the words of D W D Comins, the Inspector General of Prisons in Bengal, 'no respectable native family would consent to take such a boy'.[52] Comins acquired this insight from the Indian members of the management committee of the reformatory, revealing how indigenous elites like Mitter had inserted themselves into assessments of the success or failure of the experiment, and into the 'public' that white administrators had sought to imagine on their own terms.

The layered mediation that was involved in the provision of native opinion introduced barely manageable opportunities for the communication of dissent, for the introduction of autonomous civilizational, professional and political agendas, and for the subversion and appropriation of colonial subjects. The apparent indifference of 'respectable' natives also indicates a disjuncture between British and elite-Indian visions of reform. Whereas the British would have seen their own intervention (the reformatory itself) as altering a boy's social and moral location sufficiently that he would be acceptable to the native elite as a subordinate associate and employee, the elite in question would have felt a need to distance itself from the boy, seeing the reformatory not as a site of moral improvement, but as the antithesis of its own moral unimpeachability.

Baldly put, assessments of ownership determined the elite-Indian response. When the reformatory was their 'own' (as was the case with Sassoon), Indians were inclined to be relatively enthusiastic in their support of state-sponsored child correction. The civilizational calculations were quite different when the government owned the experimental site. Affluent Indians in Bihar, including the Raja of Darbhanga, contributed early and liberally towards the industrial school that was used as an improvised reformatory in Patna. In 1858, however, it came to light that W Taylor, the commissioner of Patna, had coerced donors into contributing, while insisting that it was their duty as 'men as standing' and hinting that contributors would be rewarded with official titles.[53] The putative donors eventually complained that the school had become an engine of their oppression. Taylor was sacked, protesting that he had 'saved' Patna during the Mutiny, and hinting that his new troubles constituted a retaliatory rebel ambush.[54] The incident highlighted the ambivalence within Indian responses to the colonial reformatory — the institution was not for children alone, but for political actors engaged in a broader range of confrontations.

By the 1890s, officials like Comins had become vehemently opposed to private reformatories in which Indians would have a greater say. A D Larymore, the Vice President of the board of management at Alipore, dismissed his Indian colleagues' proposal for private institutions by declaring, 'The country is not at present fit for such a measure. No school in India...is conducted with sufficient discipline.'[55] Yet the native expert had already become an insistent and competing presence within the reformatory. In the afterglow of the Ilbert Bill affair[56] and the foundation of the Indian National Congress, this was inevitably an intrusive presence. By 1885, Indians were included among the inspectors of reformatories in Bengal and their voices were occasionally featured in the annual reports.[57] Four of the thirteen men who signed the

Visitors' Book at the Chingleput Reformatory in Madras in 1892 were district level Indian officials. Mohammed Raza Khan, Acting Sub-Collector and Joint Magistrate of Chingleput, made a surprise visit, toured the kitchen, and thought the curry smelled nice. He added:

> I was quite delighted to find a number of Muhammadan youngsters at work at their several industries. [The Deputy Superintendent] Mr. Lewis told me that they were smart, intelligent and obedient, save one. I have reprimanded him severely.[58] [He meant the boy, not Lewis.]

Another surprise visitor to Chingleput that year was M R Pantulu Garu, the Municipal Commissioner of Madras. Pantulu Garu's interest in modern penal institutions extended beyond the reformatory; he was also an unofficial visitor to the Madras Penitentiary. He was pleased by what he saw at Chingleput, writing:

> I will not be doing justice if I cannot express the great surprise…and the great satisfaction I felt in inspecting the several industries taught here, the discipline of the boys, and the educational courses they have gone through.[59]

He praised the workshops, the drill, the singing and the handwriting, lavished praise on the superintendent's dedication to 'making this novel institution a great success' and noted that similar institutions had failed in other places and under less inspired leadership.[60]

In the years that Raza Khan and Pantulu Garu toured the reformatory, the more 'reformed' children at Chingleput were awarded prizes in ceremonies presided over by K R Aiyar the District Munsif. Aiyar used one such occasion to make a speech about 'the eternal truths of morality common to all mankind', by which he meant industrial education and 'due observance of the laws of sanitation'.[61] The superintendent of Chingleput agreed heartily. This much appreciated native support was not, however, entirely comforting. By emphasizing the universality of institutional morality, Ariyar had expressed a subversive identification with the ruling civilization on behalf of the Indian elites who were conscious of the moral critiques to which they were subjected. Raza Khan, Pantulu Garu and Ariyar were asserting a measure of authority not only over incarcerated juveniles, but over the reformatory administrators as well. This authority flowed from their positions as government officials, but it flowed also from their appropriation of the moral vision of juvenile reform. The ability to make surprise visits and praise British administrators for doing a surprisingly good job is not an insignificant power. It is almost as significant as the power to criticize. Due to the unstable nature of praise, it might be seen as an 'implicit' or 'potential' critique.

By the turn of the century, a tentative Indianization of the reformatory administration is evident, with natives occasionally officiating as superintendents.[62] Just as importantly, the amendment of the RS Act in 1897 invited more Indian intrusion into the punishment of children. Pandit Bishumber Nath, the sole Indian member of the committee that drafted the amended law, obliquely criticized his co-legislators' desire for long terms of incarceration:

> The idea that it is better to sentence a youthful criminal to be detained in a Reformatory School for a long term, instead of giving him a short term of imprisonment is, I understand, opposed to Indian feelings. The general opinion decidedly is that...if youth is to make any difference, it should be in the way of shortening the length of the imprisonment.[63]

Bishumber Nath cites 'Indian feelings' without identifying himself with them. In the process, he positions himself as a mediator and articulator of native responses to colonialism — himself undeniably a native (and valuable and empowered for that reason alone), and poised precariously between what might be considered colour of skin and colour of intellect. He is the native talking about natives as if he were white, when he knows, and his white listeners know, that he is a native and speaks as one. This knowledge must be left unstated for the performance (and the knowledge it conveys) to be 'successful', i.e. beneficial and pleasurable to both speaker and listener. At the same time, by introducing a new and non-consenting 'public' into the reformatory, Bishumber Nath disrupts the exclusive circle of colonial expertise.

Other Indian observers of the impending legislation consistently showed their determination to shape the disciplinary regime and its products. Nihal-ud-Din Ahmed, the deputy collector of Gorakhpur, told his superiors that reformatories must instruct their wards 'in their respective religions', adding, 'To bring up these youths without any religious training will be a calamity, for their principles of morality will be on no sound basis and their reformation therefore will be incomplete.'[64] Nihal-ud-Din's recommendation, which was by no means isolated or unusual, represented a complex ideological response to a colonizing institution. By grounding his advice in the evangelical idea that the reform of children must be informed by religion, he created a space for dissent and decolonization. By the mid-1890s, the influence of evangelicals like Carpenter — which had never been especially strong — had faded almost completely from Indian reformatories; the regime had developed along largely secular lines, with a wistful Christianity audible in its margins.[65] By challenging this regime, Nihal-ud-Din claimed the reformed child for a communal identity that was defined by neither Christianity nor religious indifference, and that was positively and assertively extra-colonial.

A not altogether different attempt at negotiation came from Dayaram Gidumal, the Acting District Judge of Shikarpur. Gidumal wrote to the Bombay administration that a revised RS Act should provide explicitly for the 'physical exercise' of incarcerated children and not just for industrial training.[66] The suggestion was immediately opposed by R L Johnston, the Judicial Commissioner of Sind, who remarked:

> I would suggest the words 'bodily labour' instead of 'physical exercise'. The labour of the boys might be thus profitably employed while giving them at the same time the physical exercise necessary for their health and strength in producing some…return to the State from their labour in consideration of its supporting them and training them for so many years from criminals to possibly future good citizens.[67]

Evident here is Gidumal's status as a native administrator engaged in a debate with white administrators about the physiological and ideological products of colonial administration. By asking for 'exercise' in the reformatory at a time when middle-class Indians participated obsessively in the search for a strong national physique,[68] Gidumal displaced the native elite's gender anxieties on to other colonized native bodies, in what might be considered an absent-minded identification with the children of the criminalized poor. This implicitly anticolonial agenda was, for him, an essential aspect of the 'reform' that a disciplining institution might accomplish.

Johnston, on the other hand, was clear that the boys were being 'reformed' to be orderly members of the laboring class. Exercise and strength for their own sake are prerogatives of those who have the political agency to put exercise and strength to imaginative and ideological use, and who have legitimate leisure for recreation. Ironically, it was Johnston who used the word 'citizen' to describe his worker boys — a slippage from the metropolitan context of reformatory discipline. The exercise-labor dichotomy was, of course, also a child-adult dichotomy by this time, especially in the metropolitan discourses of athletic education and child labor prevention.[69] In the colonial periphery, Johnston could experimentally dilute the content of labor-free childhoods. Gidumal, however, saw the colonial reformatory as central to an emerging archipelago of national assets and felt impelled to insist upon a notion of childhood that was not only in concert with metropolitan modernity, but subversive of the imposed inequities of the colonial political order.

Gidumal's desire for exercise in the reformatory was anticipated by another Indian observer's insistence that incarcerated children be taught English.

Besveswar Mukerji sat on the board of managers at the Hazaribagh Reformatory. English was in fact taught in Bengal's reformatories until 1896, existing uneasily in the grey area between prison and school. In 1893, when the reformatory administration began a discussion of the merits of teaching English to boys slated to become laborers and artisans, Mukerji took it upon himself to argue that learning English was 'essential' to a 'useful' education, even in the reformatory.[70] His fellow manager C Garbett disagreed, calling English-language education 'time wasted'.[71] Garbett was echoing E V Westmacott, the former Inspector General of Prisons in Bengal, who had contemptuously dismissed the importance of English to the reform of juvenile criminals.[72] In 1897, Garbett and Westmacott won the skirmish and English was discontinued in the reformatories of Bengal.[73]

Following Viswanathan's point about the disciplining effects of English education in the colony,[74] English might have had a place in the reformatory curriculum, where discipline was an acknowledged necessity. That need, however, was outweighed by the greater need to maintain the hierarchies of race and class, which were more often destabilized by English-educated natives than stabilized. It is unlikely that Mukerji seriously imagined, or desired, that juvenile offenders might become English-literate members of the native elite. Wiener's argument that middle-class Indians have a peculiarly antimodern and culturally determined (crudely put, caste-based) disinclination to committing the state to the education of poor children ought to apply in Mukerji's case.[75] Among the various reasons that it does not[76] is that the modern Self is not so watertight that it would generate a uniform set of institutional priorities. English education for incarcerated children reflected a larger political conflict over Macaulayan education, identity, authenticity and political rights for Indians in colonial society. While denigrating the English-educated native came easily to white administrators, articulating an effective response was difficult for people like Mukerji if they had to refer to themselves. The juvenile offender could, in this limited be an alternative 'borrowed' self that was useful in more ways than one — his utility, or conversely the time that he wasted, were actually Mukerji's own.

K N Panikkar has argued that the pedagogical agendas of Indian intellectuals in the nineteenth century were driven as much by a rejection of their provinciality in the colony as by a critique of 'tradition.' Both struggles were regenerative, Panikkar argues, and while he implies that there was something 'decayed' to regenerate (rather than something that might simply be generated), it is undeniable that the Indian child and expert both embodied a re/generated nation.[77] The subversive assent that natives like Gidumal and Mukerji brought to the colonial reformatory was ubiquitous, as was the resentment it provoked. In Calcutta, Mitter protested to Larymore that legal provisions for the punishment of children made insidious distinctions between native and European magistrates (privileging the latter), and demanded that this injustice be addressed through new legislation.[78] R Obbard, the Judicial Commissioner of the Hyderabad Assigned Districts, complained to his superior in 1896 that a major weakness of the 1876 reformatory law was that it gave too much discretion to junior magistrates; this had allowed native judges to undermine Obbard by sending convicted juveniles to the reformatory even when he had expressed his preference that the boys be sent to jail.[79] A similar problem was apparent to British officials in Burma, where Burmese magistrates showed a 'mischievous' inclination to release convicted boys to their parents instead of locking them up in the reformatory or the jail.[80]

The tension between the court and the executive reflected the different racial, political and moral make-up of two sites at which knowledge about native child criminals, and the child criminal himself, were produced and deployed. Clearly, the invention of the juvenile delinquent had exposed moral ruptures and generated new avenues of resistance within the colonial regime. Consequently, the state's handling of the native child was equated by Obbard with a colonization of the native adult. As delinquency became more expansive, it became increasingly urgent (and hopeless to expect) that the machinery for the identification and punishment of juveniles would be controlled by white experts, civil servants and surrogate parents located in the upper and middle levels of the government, rather than by natives pretenders to disciplinary, governmental and parental expertise. An extended and rigorous period of punishment for the juvenile delinquent thus marked an attempt by the colonial state to extend its authority over multiple loci: children, native elite, parents, the meanings of civilization and reform, Burma and Hyderabad, Madras and Bengal.

By the 1920s, this authority had become threadbare. Indian participation in the administration and interpretation of juvenile punishment had changed both quantitatively and qualitatively since the days of Gidumal, Aiyar and Mukerji. When the provincial governments began to introduce a new set of laws and institutions — Children Acts backed up by age-graded 'certified schools' (a new term for 'reformatory'), Borstal Acts for the newly congealed category of the adolescent offender, juvenile courts, social work bureaucracies and probationary release — the white expert was relegated to a periphery where he did not control the boundaries, even as colonial systems moved closer to metropolitan models. Like the legislative activity of the 1870s, the new initiatives began in Madras and were refined in Bengal, after much additional discussion and argument. They were, however, promoted by Indian legislators who had been empowered within the provincial administrations by the Montague-Chelmsford regime, and who were eager to circumvent what they perceived as the bureaucratic and ideological inertia of the British-controlled central government.

In 1928, the Madras legislature began debating an amendment to the Children Act it had passed in 1920. That earlier law had been the first attempt by Indian legislators in the era of dyarchy to reach for a 'universal' model of modern child correction that seemed to exist in the metropole but not in the colony, by incorporating the features of the landmark English Children Act of 1908 into the Indian reformatory.[81] The 1928 amendment was also intended to bring the Children Act into better alignment with the Madras Borstal Schools Act of 1926. It codified the circumstances under which relatively young children could be transferred to institutions for older juveniles; these included disciplinary problems posed by individual children, overcrowding in the junior certified schools, and the availability of specialized vocational training programmes in the senior certified schools. During the debate, unexpected issues surfaced within this seemingly uncontentious agenda. J A Saldanha, who was one of the movers of the amendment bill, declared:

> We have to guard against...the period of imprisonment. During the discussion of the Borstal Schools Bill we...pointed out the dangers of the authorities having enormous powers of keeping young men for a longer period than could ever have been dreamt of by imprisoning them in Borstal schools in the name of a school. To be in a Borstal school is practically the same as imprisonment. By transferring a youthful offender already kept in a Children's School to a Borstal School his period of school is extended for another two years...if not for a longer period. I would [include] certain restrictions and conditions so that the Inspector General of Prisons would not have indefinite power to do what he pleases.[82]

Unlike his predecessors of the 1890s, Saldanha was not reticent about his perception that the reformatory was a political weapon in the hands of a colonial state that was itself bitterly contested. He was prescient; the juvenile delinquency apparatus was used by judges in the early 1930s to punish young participants in the Salt Satyagraha.[83] Saldanha's protest, couched within a debate on a bill that he had himself sponsored, was to point out that the colonial reformatory distorted childhood — the Indian Borstal was an adult jail rather than a children's institution, and the *mis*placement of adolescents in this institution could only be a perverted punishment that reflected other political perversions.

These issues were replayed with additional twists in Calcutta the same year during the passage of the Bengal Borstal Schools Act. The law enabled the courts to send convicted boys between the ages of sixteen and twenty one to

Borstal Schools for industrial training and 'such disciplinary measures and moral influences as in the opinion of the Local Government will conduce to their reformation and the prevention of crime'.[84] It also mandated that the Prisons Act of 1894 and Prisoners Act of 1900 would apply to a Borstal school 'as if it were a prison and the inmate thereof a prisoner'.[85] In practical terms, this meant that the disciplinary regime of an adult jail could be imposed in the Borstal at the discretion of the Inspector General of Prisons, that the Inspector General could move an incarcerated child to a different Borstal when he saw fit, and that escape from a Borstal was a criminal offence. Terms of detention in the Borstal were to be between two and three years.[86]

This arrangement found favour, or at least acceptance, with Maharaja Kshaunish Chandra Ray of Nadia, who introduced the bill in the Bengal Legislative Council. Ray made no secret of his admiration for the Borstal school, which was derived from a Kentish prototype in which offenders in their upper teens, many of them described as physically and mentally weak, were subjected to a minimum of two years of industrial training, primary education and games.[87] At the end of their detention, the inmates were licensed into the charge of the Borstal Association, a proto-NGO that functioned with some support from the British government. For two probationary years, the association would try to find employment for the former inmates and exercise a general supervision in the capacity of 'friends and helpers'.[88] Addressing the Bengal legislature, Ray described the British Borstal in detail, noted that it 'reformed' seventy percent of its wards, and added, 'Considering the unpromising nature of the material, [seventy percent] is a fairly good achievement.'[89] In the process, he asserted not only his ownership of the law that was being debated and his mastery over a signifier of metropolitan civilization, but also his status as a participant in a supra-colonial and cosmopolitan field of experimentation.

While Ray referred liberally to metropolitan models and experiments, his immediate objectives were closer to home. Specifically, he proposed that existing civil society organizations such as the Discharged Prisoners Aid Societies (DPAS, which rehabilitated released convicts and ensured that they did not disappear from the vision of the state and its affiliates) be transformed into Borstal Associations. This adaptation had already been attempted in Madras, where the Tanjore DPAS had become the Tanjore Borstal Association. In Bengal, the task was apparently larger — the Inspector General of Prisons had already approached the Calcutta Prisoners Aid Society and been told that the Society was ill-equipped for the task — but Ray was confident that the new law would provide a framework within which the Borstal could develop.

The institutional transformation that Ray had in mind, in which a predominantly native district association became a Borstal, was a whitening enabled by the issue of juvenile delinquency — the association 'reformed' itself, presumably more than it reformed the boys in its charge. Yet, old dilemmas lingered among novel experiments. The native authority on juvenile reform found himself (and was able to place himself, not without benefit) in a position of heroic isolation, battling apathy and impossible odds. Envisioning the colonial regime as an ally, Ray appealed to his fellow legislators to 'help me and the Government to organize and build up such a school in this province'.[90]

Ray was supported by a majority of the European members of the Council and by J Campbell Forrester, a member of the Tanjore Borstal Association who had come to Calcutta to share his expertise with the legislators. Forrester called enthusiastically for 'an extension of the present system of conditional release from prison, so that the State may retain control over a lad for a considerable time after his discharge and may resume more complete control by revoking his license if he shows that he is not yet fit for freedom'.[91] Raja Bhupendra Narayan Sinha of Nashipur also backed Ray, but explained his support by arguing that existing reformatory regimes in India were 'soulless', exploitative, unscientific and counterproductive.[92] Other Indian legislators opposed Ray vehemently; to a degree, the clash was a fight between 'rajas' who clung to a precarious loyalism and 'babus' who tended to be dismissive of rajas and others.[93]

As Sanjay Joshi and others have noted, a self-conscious and public grasping for the signifiers of modernity was central to the making of the middle-class in colonial India.[94] The modern reformatory was a platform upon which elite Indian legislators and administrators constructed themselves, insisting that colonial institutions did not provide for childhoods that were adequately modern. These critics did not attack the basic ideas of the Borstal, or other contemporary narratives of juvenile reform. They attacked the colonial context within which juvenile reform was attempted in India. Babu Bijoy Krishna Bose praised 'the idea underlying the Bill', but declared that the proposed law nevertheless had 'numerous defects'. He went on to note that he would have brought these defects to light, had he not been 'muzzled and gagged' by the Legislative Department, which had told him that he could not propose an amendment without first getting the sanction of the Government of India. Bose then elaborated upon the defects that he had perceived, arguing that a single institution at Bankura, with space for two hundred and forty boys, would be grossly insufficient for the Borstal project that was envisioned by the Bill. This inadequacy would inevitably mean that some boys, who would not find space at Bankura, would have to be sent to common jails. Making a pointed jab at Ray, Bose added that the arrangements for 'aftercare' were non-existent in Bengal.[95]

For those who opposed Kshaunish Ray and his allies in the legislative council, the most objectionable part of the Bill was its provision for the use of prison-specific laws in the juvenile institution, or the convergence of the child and the adult in the colonial reformatory. The most articulate of these opponents was Jogindra Chandra Chakravarti, who argued that the Bill merely created new prisons in the name of the reformatory:

> When a young man instead of being sent to jail is detained in a Borstal school...he should at least be made to feel that he is living in an atmosphere which is free from the rigors of a prison life. The indignities generally associated with jail life can hardly conduce to the moral elevation of an individual. If a Borstal school is made only a special prison with this difference that the inmates thereof will have a special training, the necessity of having [a] separate institution for that purpose does not seem to be clear because arrangements for special training in particular arts and industries can be made in jails also.[96]

In closing, Chakravarti — in an 'expert manoeuvre' similar to Ray's — went into some detail about English Borstals, emphasizing how unlike jails they were.

Ray defended himself by retorting that his opponent had lost sight of the 'material' that the colonial government had to work with:

> We cannot surely treat them as mere innocent schoolboys, although the intention of our Bill is reformation by such a method. The school is to be a place of detention for those youngsters who had committed crime. It is regrettable that human language does not enable us...to conceal our object and intentions. The very definition of adolescent offenders gives away the real character of these people and whatever camouflage we may try to adopt, the implication of the inevitable association of ideas cannot be avoided.[97]

Ray thus indicated that he understood how the languages of childhood and adulthood, crime, delinquency and offence, and of school, jail and hospital, all shaped the law, the institution and the inmate. Language could conceal 'true intentions' and 'true character', but, Ray implied, those 'truths' also had to be concealed *from* language for the political and ideological purposes of modernity in a colonial setting.

Such insight did not save his legislative position. When a vote was taken on deleting the clause enabling the use of the Prisons Act and the Prisoners Act in Borstal schools, the pro-deletion side, led by Bose and Chakravarti, won by a count of fifty-three votes to forty-one. All those who voted to delete the clause were Indians, whereas all sixteen Europeans who voted supported the retention of the clause. In the end, the victory of those who wanted a decisive separation between the (adult) jail and the (juvenile) reformatory was short-lived. F S Jackson, the Bengal Governor, intervened to restore the deleted clause to the law.[98]

In the Central Provinces, between 1926 and 1928, we find a variation on the clashes in Bengal. In 1926, the legislature began deliberations on Act IX (1928), a Borstal law that was similar to what was being discussed in Bengal and was intended for the Narsinghpur Jail, which had been modified for use as a Borstal. It became apparent that the maximum term of incarceration was contentious and that the tensions were aligned with the racial make-up of the colonial government. The Government of India and the provincial executive wanted a relatively long maximum sentence, of five or even seven years. Indian legislators involved in drafting the Bill disagreed, arguing that such long terms would 'crush' the child, and pointing out that the maximum period of incarceration in English Borstals was only three years.[99] On this issue, the Indians won a stable victory — the maximum sentence was fixed at three years. As in Bengal, however, they were unable to prevent the application of prison-specific laws to the Borstals that they created.

The legislative debates in Bengal, Madras and the Central Provinces constituted a more aggressive attempt to decolonize the reformatory than the quiet negotiations of the 1880s and 1890s. In the interwar years, elite Indians were confident about their expertise in the field of childhood; they had appropriated not only the discourse of the colonial reformatory, but that of the metropolitan institution as well. Aligning themselves with a fully modern, scientific and medicalized metropolitan expertise facilitated their critique of the flawed modernity of colonial practice. The tension between two closely related colonial projects — the school and the jail — then became inescapable, because one was premised on childhood and mutability, and the other on a relatively immutable adulthood. Comparisons between colonial and metropolitan Borstals, made by natives, carried the accusation that English reformatory discourse was actually a sham, that the colonial reformatory 'school' was actually a jail, and that the British authorities were making illegitimate distinctions between English children (plastic, in school) and native children (hardened, quasi-adult, in jail). In the process, Indian nationalists could imply that the colonial reformatory had deformed the native child by forcing him into the institutional molds of an oppressed adulthood.

The Parent and the Reformatory

The delinquent parent, as much as the child, was a product of the reformatory. From the Napier era onwards, administrators sought to observe, theorize and manipulate the link between child and parent, by alienating the child from its biological parents and exploring the degree to which parenting might be appropriated by experts within the ideological and political constraints of a colonial experiment. The paternal role of the reformatory administrator peaked in the era of Kiplingesque colonialism. The 1898 report from Chingleput declares:

> The perfect understanding and relationship that exist between [the superintendent] Mr Lewis and his pupils form an important factor in the scheme of moral training. He is *in loco parentis* to the unfortunates who are 'far from their homes and aliens from their own friends and relations'. The pupils generally address him as Father [in formal Tamil], and he is always accessible to them. Being able to understand all the vernaculars spoken by the boys, every boy is able to represent his wishes or wants directly to him and receive a hearing. Under him the timid or bashful are cheered on by words of encouragement, the self-willed and forward receive timely check, the wicked meet condign punishment, while the good are adequately rewarded.[100]

The reformatory, in this picture, is dominated by the Great White Father, standing in for native parents who are at best ineffectual. It is not, however, a picture that convinced many and it did not resolve the problem of finding permanent parents for children who had been 'orphaned' by colonialism. Native parents, in fact, were brought back quickly and relocated on the margins of the reformatory as subjects of interrogation themselves. This location on the periphery of criminality, however, also meant that they were not fully restored to a position of authority, either over their children or over themselves, even when the reformatory had been usurped by Indians.

The colonial project of juvenile reform was closely tied to the work of rendering native parents marginal or missing, or the production of literal and rhetorical orphans. This is, in some ways, the reverse of the pattern that Elias identifies in early modern Europe, where child-rearing — defined by Elias as the supervision of a civilizational catching-up — receded from 'society' and came to be concentrated in the hands of parents who had already achieved *civilité*.[101] In India, a racially limited 'society' of experts staked a claim on the offspring of natives who had been rendered static by their ahistorical essence, and were challenged, eventually, by other experts who wanted to locate the child within a reconstituted society.

The missing parents remained visible in the archive of native natures. Thugs who found their way into Sleeman's camps provided colonial administrators in the Jabbalpur region with the first such 'orphans'[102] and others followed as part of the penological expansion that came in the wake of the Mutiny. Midnapore, in 1858–59, saw the development of a school for the children of dacoits, thugs and assorted proscribed communities like Keechaks and Bhudaks that would eventually be targeted by the CT Act.[103] Rivers Thompson, then Governor of Bengal, noted enthusiastically that the twenty-one boys in the school were responding well to their regimen of lessons, examinations, social decorum and prizes, and urged the central government to try out such 'experimental schools' on a larger scale.[104] At the local and provincial levels, institutions designated as 'orphanages' continued to spring up through the early 1860s — a school for girls in Agra, a home for juvenile offenders near Patna run by missionaries named Ribbentrop and Bauman, state run as well as privately run homes for children identified as 'famine orphans', the African Asylum in Karachi. Most children in these institutions had living parents; they had been marginalized by economic calamities, military disasters, criminal prosecution and aggressive missionaries seeking access to the Famine Relief Fund and other sources of government largesse.[105]

There was no immediate response from the Government of India to Thompson's appeal. The school in Midnapore, the older institution for the children of thugs and the various 'orphanages' represented a very rudimentary stage in the formation of a reformatory regime. Even more than the delinquents of Napier's imagined reformatory, the pupils in Midnapore were left in the charge of Indian teachers,[106] indicating the limited scope of the reform intended for the children of native criminals. There was, at this stage, considerable reluctance in the central government and even the provincial bureaucracies to adopt a long term, widely deployable posture of the parental state.[107] Nevertheless, these limited experiments show a convergence of the 'orphan' and the 'juvenile delinquent' at an institutional site that was increasingly under state funding and supervision.

The orphan was not only the cousin of the child offender, but its alter ego — in each case, the removal of the parent had enabled the intervention of other adult agents and left the child creatively destabilized. The breaking of the parental tie, in other words, had disrupted a predictable course of development in the child, opening up the possibility of manipulation and unpredictable harvests of knowledge. The African Asylum, where Somali and Abyssinian children brought to Karachi 'in a state of slavery' were taken by the police beginning in 1856, saw intensive investigations of how African physiologies adapted to the requirements of speaking English, Hindustani and Marathi, learning map reading and European geography, singing hymns and fitting into racialized hierarchies of semi-skilled labor.[108] The new 'parents' were workers of the Church Missionary Society, an organization that would develop a specialization of sorts in colonizing the bodies of native children.[109] The detailed knowledge that the missionaries produced about the physiques, minds and habits of the children, comparing them constantly with

Indians and Europeans, passed into the records of the state, as did the tactics of knowledge-gathering through surrogate parenting.[110]

Similar experiments can be identified in the asylums for European military orphans in India, such as the Lawrence Asylum in Punjab.[111] In most such institutions, 'real' orphans were joined by European and Eurasian children whose parents had dropped off the map of white respectability in the colony.[112] The Home Department was explicit that such children needed to be saved from the fate of moral and physical degeneration induced by exposure to India and Indians. Bureaucrats in the Education Branch did not share the Kipling-Nandy ambivalence about going native[113] and readily cited Lord Canning's view that ambiguously white children in India were 'dangerous to the state[,] a glaring reproach to Government, and to the [Christian] faith'.[114] The desire to rescue children from orphaned dereliction does not, however, mean that 'Indianized English [children], loosely brought up and exhibiting most of the worst qualities of both races' were regarded as useless.[115] Opportunities for studying and adjusting the intersections of climate, race, nature, socio-economic location and political affiliation were plentiful in these proto-reformatories. The orphan could be rendered accepting of filial positions in hierarchies of race, class and power: 'if cared for betimes', the Education Branch noted, '[they] will be a source of strength to British rule and of usefulness to India. They [will] serve the Government…more efficiently than the natives can as yet serve it; they are a class which…is without that deep root in…the soil of India from which our native public servants through their families and relatives derive advantage'.[116]

The reference to the native family is revealing of a perception on the part of interested bureaucrats that the adult relative stood between the native who might be molded into a docile colonial subject and the colonial state that required docility. Nevertheless, the perception did not automatically transform itself into policy. An inclination to protect the privileges of the parent appears early in the colonial reformatory. Bayley, trying to counter Napier's demands for institutions that would remove children from birth families, articulated a forceful notion of parental rights as well as cultural non-intervention. He wrote to R S Ellis in the spring of 1868:

> The ruler has no right to intervene between parent and child, unless the former has abdicated, neglected or abused his functions. It would be both unjust and cruel to interfere in other cases, and where the parent is in any degree respectable, it would probably also be a mistake. No influence which an English official can bring to bear on a convict child for good, is at all comparable in force to parental influence; it is only in default of other protectors, that Government should provide such moral

training as it can for children thrown upon its hands. But by 'moral training' Lord Napier seems to imply...'*Christian* training'; and the suggestion he justifies by a reference to the Government mode of dealing with the 'orphans of famine.' The comparison does not hold good; 'orphans of famine' are orphans in fact; the so-called 'orphans of crime' are...in most case, not orphans at all, but are still really under parental influence.[117] [Emphasis in original]

Bayley saw the desire of pro-reformatory experts to utilize the discourse of the orphan to terminate parental influence as a politically and ideologically dangerous overstepping of the terms of post-Mutiny colonialism, and of 'universal' notions of the sanctity of the family. Just as the progressives like Napier favoured a broad definition of 'orphan' to allow for a wide range of interventionist precedents, conservatives like Bayley and Ellis wanted to distinguish between 'real' orphans (in whose families state intervention might be allowed, however grudgingly) and 'quasi-orphans' (for whom intervention would be limited by parental rights).

Bayley's objections had, however, been anticipated by Napier. In the autumn of 1867, the latter had declared:

I am not able to see more cogency in the objection...that boys confined in a Reformatory would be removed from the influence of their relatives. There are...many juvenile delinquents who have no relatives, and the effect of the Reformatory would be to afford to such the parental solicitude which they never know. In cases in which the juvenile offender has respectable natural protectors...it is still most desirable not to expose him to the contact and atmosphere of older criminals. He ought to be kept under influences as little like those of a Jail as possible. Now, the Reformatory is more like a home than a prison is. Moreover, the father, and especially the mother, would be more likely to visit the child in a Reformatory than in a Jail, and they could be admitted to more frequent and intimate access to the child.[118]

Napier's lack of stridency in promoting a system of child removal is noteworthy. Even as he constructed his reformatory with an explicit parental intent, he showed no determination to shut out birth parents. As an improvised expert in an early stage of the hegemony of expertise, he was able to make such compromises. Bayley, not surprisingly, saw Napier's position as disingenuous. As the reformatory project gathered steam, he and his allies in the bureaucracy — especially Arthur Howell — fought an ideological rearguard action, arguing that following metropolitan notions of expert intervention were unwarranted in India because 'instances of cruelty, neglect or desertion of children by their parents, so common in England, are very rare indeed here'.[119]

By the mid-1870s, it appeared that Bayley, Howell and native parents had all been defeated by men who did not share Napier's hesitations. In Bengal, Lieutenant Governor Richard Temple expressed impatience with officials who resisted his determination to institutionalize adolescents for a minimum of three years or until they reached the age of eighteen (instead of the existing prescription of two years or the age of sixteen).[120] Temple was in no hurry to return incarcerated children to their homes. He was convinced that adolescents, in particular, would not be receptive to a benign parental influence.[121] Parents, in his vision, were powerless compared with institutional settings and their dominant moral agents — jails and convicts (bad), and reformatories and the British (good). In the 1890s, administrators were even more convinced of their superiority as surrogate parents. R S Aikman, a district judge in Mainpuri, urged that 'waifs' whose parents had abdicated their responsibilities (or themselves shown signs of delinquency) be taken into reformatories before they 'lapse into crime'.[122] The nexus of childhood and class retained the delinquent within a kind of original sin, from which parenting could not relocate him. The state, however, could attempt this relocation, armed as it was with the discourses and institutions of expertise.

In the reformatory that emerged from the 1860s, the parent became increasingly incompetent and marginal as the child became older, more complex and more in need of expert management. Failures of parenting and the consequently precocious independence of the child required contradictory responses from the state. On the one hand, the state had to step in as surrogate parent, but on the other, it had to recognize that the precocious child had already forfeited childhood. This contradiction could be resolved by returning the delinquent child to authority, obedience and childhood. Since the parent and the home could not be relied upon to provide these, the reformatory became the last refuge of childhood.

Nevertheless, parents did not vanish. Their presence near the reformatory was necessary to generate knowledge about their unfitness as parents; it was also mandated by the limited nature of colonial modernity, or the reluctance of the institution to absorb totally those it had encircled. Even after the passage of the RS Act, administrators continued to express their doubts about the benefits of cutting children off from their parents. F F Handley, a judge in 24 Parganas, urged Larymore that offending Bengali children be separated from their parents only late in their childhood and for relatively short terms:

> To take a child of ten or eleven from its parents and home surroundings… seriously affects the child's nervous system. Detention for four years is

quite long enough…to teach the boys discipline without breaking off all touch with home ties. It is only necessary to see how the boys and their parents hate a sentence of detention in a reformatory and how glad the boys are to leave it.[123]

Handley saw the parent-child bond as more vital to the native child than to the European. This made him reluctant to break a tie that is biological both in the sense that it is a natal tie, and also in the sense that it is basic to the child's physical health. But expertise generated opposite desires. Handley also showed an inclination to make experimental use of the parental bond to evaluate the effectiveness of the reformatory. The more parents hated it, the better — not only because it indicated successful deterrence, but also because it demonstrated the existence of a counter-morality which justified the reformatory project. In this vision, the reformatory should displace the natal family, but only temporarily and only as long as it took to defeat the revealed counter-morality of the delinquent parent.

Twenty years later, Handley's view had become dominant in Bengal's juvenile reform establishment, with the Legislative Department noting:

[The Lieutenant Governor] observes that children of very tender age are best corrected at home. Except in cases where they belong to a Criminal Tribe, or come of parents habitually criminal, or have been previously convicted themselves, or have from a very early age been employed by professional criminals to assist in the commission of crime — the Bengal Government would fix the minimum age [for institutionalization] at eleven years. In the exceptions the Lieutenant Governor would fix the limit at eight years.[124]

The Bengal government was making a distinction between two kinds of childhood: a relatively innocent one in which family supervision had temporarily lapsed but could be restored with the help of the state, and one marked by a badly damaged innocence, in which the family was itself the contaminating agent. Only in the latter case was the state to intervene early and supplant the family as the nurturing agent.

The Politics of Parenting

In spite of widespread concern that poor parenting was a factor in juvenile delinquency, Behlmer has noted, magistrates in England were reluctant to remove children from their families for extended periods.[125] Even as British discourse became less grounded in class and more focused upon an indictment of childhood itself, the culpability of parents in the crimes of their children diminished further. In colonial India, where pockets of native society remained suspiciously marginal to the moral and political circle of British rule, there was before the 1920s no corresponding movement away from a criminality that was rooted in readily identifiable cultural units, including the family. A M Dallas, the Inspector General of Prisons in Punjab, was explicit in his perception of the problem:

> The children concerned in the crimes are not the only persons to blame — they are urged on to them by their parents. Until, therefore, they can be for a lengthened period removed from these pernicious influences, it is vain to hope that they will be deterred…from the committal of crime.[126]

A successful reformatory regime in the Indian cultural environment therefore required a constant, prolonged segregation of juveniles from families and adult criminals, so that the state and its allies could bring their influence to bear upon captive children, create models of the native subordinate and the insubordinate native, and generate a discourse of the native family and inferior parenting without competition from adults with different moral and political agendas. Indian agendas, however, proved difficult to ignore. On the one hand, Indian observers of this intervention in the native family resented the intrusion and the critiques; on the other, they sought to position themselves in the roles of intruders and critics, and to exclude Europeans from the processes by which a post-colonial relationship between child, family and state might be delineated.

In 1928, the Central Provinces legislature passed a general law for the treatment of juvenile offenders — the Central Provinces Children Act, or Act X. Seeking to improve upon the RS Act of 1897, the framers of the new law — all but one of whom were Indians — adjusted the boundaries of reformable childhood. A 'child' was now defined as being under the age of fourteen, a 'youthful offender' was younger than sixteen years old and a 'young person' was between fourteen and sixteen.[127] Quite apart from restructuring the language by which a child might be precisely identified and correctly punished, the law also specified a set of links between the family, juvenile delinquency and the reforming state. Before discussing the implications of the law, it is worth examining its particulars.

Act X authorized police to bring before the court (including but not limited to juvenile courts) children and young persons 'not subject to proper care and supervision'. That phrase included any child who

> is found wandering and has no home, settled place of abode or visible means of subsistence; or is found wandering and has no parent or other

guardian, or, in the case of an illegitimate child, his mother or other guardian is undergoing transportation or imprisonment; or is under the care of a parent or guardian who, by reason of criminal or drunken habits, is unfit to have the care of such person; or frequents the company of any reputed thief or prostitute; or is lodging or residing in a house used by a prostitute for the purposes of prostitution.[128]

Courts were permitted to ask the parents of such children to pay security bonds (reformatories awaited children whose parents had no money), to show cause why their children should not be removed from them, to send the children to reformatories and industrial schools, or to place the children in the custody of alternative guardians (including relatives) until they turned sixteen.

The law also criminalized specific 'offences against children', penalizing any parent or guardian who 'abandons, exposes or wilfully neglects or ill-treats such child or young person in a manner likely to cause...unnecessary suffering or injury to his health'. Negligence included the wilful failure to provide food, clothing, shelter and medical care. At the same time, the Act was explicit that parents and guardians did have the right to 'administer punishment'. The use of children for begging was criminalized, as was being drunk while in charge of a child under age of seven, giving alcohol to children, encouraging children to gamble, accepting pawned articles from anybody under the age of sixteen, and allowing a child (of either sex) to live in or frequent a brothel.[129]

Police were authorized to take children who had been victimized in any of the above ways temporarily to 'places of safety', which were defined as 'any orphanage, hospital, surgery or other suitable place or institution, or...in the case of a male child or young person only, a police station'. Judges who had information about the ongoing victimization of children were authorized to 'cause the child or young person to be arrested and then detained in a place of safety'. Parents were required to attend their children's court hearings, unless the mother was prevented by 'the customs or manners of the country'. Reformatory regimes were also modified along the lines of gender and race — inspectors were to be men (except in institutions for girls, which did not exist in the Central Provinces), all reformatories were to instruct their inmates in their respective religions and court-appointed guardians were either to be coreligionists of their wards, or to promise to educate the child in its own religion.[130]

Act X was thus a large, sweeping measure, part renovation and part innovation. With its attempt to shut European women, Christians and others out of the reforming process, it was an attempt by the authentically national to assert their claim on surrogate parenting. Some old tools of the reformatory acquired new uses: while advocating religious education, the Indian legislator-moralists were less concerned with constructing discrete communities than with asserting discrete communal identities, and critiquing the miscegenating/proselytizing reputation of colonial institutions. The law was also an assertion of disciplinary confidence, i.e. of expertise. The different ages at which children were legally protected from exposure to alcohol, prostitution, gambling, etc. showed an inclination to define childhood differently depending upon the moral context. The definitive innocence of the child was no longer a uniform quality. It had become reliant upon particular stages of the parent-child relationship. The law was, in fact, an ambitious attempt to expand the idea of delinquency, to connect it with parenting and to bring both under the management of a partially decolonized state. It reconfirmed the birth parent as a delinquent that must be brought under juridical supervision, and simultaneously recreated the victimized child as a delinquent (and *vice versa*) in need of rescue.

The manoeuvre and its concomitant merger of rescue and arrest allowed for a much wider discursive, judicial and institutional net than earlier administrators had been willing to create. Victimized children were easier to find than children who had actually been convicted, especially in criminalized adult milieus such as the brothel or the gambling house. If delinquents were defined as the victims of parents who were themselves constituted as delinquent, then there were many more delinquents. Ironically, a legal-institutional mechanism of delinquency that had first been imagined in the 1860s, with the children of the CTs at its centre,[131] was realized only in 1928, when the idea of large criminal communities had been eroded and Indians had substantially taken over the making of child-correction policy. It is, however, a comprehensible irony. The requirement that parents attend their children's court hearings, for instance, carried a pedagogical function within a middle-class attempt to shape a set of national norms. It constituted an attempt to teach a new relationship between child, parents and state, privileging a strikingly nuclear family and its relationship with the judging/punishing state.

Parents were not, however, crushed into penal fodder by the 1928 law and here, the racial Self of the lawmakers is apparent. Act X created a more bureaucratic, but also a more individualized system for state intervention in the native family. In her perceptive study of punished bodies, Anderson has noted that colonial prisons created individuals as well as the collectives within which they might be located.[132] She has explained this in terms of the British obsession with caste, but historicizing the relationship between the incarcerated individual and the delinquent community requires sensitivity to the evolving political context of colonial punishment. As nationally identified Indians took over the prison, parents were viewed more as individuals with natural claims upon the child, than as representatives of proscribed social groups. In the process, the offending unit of native society became the particular family, rather than the tribe/caste. It is not a coincidence that probationary mechanisms expanded quickly from the 1920s onwards, and that probation officers were instructed to pay close attention to the 'home conditions' — and not the communal conditions — of the children in their charge.[133] References to communal criminality did not become extinct, but they became the ideologically hollow means of casting a wider penal net, reflecting a decay in the discourse of the criminal collective.[134] With the emergence of the individually delinquent parent, the exclusion of entire communities had become less urgent. There is, at this point, a discernible movement towards the metropolitan model of parent-state relations.

In the mid-1890s, when the Legislative Department was drafting the amended RS Bill, such a movement was assumed by colonial administrators to be impossible. Officials across the country undertook surveys of 'native opinion' on the issue of juvenile delinquency and reformatory procedures. Such attempts to gauge the views of the colonized elite had become common practice in the formulation of 'social' legislation in the decades after 1857, and when the initial RS Act had been prepared in the 1870s the government had sought to 'consult such leading members of the Hindoo and Mohammadan communities as are likely to take an interest in the subject'.[135] In the 1890s, as on the previous occasion, the provincial surveys threw up a confounding mixture of indifference, support and obstruction for a legislative measure that promised to remove children from parents and associate them with strangers.

The reports that filtered into the Northwest Provinces and Oudh administration are typical. J S Mackintosh, the Commissioner of Lucknow, reported with frustration that he had found it extremely difficult to 'ascertain the native view of the Reformatory question', because Indians neither knew nor cared about reformatories.[136] Similar reports were filed by P Gray (District Magistrate of Lucknow), H M Bird (Magistrate of Allahabad), and J Hooper (Acting Commissioner of Allahabad).[137] A W Trethewy, the Collector of Kanpur, however, reported that 'native opinion is in favour of Reformatory Schools', as long as it did not associate the children of the respectable with the offspring of professional criminals.[138] In Allahabad, Bird qualified his remark about indifference by noting that those Indians who did take an interest in the experiment were in favor of reformatories. Hooper also declared that 'the more intelligent ones whom I consulted' were enthusiastic, and added that they were especially keen that the thieving children of the 'criminal and quasi-criminal classes' be locked up, provided that they were kept separate from the children of the respectable.

These complicated conversations cannot be taken at face value. Trethewy chose a particular set of Indians, phrased his questions carefully, and then interpreted the answers according to his own categories. When his correspondents expressed anxiety about the contamination of their children by 'professional criminals', they may have been thinking in terms of class or caste, whereas Trethewy would have heard an echo of the colonial fear of the CT. The *Gopal/rakhal* dichotomy that Shivaji Bandyopadhyay has noted in Bengali children's literature indicates that some Indian elites had constructed their own delinquent child in the countryside,[139] but even if a central-Indian equivalent of the *rakhal* existed dialogically with the CT child, they cannot be assumed to be coterminous. They expressed different desires and anxieties; they spoke, and were spoken in, different languages.[140] Given the difficulties of 'translating' across such differences of language, class and culture,[141] it is unlikely that the 'intelligent' Indians who communicated with Trethewy and Hooper accepted the argument that reformatories were prisons for the 'better sort' of juvenile offender, and that officially demarcated CTs were a class apart from those redeemable children who might be sent to the reformatory. They would have seen them as parts of a generalized population of the children of social inferiors and troublemakers, worth segregating from the children of 'gentlemen', but hardly from each other. Trethewy's reading of native 'favour' is therefore unreliable. The remarks by Bird and Hooper that those interested were also in favor indicates the tautological nature of 'favour' and 'interest' — the issue was framed in such a way that it was impossible to be both interested and opposed.

Yet opposition there was, because the native gentlemen were telling the experts that the reformatory was, at the most, a dumping ground for the incorrigible children of those who existed on the margins of respectability : the children of the Others. It is useful to look closely at Mackintosh's report from Lucknow. The Commissioner wrote:

> The main idea underlying the English Reformatory system seems to be that where a youthful criminal either has no relatives or where his relatives are of such a class that it is not likely that they will bring him up decently, it is better, instead of giving him a short term of imprisonment, to sentence him to a long term of years in a Reformatory. The main object...is to separate the youthful criminal from his family, and ultimately to give him a fresh start in life. This principle is entirely opposed to all Indian feeling and religion. A man who deliberately cuts himself off from his family, however worthless that family may be, is looked upon much in the light of a pariah dog. It is thought that to live with one's own family — and there is almost no native of India who has not a home and relatives, though he may have lost his parents — is better for a youth than to spend any number of years in Reformatories in on European

principles and plans and supervised by European officers. It is usually thought that the best plan of dealing with [convicted juveniles] is to make them over to their families on security, and that their families will take care that they are properly punished. The above is what appears to be the general view…taken by educated and intelligent natives.[142]

Obviously, the reformatory had generated skepticism not only in 'native opinion', but also in white administrators' opinion of native opinion. Mackintosh perceived an ideological clash between English morality and Indian perversity; radically different views of the relationship between individual, family and society; disagreement about the roles and relative effectiveness of the native family and the alien state as agents of reform; and to some extent, a conflict between reason and 'habit'. Much of this tension is the apparent inability of native parents to see youthful delinquency as a distinct condition that must be treated in specialized institutions. This reflected an indifference towards the liberal faith in the ability of institutions to transform the nature of the individual. Moreover, in the view of even those Indians who were 'educated and intelligent', the *budmashi* of the child was either childishness (which fades with childhood), or the early sign of an abiding *budmashi* that would persist into adulthood. In neither case was there a sense that childhood is a peculiar moment of peril and opportunity, when the juvenile *budmash* might (and must) be corrected, so as to pre-empt the emergence of the adult *budmash*. Mackintosh, however, also perceived that because the idea of the corrupting family was alien to India, institutions based on segregation from the family and aimed at creating individuals largely autonomous of the native family would be either resisted or ignored.

Mackintosh himself was not hostile to the idealized images of native familiality — an ambivalence not rare in colonial bureaucrats who tried to sustain the family ties of institutionalized children even as they sought to assert their supervision over those ties.[143] By the mid-1890s, when Mackintosh conducted his survey, reformatory administrations in the Northwest Provinces and Oudh permitted parental visits, and parents of sick children had acquired additional access to their sons.[144] These were significant departures from the reformatory that had imposed itself between parent and convicted child in 1876. In the 1890s, the native parent had become an undeniable material and discursive presence at the doorstep of the reformatory, in the blank space that had been vacated by the progenitor of the colonial orphan and not completely filled by the expert and the state. While it was not yet a 'national' parent, it was nevertheless defined by a willingness to articulate its opposition to the parental priorities of the expert state.

Parents and Rehabilitation

The native adult that materialized in the reformatory was a schizophrenic entity: it was present in the discourse as an absence from the lives of its children, but it also gained substance as an active agent of corruption. The absent parent and the corrupting parent required different determinations of whether the expert should suspend, terminate or reinforce the authority of family members. Negligent parents could conceivably be 'reformed' like the child itself, but corrupting parents had to be permanently separated from their offspring. In India, until the innovations of the late 1920s, a single set of legal and institutional measures were expected to deal with both realities. This reflected and shaped the chronic uncertainty among administrators about the colonial state's relationship with the offending native family, both during and after the punishment of the child. Within this uncertainty, a historical curve — by no means regular or uninterrupted — can be identified, beginning with a suspension of the active involvement of the parent in the life of the juvenile offender and progressing towards a rediscovery of the parent, a reassertion of the legitimacy of familial authority over the child, and the reinforcement of that authority by the state. The last step, in particular, was vital to the idea of rehabilitation. The state, however, could reinforce the family only when it achieved a degree of identification with the relatives of the child — a step that was beyond the ideological abilities of the colonial regime.

In the 1860s, when the discourse of the 'orphan' was still prominent in the reformatory, juvenile candidates for institutionalization were perceived by experts as victims not so much of harmful parenting as of non-parenting. In the mid-1870s, however, non-parenting was partially supplemented by a new emphasis on antiparenting.[145] Both visions of the delinquent parent are perceptible in the remarks of J D Gordon, the Judicial Commissioner of Mysore, who softened his opposition to the first RS Act by assuring his superiors that he supported the disruption of the family 'if the [child] belongs to the criminal classes, such as the Kormurs, Korchurs, Lumbanees, or what are called the Street Arab class, or if the offender has no parents or guardians, or has been deserted by them, or if there is reason to believe that the offence has been committed at the prompting of parents'.[146]

In the 1890s, experts continued to highlight the actively delinquent adult, showing less interest in the missing. In a period of heightened interest in the mechanisms by which criminality is transmitted across generations, the Bengal government urged the Legislative Department to provide for the institutionalization of very young children, whose actual involvement in specific crimes was ambiguous but whose parents' proclivities seemed straightforward, writing that it was 'the duty of Government to endeavour to rescue such children from criminal courses, the result entirely of their association with criminal parents'.[147] In the 1920s, however, with juvenile crime redefined as an urban phenomenon, the family was in some danger of becoming entirely ethereal as the delinquency of children was located in their bodies and in urbanity itself.[148] The loss of materiality posed the problem of rehabilitation — to whom might the child be returned? — that Indian experts were able to resolve ideologically and legally by differentiating between 'good' and 'bad' relatives, recovering the former for reinforcement and the latter for punishment.

A relationship between geography and bad parenting can be identified within these fluctuating emphases. While delinquent parents were actively corrupting in the countryside (where, from the 1870s on, Criminal Tribes lurked), their counterparts in the city (which was marked by the echoed discourse of the Street Arab) were delinquent by virtue of their absence from the lives of their children. The lack of parents made the urban juvenile delinquent potentially incorrigible. The juvenile member of a CT was worse precisely when the opposite was true, i.e. when he had parents. In the countryside there appeared a surfeit of perverse parental agency for administrators to confront and displace: gangs of parents and the gang-as-parent. As Lyall remarked in 1874:

> We want some way of detaching the children of the thieving tribes, when they are caught, from the parent gang. Now and then a whole covey is caught and lodged in jail. We can't teach them morals, as we have no religious agency at hand; but I still think we might do more toward providing them with an occupation and a settled life.[149]

Such provision was difficult to organize when parents appeared uninterested in the reform of their children, as was often the case with urban delinquents. In 1892, the superintendent of the Chingleput reformatory lamented that children were often released into the care of relatives who abandoned their charges.[150] W F Thomas found himself confronted by a dilemma: he saw the family as a malignant moral influence that threatened to reverse the effects of the reformatory, but he had no doubt that without reintegration into a social and economic world untouched by the stigma of punishment, the child reverted by definition to being a delinquent.[151] As late as 1928, prison reformers in Burma declared that 'owing either to the shiftlessness of the parents, [or] the undesirable nature of the home surroundings, a delinquent child cannot suitably be left in the parent's or guardian's home'.[152]

Thomas' dilemma was, however, also partially resolved in the 1920s. When the family was restored to the life of the rehabilitated juvenile delinquent in the interwar period, parents were not necessarily key players in the reintegration. Rather, children were 'returned' to other family members, whose authority was then bolstered by newly powerful agents of the state, such as probation officers and juvenile courts. This, in effect, was the solution that Indian legislators and professionals devised to the problem of the relationship between the state and the family in the life of the delinquent child — the Indian family could actually be protected by the marginalization of the delinquent parent.

The Indian legislators who shaped the Children Acts and Borstal laws in Madras, Bengal and the Central Provinces did not share Bayley's qualms about cultural interference; with their location in race, class and expertise, they owned the culture that required their expert intervention. At the same time, they were unwilling to engage in blanket criticisms of the social environment in which the child might be rehabilitated, although their own identification with this environment was contextual at best. C S Devadhar and S Rangnekar, who oversaw probation schemes at the Dharwar Borstal and the Sholapur reformatory in the 1930s and 1940s, consistently attempted to place children with older birth relatives when the boys were released on license (probation), indicating a perception that reform includes the preservation and resuscitation of the family tie.[153] This was superficially aligned with metropolitan practice and reinforced the Indians' attempt to follow a 'universal' expertise.[154]

The new friendship between the expert and the native family coexisted with a chronic conflict between juvenile courts and probation officers on the one hand, and the parents of released children on the other. Parents were routinely described as uncooperative, obstructive, difficult and 'of doubtful character', especially when probation officers interfered in the employment of their sons and the marriages of their daughters.[155] Since marriage was a site of the authority of adult family members, parents resented the state's attempt to capture it. For their part, probation officers saw birth parents as unreliable and competing influences that complicated the process of teaching models of adulthood that were appropriate to class and gender.

This tension had surfaced as soon as probation became systematized under the new reformatory laws of the 1920s — in 1922, Burma's Departmental Committee on Probation had observed that probation derived its value from 'influence which a man or woman of strong personality may exercise over one of weaker or immature character'.[156] The 'immature character' could be the parent, relative to the probation officer, as easily as it could be the child, relative to the parent or probation officer. This formulation made conflict with parents almost inevitable. Over the next two decades, few 'successful' licensees were returned to their parents anywhere in British India, and 'domestic life' was routinely cited as a factor in the criminality of those whose probation had apparently failed.[157] Thus, the family tie was both valued as a part of a healthy childhood that does not end when the child has graduated from the state institution, and altered through state intervention. As delinquency became individualized, an increasingly Indianized state became better equipped to make distinctions between bad parents and good relatives, and more ideologically invested in those distinctions.

Conclusion

The colonial reformatory was a modernizing experiment with material that was not intended to leave the periphery of modern society. The children, the parents and even the experts it produced existed at a distance from the 'real thing': the orphan, the delinquent, the specialist, true public opinion, metropolitan example, the citizen and so on. This distance marked native children and colonial experts as species in their own right, safe from the intervention of metropolitan child reformers. It did not, however, protect them indefinitely, because metropolitan references could be accessed and deployed effectively by those Indian elites who partially inherited the reformatory in the years after the First World War. For these elites, the distance from metropolitan models was a metaphor of the central deception of liberal colonialism — the 'not yet' premise that restricted them to the margins of political power and racial worth.[158] The native child offender and his parents were transformed by this political misalignment, becoming increasingly individual in their identity and delinquency. They did not become absorbed into the national circle of those who had usurped the reformatory, excluded as they were by the middle class' broad acceptance of the dominant British reading of the relationship between class and criminality. For the same middle-class Indians, however, the delinquent child became a symbol of a national Self that might be 'corrected' and recovered from the damage done by the non-modernity of subaltern parents and the false modernity of colonial rule.

2

THE NATURE OF THE BEAST: THE CONTENT OF INSTITUTIONALIZED CHILDHOOD

Alongside the expert on native children, the colonial reformatory produced the native child, or at any rate, a widening set of arguments about its boundaries, content and varieties. Childhood was partially delinked from age, and constructed with reference to a 'nature' that was revealed by encounters with the judicial system and articulated in terms of plasticity and hardness. By interrogating nature, child-correction professionals sought to differentiate the plastic child (that might be detained) from the hardened adult (that must be rejected or released). The hardness or plasticity of nature was reflected in the inmate's natal society, in the crime itself, in the punishment, in the response to punishment, in sexual behaviour and in the juvenile body. Between child and adult, in the 1920s as in the 1860s, there existed not so much a line as a process — a zone of discipline, investigation and uncertainty. The reformatory, along with experimental concepts such as adolescence and precocity, lay within this gap of productive uncertainty.

As a penal institution, the juvenile reformatory was of course a part of the 'carceral archipelago' of colonial India. Its inmates entered not only as children but also as criminals. The two categories are closely related — Nasaw has pointed out that the pedagogical focus of modern child-saving requires the construction of children as delinquents.[1] Due to the fact that nineteenth-century colonial discourses of native criminality placed great emphasis on crime as a communal identity, and because the child was assumed to be a sponge that absorbed and replicated parental influence, the reformatory provided penal administrators with unique opportunities to study, and disrupt, the processes by which criminality was transmitted. Even in the heyday of H H Risley and biological-racial perspectives on native deviance,[2] the colonial reformatory preserved a faith in social mechanisms of character formation, because the hardness of the biologically determined adult native was substantially balanced by the malleability of the child.

There can be little doubt that the reformatory experts' attempt to isolate the processes by which children inherited their criminal tendencies was a successful project. It could hardly fail, since 'success' was measured by the quantity of knowledge produced. A broad generalization might be made about pre-war expectations of the child, the institution, heredity and external influence. Before the juvenile offender entered the reformatory, his character (an identifying stability of habit, as it was subsequently constructed by penal administrators) was essentially that of his social environment. Within the reformatory, the offender was defined by the plasticity of the child, or the absence of character. (If he demonstrated something approaching character, he compromised his childhood and was liable to be transferred to jail, and that transfer was itself a worthwhile revelation.) When the offender left the reformatory, he again acquired a character and an adulthood of sorts — one that had been fostered by the colonial institution, one picked up from native society upon release, one that had survived colonial intervention, or one that had been acquired illicitly within the children's prison. The reformatory, in this scheme of things, was a space where character might be suspended or rendered fluid, so that the questions of inheritance could be reopened.

An abiding ambivalence within the colonial reformatory was whether it was in fact an institution for delinquent children, or whether its inmates were merely young criminals. The criminal and the delinquent are different creatures,[3] and child-correction experts in India struggled to decide whether the offences of their wards could be managed as delinquency. In the process, the reformatory and the child inmate became sites of investigation into marginality in native society. Where might the delinquent be located within and without the institution? A significant subsection of colonial child-correction administrators believed that delinquent children did not belong in the reformatory, because their 'habitual' criminal tendencies would inevitably defeat the adults and infect other children. Like the child of the criminalized community, the 'habitual' child was constructed as quasi-adult and consigned to the margins of the juvenile institution. Their marginal status was enormously productive as a source of knowledge about children, criminals and the possibilities of colonialism. At the same time, debates on whether unconvicted children should be routinely institutionalized on the basis of criminal habits (as opposed to acts) were generally unresolved. An experiment initiated as a demonstration of colonial authority and an investigation of difference was, once again, a self-limiting project. In the early decades of the reformatory, certainly, delinquency was too modern and metropolitan a concept to apply to native society, and the limited encounters between white adults and native children served to underscore the importance of preserving the peripheral location of a colonial discourse.

The last phenomenon is evident when adolescents who committed thefts and other offences while out on probation were labelled 'confirmed criminals' incapable of making 'progress,' and sent from Borstal schools to jail over the protests of Indian legislators.[4] The accelerated, premature adulthood is also, paradoxically, a condition of stasis, i.e. an inability to progress. In this sense, the premature adult is frozen in a permanently unreasoning, childish state. The reformatory could thus produce not only the native child, but also its adult versions and counterparts — occasionally the useful subject and a model of citizenship, but more often the criminal, the delinquent, the precocious and the retarded.

Before the passage of the first RS Bill, it was already apparent to experts that the reformatory might actually close the distance between the child and the adult criminal. The Heeley-Mackenzie-Lambert committee on juvenile punishment had observed in 1874:

> The actual desideratum is an institution for confining juvenile criminals who have so conducted themselves that, if they were adult, they might be brought under [Section 504 of] the Code of Criminal Procedure, which provides for the exaction of security from persons of bad repute and character. The [existing] law is defective, [in] that reformatory treatment is confined to those who have committed an offence, while imprisonment is frequently given in the case of adults to persons who have not been convicted of any special offence, but who are...without ostensible means of subsistence, or...by repute robbers or thieves or of notoriously bad livelihood. Such persons, when children, are quite as suited for a reformatory as any others, and the interference of the State with them is quite as much justified. Even in England, where the doctrine of liberty of the subject is perhaps pushed as far as in any country, such persons are placed under control by the law.[5]

In this vision, the reformatory not only reified a particular vision of the child, but bridged an existing gap between the child and the adult delinquent. By doing so, it furnished the state with the legal and institutional mechanisms for converting the child into a counterpart of the adult delinquent. By claiming that juvenile delinquents and assorted unconvicted adult prisoners were essentially the same individuals at different stages of their lives, the committee was able to affiliate the reformatory with other colonial institutions for dealing with problem populations. English precedents were brought into the frame of reference, but without conceding that the problem was identical.

In the 1890s, the convergence of the native adult and child as inmates of colonial penal institutions continued even as the child acquired an increasingly separate identity as an object of knowledge and legislation. As the Legislative Department prepared the amended RS Bill, it shied away from creating a rigid definition of juvenile offender, noting that 'elaborate definitions are very dangerous' because they tended to be exclusive.[6] This inclination had informed the original law also. The RS Act of 1876 had originated in a highly open-ended definition of juvenile offender, incorporating a fear of adult habitual criminals, the peripatetic and those without legitimate work, downplaying guilt in favour of delinquency, and reflecting the tendency to rely upon reputation and association in constructing criminality.[7] By refusing to move away from this relatively unsegregated definition of the child offender, the legislators of 1897 chose not to distance children from the institutional world of the criminalized adult. That this was very much a phenomenon of the periphery was acknowledged by at least one lawmaker (A E Miller), following a discussion in which his colleague S Harvey James argued that in the English law that inspired the existing Indian RS Act, curative detention in the reformatory was clearly distinct from the deterrent objective of imprisonment.[8] Miller responded, 'It is clear that a reformatory is not a prison. Whether [an Indian] Reformatory School is a reformatory is not so clear.'[9]

Provincial and district level administrators agreed with Miller, especially when children in their reformatories exhibited quasi-adult characteristics. The Chief Commissioner's office in Burma was unequivocal:

> When an inmate of a Reformatory School commits a fresh offence and is sent before a Criminal Court for punishment, it is in most cases clear *ex hypothesi* that reformatory discipline has failed in his case and that the proper place for him is the criminal jail. In this respect...there are not sufficient grounds for treating youthful offenders differently from adults.[10]

Distinguishing between adults and children in such circumstances not only revealed a failure of knowledge, but it also undermined the colonial state's power to punish effectively. D Duncan, Director of Public Instruction in Madras and a frequent inspector of the Chingleput reformatory, agreed that children with unchildlike 'habits' were better suited to the prison than to the reformatory, although Duncan was eager to utilize his expertise to discriminate between habits: habitual property criminals might possess a dormant childhood that he could revive, whereas the habitually sexual were too adult to benefit from his intervention.[11]

The refusal to make a decisive separation between the punishment of children and that of adults, and the inclination to use courts and reformatories to discover new 'adult' qualities in the child offender that would warrant his incarceration in jail, continued into the 1920s, and even the overtly modernizing

Jails Committee of 1922 did not deviate significantly from the pattern. While the committee and its correspondents agreed generally that juveniles should not be sent to jail, the conviction was superficial, with serious reservations persisting below the surface about whether metropolitan models of separate punishment were applicable in India and to native children.[12] The committee members' expectations of the reformed adult that might be produced by the reformatory actually served to exclude large numbers of children from the juvenile institution, sending them directly into prison — deformity and 'weak intellect', for instance, were identified as qualities that could not only render the child resistant to reforming influence (and thus unchildlike), but also render the future adult economically useless (and ironically, childlike). Under the circumstances, when Indian professionals and legislators moved to widen the distance between the incarcerated child and adult offenders, it constituted a partial decolonization of the reformatory.

Broadly speaking, captive children provided European observers with opportunities and specimens for investigations of the nature of the native, which could be filtered from the natures of the universal child and of the delinquent. While nature was not necessarily envisioned as congenital, it nevertheless possessed a biological component: it was widely assumed that children passed through a stage when plasticity was lost and social inheritance congealed into biological nature. This nature could be laid bare if experts in the reformatory investigated whether native childhood was marked by innocence, the loss of innocence, the absence of innocence, or the positive presence of something dark and cunning.

The innocence of the native was, perhaps obviously, not an unambiguous or apolitical virtue, and the imperative that it be preserved was at odds with the imperative of reform. This brings us to a critical tension within the reformatory. The experts in the colony could not agree whether their experiment was intended to mold deviant children into a redeemed adulthood, or to recover deviant quasi-adults into a redeemed childhood. The pervasive uncertainty about the impact of incarceration upon the native child was, however, not entirely frustrating. The results of the experiment were sometimes unknowable, and that absence of knowledge could be pleasurable. The child who left the reformatory and vanished into the jungle of native society could be imagined as a native upon whom the colonial institution had left a mark, and it was pleasing to envision that mark as redeeming, rather than corrupting or inconsequential.

Marginality

As the reformatory project gathered steam in the 1860s and 1870s, colonial administrators felt compelled to ask — and occasionally to answer — just which children were 'delinquent' in India. While the bureaucracy hesitated to embrace an expansive vision of delinquency, they flirted constantly with the idea that large numbers of Indians were in fact predisposed towards criminal behaviour without having committed a specific criminal act. They identified various discursive and institutional spaces where the Indian child offender might be found, including the Criminal Tribe (CT) in the countryside, an urban jungle inhabited by 'habitual' criminals, and the reformatory itself. Together and separately, these were the margins that promised to reveal the nature of the native child, the native criminal and the native.

By the end of the 1850s, when R E Ravenshaw was campaigning for a school for the children of dacoits and other administrators were engaged in institutionalizing European and African orphans, four kinds of marginality had been established within the discourse of Indian child offenders.[13] These were the marginality of all children in the world of adults, the marginality of native children (including delinquents) in the world of ideal (European) children, the marginality of criminalized children in the world of children, and the marginality of the incorrigible child in the world of criminalized children. When the first RS Act went into effect, these marginalities overlapped, albeit imperfectly, with more concrete bureaucratic categories which were created for children who were to be the inmates of the new institutions. The Northwest Provinces administration noted that reformatory was best utilized in the correction of '(1) the offspring of habitual criminals, (2) children driven to crime by want, (3) children guilty of crimes arguing great depravity, and (4) children of respectable parents guilty of crimes not indicating great depravity.'[14] While this reflected an attempt to create a rationally differentiated model of native delinquency, it also underlined a perception that some child offenders were more marginal than others. For the most part, in spite of the existence of the second category, colonial child-correction experts had little interest in exploring the relationship between poverty and crime.[15] Overwhelmingly, they were interested in children whose offences were rooted not in mundane economic misfortune, but in their normative social environments, and in the circumstances of biology. Also, as in penal transportation, depravity — understood as the combination of opprobrium and incorrigibility, and thus a fact of nature — was associated with property crimes rather than with violence.[16]

The children of CTs constituted the fifth, unstated client of the reformatory, because although they were officially excluded from the institution, they were in fact present conceptually as well as physically. The reformatory administrators' concern with inherited criminal tendencies was derived substantially from the discourse of the criminal tribe.[17] This was not only because the children of criminalized communities were sometimes seen as natural candidates for incarceration in the reformatory, but also because the CT provided a model of delinquency, intervention and salvation[18] that could conceivably be applied to a wider category of offending children, including those that had not actually committed a crime, and those that had completed their punishments but not their childhood.

As the RS Bill took shape in the mid-1870s, A C Lyall had speculated that the institutionalization of the children of the CTs was essential for the success of the child reform project.[19] Disagreeing vehemently, Bayley had responded:

> Everybody knows that in India certain classes of crime are hereditary among certain tribes. Among 'Pasis', 'Sansis', 'Boureahs' and such like, and even among the slightly more respectable classes, such as 'Goojurs', 'Minas', 'Meos', etc. it is almost morally certain that from nine in ten, to ninety nine in one hundred of the children of the tribe are being trained to evil courses of some sort. If we are entering on a system of reformatory action, is it logical to confine ourselves to the rare cases in which, as Mr Lyall describes it, a 'covey' of men, women, and children are lodged in jail? The real excuse in such a case is not their *specific crime* [emphases in original], but the general character of the tribe, and the tribal character of those at liberty is quite as bad as those arrested by an accident. I can understand a sweeping measure of taking away and educating the children of all criminal tribes declared by law to be such, but I doubt if Government would be prepared to accept such a policy, or to face the practical difficulties of putting it in force.[20]

The spat between Bayley and Lyall is about the scope and the practicality of the experiment; it is also a disagreement about the illegality of delinquency. Both agree that CT children ought to be institutionalized, but they disagree about the circumstances. Lyall is optimistic because he wanted to 'detach' relatively small numbers of children who had actually broken the law. Bayley proceeds from the assumption that it would, in theory, make sense to remove all CT children from their parents and place them in reformatories, because education might erase their inherited delinquency. While this vision of wholesale child removal from delinquent communities foreshadows, in some ways, the state-sponsored kidnapping of Aboriginal children in Australia,[21] Bayley is pessimistic — India is politically not Australia, and Bayley is himself shocked by this 'logical' extension of the scope of the colonial reformatory. In other words, Bayley is reluctant to sanction reformatories because he believed that CT children do belong in the reformatory and that it is practically and perhaps morally impossible to place them there. (The moral hesitation is based on Bayley's sense of the rights of the parent, rather than those of the child. The coexisting beliefs in collective criminality and individual rights — an early version of the conflict between a 'discourse of policy' and a 'discourse of rights'[22] — generated much of the paralysis that marks Bayley's attitude towards the colonial reformatory.)

While CT children continued to be officially excluded from the reformatory in the 1890s, the modular applicability of the CT only grew, and local rules proliferated in open violation of the broader proscription. F W Edgerton, the Deputy Commissioner of Sialkot, declared that he and his colleagues believed the exclusion of CT children to be misguided and shortsighted:

> The separation of youthful members of Criminal Tribes from the degrading influence of their parents is the only method by which it may be hoped to reclaim these tribes at some future date. The Sansi, Pakhiwara, Harni or Bhat removed from the influence of tribal traditions would…become a useful member of society, and when the present generation has dies out…the Government would find itself relieved of the responsibility of maintaining criminal *kots* and of the determination of a social problem of great and increasing difficulty, viz. what is to be done with the Criminal Tribes eventually when their population is increasing, the land of their villages insufficient for their support, and when all efforts at reclamation have proved unsuccessful? It therefore appears to me undesirable that until any youthful member had actually committed a crime he should be excluded from the benefits of such an excellent institution as a Reformatory School.[23]

There was literally much shared ground between the discourses of the CT and juvenile delinquency. The CT could be seen as a ticking time bomb, but the 'problem' existed in the specific context of restraining/categorizing institutions — the camps and closed villages. If the CT could exist only within these physical and conceptual enclosures, then the 'problem' threatened to burst its boundaries. The reformatory, however, could be imagined as a theoretical, methodological and spatial extension of the CT camp, receiving and treating the overflow. It could also be imagined as a moral-political space that might invade the delinquent structures of native society. The hostility of penal administrators towards the CT should not be overstated; the idea of a tribally organized native society was not without value in the romantic imagination.[24] E V Westmacott, Inspector General of Prisons in Bengal in the mid-1880s, felt that cattle-poisoning societies could be saved if they were infiltrated by CT boys who had learned legitimate leather work in the reformatory, who were driven by 'habit' but whose habits had been decriminalized, and who were politically and economically affiliated with the colonial state.[25] The peripheral reformatory existed to colonize the habit and its social location, but it also aimed to 'preserve' what it colonized.

In the Judicial Department of the Northwest Provinces and Oudh, R Greeven insisted that reformatory administrators needed greater discretionary power to admit the occasional CT child, and drew attention to ongoing efforts to reform Sansi children in the CT camp in Fatehgarh. Greeven argued, moreover, that some children who were not actually from a CT ought to be excluded from the reformatory because they were similar to CT children.[26] The CT and the CT camp thus provided a model of 'habit' — synonymous with delinquency, and a symptom of socialization hardening into nature — that had relevance beyond the CT Act, and that could be extended to a wide population of native children. At the same time, the debate about CT children in reformatories advanced the idea that some children, whose delinquent nature had already been reified by the colonial state, its laws and its institutions, were too strong and perverse for institutions intended for more 'normal' juvenile natures. For the CT child, childhood had been fatally compromised by the adult nature of the discourse of hereditary collective criminality. This compromised nature, however, made him irresistible to 'interested' experts engaged in investigations of marginal childhoods. Small numbers of CT children were present in practically every reformatory,[27] serving longer sentences than non-CT inmates[28] and generating a contrary knowledge about natives and colonial institutions. They supplied the explanations for why colonial reformatories were not especially reforming, how parents and natal societies affected the released delinquents and, paradoxically, why CT children should not be allowed into the reformatory.

If the CT represented the rural margin, the 'habitual offender' was his urban counterpart. Habituality became a concern in India significantly before it came to preoccupy metropolitan jailors, and habit was not simply a matter of recidivism as Garland has implied.[29] In the mid-1870s, the juvenile urban pariah was constructed by J D Gordon in Mysore as a parallel society of the CT, with protectors who nurtured habits based on idleness and an indifference to the authority of the state.[30] As with CT children and 'street Arabs', there was an abiding ambivalence in the reformatory about whether such marginal children were suitable inmates.[31] Both RS Acts excluded the 'habitually criminal' from the children's institution. Nevertheless, many administrators shared Gordon's regret that this left a valuable specimen out of the experiment, and most reformatories continued to categorize their inmates in a manner that replicated the order of collective criminality.

W F Thomas, who superintended the Chingleput reformatory in the early 1890s, was not atypical in trying to identify 'thieving castes' in the registers of his institution, and in speculating on how such boys might be 'regenerated'.[32]

Thomas shows a strong faith in a biologically transmitted criminal nature in the child. This nature is not, however, independent of learned habit; it can be reinforced or undermined by the environment. Inspecting the Delhi reformatory in 1906, W Bell, the Inspector General of Education and Reformatory Schools for Punjab, came to a similar conclusion about 'those boys who appear to have marked criminal propensities, or whose parents are habitual criminals'. Bell wrote, 'All such boys on admission are given a blue cap, as distinguished from the white of others, the significance of which they readily understand when it is explained to them that a change from the blue to the white cap can only be effected by…good conduct and industry.'[33] The conceptual and sartorial separation of the relatively plastic from those whose natures had already frozen into the 'marks' of inherited habit distinguished the child from the quasi-adult.[34] As a miniature replica of his parent, the 'habitual' child was a small adult without 'good conduct and industry'. He was an ideal client of the experimental reformatory, not so much because he might be 'unfrozen' to demonstrate a capacity for reform, as because he could be discovered as a fraudulent child. This also made him a challenge that threatened to defeat the colonizing institution, and that could not be acknowledged explicitly in the law.

The colonial reformatory thus made room for the delinquent child, in spite of official proscriptions, a foundational resistance to the notion of delinquency, and a general skepticism among experts about whether 'habit' could be interrupted once it had been produced. Also, while the juvenile periphery shifted to the city in the 1890s, the countryside continued to be implicated in delinquency. The governors of the Sassoon reformatory believed that most urban child offenders had drifted to Bombay from villages and mofussil towns, and administrators at Chingleput had the same to report about troublesome children in Madras. They saw displacement from a normative geography of native life, with its built-in fantasy of a hierarchical and stable caste-peasant society, as a major aspect of delinquency in India.[35] The idea of a criminalizing dislocation persisted into the 1920s, when it was supplemented, but not replaced, by a vision of the city as an autonomous engine of disorder.

Urban juvenile delinquency was a metaphor of a broader problem of colonialism — the metropolis as an unnatural civilizational space inhabited by natives who had slipped from dependence, deference and place. Reformatory men in the twentieth century nursed fantasies of restoring their wards to rural utopias on the margins of the modern. Penal administrators in Burma imagined rustic reformatories in which expert Englishmen with plenty of colonial experience might preside over natives with 'rural tastes and a large hearted sympathy for village folk', who would, in turn, supervise a reparative regime of agriculture and cottage industry.[36] The colonial city was the margin of the native village as well as of the metropolitan city, its marginality spilling over into the reformatory. The objective of the reformatory was to investigate the effects of these multiple marginalities in the children who appeared to be its products.

The Native Child

The first colonial ideologues of the reformatory, like their metropolitan counterparts, began with an assumption that the child was a plastic entity amenable to both corruption and reform. In 1875, Richard Temple wrote evocatively of scores of convicts 'of tender age...growing up in vice and ignorance, and mixing with older criminals' in the jails of Bengal, while the state neglected to mold them into useful workers and disciplined subjects.[37] Temple's language reflected not only the Victorian cult of innocent and sentimentalized childhood,[38] but also a normatively impressionable pre-adulthood that might prove to be an ideological asset in a faltering utilitarianism. The previous year, Lyall had written to the Viceroy (Baring) that as an experiment in the transformation of individuals, the adult prison had largely failed. Only the juvenile reformatory still held out the hope of redeeming a major plank of metropolitan civilization and its extension in the colony.[39]

At the same time, the reformatory in the colony seemed perfectly positioned to discover the fundamentally unnatural character, or the lack of plasticity, that some native children concealed. Roughly contemporaneously with Lyall and Temple, S Lynch wrote about redesigning the juvenile ward of the Alipore Jail:

> [Only] when cell accommodation is provided...can the influence of hardened, vicious nature amongst the children be counter-acted. A totally depraved mind is often found amongst offenders undergoing their first sentence, and these under the existing system mix for a long time with others less vicious, doing much harm before they are detected.[40]

By arguing that some children have 'hardened, vicious' natures from which other, relatively innocent, children had to be insulated, Lynch set out two distinct models of the child that was incarcerated in the Indian reformatory.

By the end of the century, both models had been reified by institutional practice. When the new RS Bill was drafted in 1897, Greeven was chagrined to see that the new law did not allow child inmates to spend their pocket money on sweets and toys (the 1876 law had encouraged reformatory administrators to facilitate that habit). He complained:

> It is absolutely essential, as an incentive to good behaviour, that, until the inmates are finally discharged, they should feel that they are enjoying

the benefit of an experiment *quamdiu bene se gesserint*, with the alternative, in case of misconduct, of having to serve out their sentences. The novelty of the surroundings naturally induces more or less orderly conduct for the first few months of confinement; and even in the case of an unruly spirit this period can best be regarded as a term of probation. When 'such sentence would have expired by effluxion of time', the inmate has become habituated to his surroundings; and for the remainder of the period of his confinement the Local Government…will be in the dilemma of having to retain him as a danger to his comrades or to reward his misconduct by setting him at liberty.[41]

The childhood that Greeven envisioned is marked on the one hand by sweets and toys, i.e. premised on innocence and indulgence. On the other hand, it is marked by something clever, even devious: a nature that is malleable, but that has a will of its own and that adapts in its own interests. The reformatory expert had constantly to manipulate those interests and the two models of the child by holding out rewards and threatening to withhold them. Not coincidentally, Greeven (along with other white officials in Allahabad) was deeply troubled by the case of a twelve-year-old murderer named Anrudh Singh who had been sentenced by an Indian magistrate to five years in the reformatory rather than twenty years in the Andamans.[42] A twelve-year-old murderer was undoubtedly a child, but only very questionably a child of the first, tenderly impressionable, variety.

Early in the history of the colonial reformatory, this schizophrenic model of the native child was recognized as a peculiar entity that existed in a dynamic relationship with the metropolitan child that supplied the discipline of child correction with its normative procedures. The peculiarity was essentially the doubt that hung over the plasticity of the native child and the uncertain location of the boundary between child and adult in India. It was a remarkably durable influence upon policy — it was common in the 1890s for the administrators to observe, as the Deputy Commissioner of Multan did, that the colonial reformatory would fail if it did not take into account 'the early age at which maturity of understanding and proficiency in vice are attained [in India]'.[43]

Native peculiarity was not a uniform or uncomplicated quality. After the First World War, Indian and white experts on colonial juvenile delinquency both moved to locate the delinquent in a wide, transnational discourse of the child and the modern that included American progressivism.[44] The Indian Jails Committee of 1922 formulated its plans for a system of probation with direct reference to 'a great development in America in recent years'.[45] In this late period in colonial child correction, the unease within the expert-bureaucratic establishment with an emphasis on the peculiarity of native children is increasingly discernible. The ideological pressure to distinguish between children and adults and not between natives and Europeans had grown simultaneously in the interwar era. When bureaucrats in the United Provinces complained that the expense of creating a new regime of laws and institutions would present 'a real difficulty', they could not deny that the merger of juvenile and adult penology in the colonial reformatory was embarrassing and contentious.[46]

The developments of the 1920s were not unprecedented. The RS Act of 1876 drew its power from a closing of the gap between European and native childhoods. Colonial experts of the era based their authority on their ability to recognize the universal; Napier, Lynch and Mouat sought to locate themselves and 'their' children within molds that were familiar to metropolitan child-savers. Napier, for instance, was clear that English and Indian children could be reformed through similar disciplining strategies if the strategies were adapted to colonial and native social realities. He drew an explicit parallel between English and Indian 'strays', seeing both as unsocialized, non-nurtured *tabulae rasa* upon which the child-saver might inscribe morality and modernity.[47] By seeking out such 'untouched' children and forming (rather than reforming) them, Napier implied, the natures of the child, the delinquent, the native and the European could all be investigated. Lyall assumed that reformatories could be the salvation of modern penology in both India and England.[48] He borrowed readily from metropolitan precedents, citing the experience of Preston Jail administrators while arguing for long periods of detention in specialized institutions.[49] Even at the end of the century, self-consciously modern administrators remained reluctant to deviate drastically from the English example. When the government of the Northwest Provinces and Oudh urged the central legislature to provide for the incarceration of boys between seven and twelve years of age, the Lieutenant Governor of Bengal intervened, pointing out, that children under the age of twelve could not be detained in English reformatories.[50]

This does not mean, however, that Lynch and Mouat saw the native child as the same as its English counterpart. Their inclination to apply a universal model of the reformatory was based on the assumption that the institution would tease out the differences that existed between racially constituted childhoods, such as the curious inclination of Bengali children to study in their cells when offered the chance.[51] As late as 1922, the government of Burma issued a vehement statement of native peculiarity. Rejecting the Jails Committee's recommendation that colonial child-correction be made more like the English and American models, and equipped with juvenile courts and probation systems, the provincial executive told the Home Department:

> The assimilation of Indian to English practice [is] not...justified by a comparison of the ages at which children in the East and the West attain maturity. Life in oriental countries is such as to develop much more rapidly both the bodily and mental faculties of children. They are not surrounded by...influences which preserve a native innocence and produce a high moral tone. Many boys between the ages of twelve and sixteen are as fully grown in their knowledge of the world as mature men in other countries. They begin to seek work...much earlier than they do elsewhere and are tempted to add to their earnings by devious methods. The suggestion [for] remand homes...borders on the fantastic. Even in a city like London, remand homes have been found to be unsuitable. When...the ease with which a criminal can conceal himself in this country is remembered, the proposal stands self-condemned. The inevitable consequence of any marked laxity in the punishments of offences would be a similar increase of crime to that recorded in America; for, children in the East...are likely to misapprehend the reasons for indulgent treatment and regard them as indications of weakness on the part of the courts. When the accepted maxims of the ages are under the critical examination of modern theorists, the tendency [is] to swing to the opposite extreme and to reject the wisdom of a Solomon for the pulling sentimentalities of a humanitarianism, which refuses to look life in the face.[52]

Following up in another letter to the Home Department, the Burma administration pointed out that the Jails Committee's report was based on Indian conditions that did not necessarily apply to Burma.[53]

The dissidents in Burma were concerned with limiting the scope of childhood by blocking its escape from adult penology. They rejected the universality of childhood, and English children were not the only Other — Indian children also underlined the peculiarity of young Burmese. The relevance of metropolitan models to the colonial context was denied on grounds of cultural difference: native society was too morally lax, too indifferent to the need to create upstanding citizens, and too tolerant and indulgent in its parenting, to be engaged through metropolitan institutions of juvenile correction. The problem was also located in the colonial regime — it was the weakness of the colonial eye that limited the state's ability to replicate London in Rangoon, although it was acknowledged that Rangoon and London shared similarly manifested problems of juvenile delinquency. Thus, even as the validity of the East-West comparison was denied, it was made anyway, to justify what can and cannot be done in the East. In the process, difference and similarity were both established. Such revelations became practical academic knowledge, allowing for a proliferation of childhoods and children's institutions, and modifications and experiments that added further dimensions to the native child, to native criminality, to legislative and infrastructural responses, to Selves and Others.

Boundaries of Childhood

Early in the evolution of the colonial reformatory, it was apparent to child correction experts that the penal institution could produce native children with a flexibility that might accommodate the differences with metropolitan material. The apprenticeship and ticket-of-leave regimes based on Act XIX of 1850 are cases in point. Boys with tickets of leave were kept apart from other children at Sassoon, indicating not only a perception that freedom could introduce a premature and corrupting adulthood, but that the onset of this corruption could be managed by the expert.[54] Apprenticeship, which functioned as a controlled termination of dependence, produced its own boundary of childhood. By the 1870s, it was an established assumption among progressive administrators like Richard Temple and his allies in Bengal that the reformatory could either generate the childhood of the native by prolonging detention as a 'juvenile', or consign him early to the 'adult' prison, based on what the experts discovered about him.[55]

The ideological basis of the extension of childhood can be glimpsed in the Alipore reformatory in 1880, when a boy was given five extra years of detention for 'stealing and selling sugarcane to a stranger [in] the Reformatory Garden'.[56] In this instance, the extended sentence does not reflect a belief that the offender will be reformed in the extra time. Rather, it is contradictory and almost purely punitive, reflecting a perception of incorrigibility — a pathological freezing of childhood — in the individual child. In that sense, it reflects the proximity between the reformatory and the orphanage or asylum, rather than that between the reformatory and the prison. Childhood could, however, also be extended in a relatively optimistic expectation that extra time in the institution would reform the inmate who had hitherto been resistant. In 1890, the Court of the Judicial Commissioner of the Central Provinces moved to block a perceived loophole in the RS Act. The court observed that 'precocious young criminals' aged nine years or less were occasionally encountered by magistrates, and that such children remained unreformed when freed at the age of sixteen. (The RS Act mandated that children under ten be detained for a maximum of seven years.) It then urged that very young children be detained until they were eighteen.[57] J G Kirschner had made a similar recommendation in Bengal in 1880, insisting that the reformatory must address the childhood of the inmate rather than the gravity of the crime.[58] To let the child leave the institution 'early' because he had exhausted the punishment mandated by his crime allowed other agents to colonize or harden his nature; when this hardened child re-entered the reformatory, the institution itself lost its juvenile nature and became analogous to a jail.

These juvenilizing agendas coexisted with the parallel, but opposite, perception in which the reformatory produced an attenuated childhood in native delinquents, hastening the transition to a perverse adulthood. C E Fox, the Government Advocate of Burma, wrote in 1892 that while sending resisting children from the reformatory to the prison would be contrary to the intention of the 1876 law, it was possible that 'a boy might even, after being in a reformatory for some time, be still so unruly that punishment in jail on his original sentence would be the only appropriate punishment'.[59] In such cases, the peculiarity of native material would have defeated the colonial institution, but not before the institution had revealed the peculiarity.

Since such manipulations of the lines between child and adult were imbedded in an institutional setting, reformatories facilitated the development of mathematical formulae by which food allowances for adult prisoners could be converted into diets that signified the needs of children,[60] and jail sentences (i.e. criminalized adulthood) awarded by the courts could be converted into terms of childhood in the reformatory. In Bengal in the 1870s, a six-month sentence of rigorous imprisonment could translate as six years in the reformatory,[61] and the Legislative Department invested much effort in finding a satisfactory table of conversion.[62]

Such devices were never 'acceptable' in the context of an ongoing experiment. The failure to come up with a broadly satisfactory reformatory, however, constantly threw up new, experimental boundaries for the childhood of the inmate. Resistance within the institution, for instance, generated problems as well as knowledge. Incarcerated juveniles could coopt the rules that determined their suitability for the reformatory — in 1890, a convicted boy declared that he was a member of a Criminal Tribe and to the great frustration of the disbelieving Deputy Commissioner of Hardoi, insisted that he be sent to jail instead of the reformatory.[63] Jail sentences were typically shorter than reformatory sentences. The claim to a perverse adulthood, in this case, reinforced the childish nature of the native who was unable to recognize his own best interests, and who had no regard for rightful authority. The production of childhood in the reformatory was inseparable from this generation of its opposite: the child was produced as quasi-adult, and the adult as the quasi-child, limiting both childhood and adulthood in the process.

In each case, the reformatory did not so much identify or allot stable boundaries for the native child as play with slippery numbers, i.e. ages, produced, tested and revised by it. By the 1870s, it was already evident to child-correction experts that age was an unreliable signifier of native childhood. To a degree, this was because Indians seemed ignorant, uninterested or unforthcoming about the concept of age. (The uncertainty kept prison and reformatory doctors busy for much of the late nineteenth century, trying to guess the ages of convicts by examining their bodies.[64] One administrator in the Central Provinces grumbled that the reformatory regime actually contributed to the difficulty, because an inmate who had been fed by the colonial kitchen 'looks considerably older than appears from the judgment of the sentencing court.'[65]) It was, however, also because European assumptions about age and childhood appeared unsuited to the task of identifying children in India: Indians did not become 'children' or 'adults' at the ages at which Europeans did, and juvenile delinquents, in particular, seemed to acquire the marks of adulthood early in life. This did not mean that age lost its significance in the reformatory, which continued to gather and organize its wards with reference to age. If anything, age became all the more important as an area of investigation, experimentation and productive failure.

Metropolitan notions of the ages of childhood were themselves historically determined, and a wide range of forces went into the process of determination — industrial labour and its regulation, the bureaucratization of schooling, the growing disciplinary authority of medicine and psychology and juvenile penology, to name a few.[66] The knowledge these generated could be tested in the Indian experiments, but the results by and large indicated a 'failure' of metropolitan knowledge, or the conclusion that whereas the methods of investigation were sound, there were additional, purely colonial factors which would have to be factored into the experiment, and which would produce a result — a child — that was peculiar to the periphery. Broadly speaking, while age as a biological-numerical-bureaucratic phenomenon remained relevant and necessary in setting boundaries for native childhood, it became evident that the location of those boundaries was dependent upon culture and upon the colonial experience itself — sexual permission and precocity, location within native society, and the encounter with the reformatory.

In 1922, the Jails Committee attempted to establish a set of guidelines for the ages at which children might be incarcerated in India. It stated:

> The Committee deprecate the committal to prison of children (i.e. persons under the age of fourteen years) and young persons (i.e. persons who are over fourteen years but under sixteen years of age), whether after conviction or while on remand or under trial, as being contrary to public policy, and are of [the] opinion that imprisonment should in their case be made illegal as in England.[67] [Parentheses in original]

Borrowing its categories from the metropolitan Children's Employment Commission of 1842,[68] this declaration might be seen as a milestone in the colonial penal bureaucracy's outlook on the relationship between age and childhood. The committee was calling for a definition of childhood that was based on age alone, and not on the 'depravity' of the individual child, the 'heinousness' of the offence, the notoriety or poverty of the child's social environment, or the discretion of the judge or local government, all of which had been factors in the constitution of the native child in the years since the Napier-Bayley debates and the passage of the RS Act. On the surface, it marked a return to the simplicity of the early 1860s, when the colonial government, faced with 'famine orphans', had found it convenient and natural to use the age of eighteen as the line between child and adult. All those under eighteen were entitled to government assistance and constituted an undifferentiated category of children.[69] This policy was consonant not only with an emerging metropolitan model of political maturity, but with the idea that financial independence marked the end of childhood.

Below the surface, however, the 1922 position was much more complex than the assumptions that guided the government in 1860. It presumed not only a lower threshold of childhood, but also proliferating subcategories of the child that might be subjected to different disciplinary regimes. Under the Children Acts which legislators in Bengal, Madras, the Central Provinces and Bombay passed following the Jail Committee's report, offenders below the age of fourteen were to be sent to 'industrial school', and those between fourteen and sixteen to 'reformatory school'.[70] The ceiling for incarceration in the reformatory was raised to sixteen (as it had been in the original RS Act), allowing for a longer childhood within the colonial institution. Further extensions and elaborations followed — boys over the age of sixteen would be sent to the Borstal, and the Central Provinces decided that boys under the age of eight could be sentenced to the reformatory but boarded with 'any suitable person' until they reached the age of ten.[71] All of these age groups had been covered in the past (by unreformed jail regimes and the two RS Acts), so the incarceration of children of these ages was nothing new. Whereas the old reformatory regimes had sought to restrict the boundaries of criminalized and institutionalized childhood, however, the new laws re-expanded the boundaries, while making internal differentiations between age groups and institutions. The contradictions between age and childhood in the colony were dispersed over multiple stages in the life of the native child.

Sex and Institutionalized Childhood

The sexual life of the child was particularly rich in such contradictions. The relevance of sex to the concept of majority in British India has been noted by scholars of age-of-consent controversies.[72] This work, however, has not taken into account the degree to which the intersection of sex and age marked an active zone of investigation into native childhood. In 1872, as the colonial government debated whether to criminalize sex with prostitutes under the age of sixteen,[73] district level and provincial administrators disparaged the idea, arguing that in much of native society, a sixteen year old female was neither biologically nor morally a child.[74] By locating minority in social and sexual habits that are themselves located in caste, officials like R L Mangles in Mysore and William Muir in the Northwest Provinces made the case that children from different sections of Indian society 'matured' at different ages that signified their levels of civilization.[75] By preserving, manipulating, applying, or ignoring minority laws based on sexual awareness, Mangles implied, the colonial government could preserve or destabilize the boundaries between child and adult, civilized and savage, whore and respectable female, minor and child, in a particular native community.[76] 'Minority' and 'childhood' are not the same; the latter is a moral concept while the former is legal, and subject to a different set of negotiations. It was necessary, therefore, for colonial experts to separate childhood from minority in the community of inmates, because incarcerated delinquents could be minors without being children.

Not surprisingly, there was much sex in the reformatory, not only in the sense that incarcerated juveniles engaged in various kinds of sexual behaviour, but in the Foucauldian sense that the appearance of suppression by adults in charge of the reformatory barely disguised a vigorous generative enterprise.[77] Sex pervades administrative procedures, architectural priorities, the historical archive, and the child itself. In Burma in 1869, jailors expressed relief that teenagers in their wards were not given to 'the nameless vice which disgraces the Gaols of other countries' and thanked the moral influence of monastic Buddhism; this led them to conclude that the young males were in fact children, but it also allowed them to declare that reformatories were not needed in Burma.[78] The implication was that reformatories were for children whose childhood was imperilled by sex, which was further linked to a precocious adulthood.

This set up a productive tension within the reformatory as it emerged in the late 1860s. In Calcutta, Fawcus wrote about children who were imperfectly segregated in the juvenile ward of Alipore Jail:

> Much...can be done to prevent their contamination by each other and by older prisoners, and it appears to me that it is in this direction that endeavours should...be made. There is a strong objection to allowing youths who have even attained the stature and strength of men, unreserved intercourse with men who have disgusting propensities.[79]

The problem, however, was larger than simply preventing sexual contact between men and boys. Fawcus recognized that age was in itself not a satisfactory indicator of where childhood ended in the prison wards — not only because natives were vague about age, and physical development was inadequate as the signifier of a moral idea, but also because in British eyes, the 'normal' next phase for the free native who became an adult would be heterosexual marriage. When this phase was precluded by imprisonment and the likelihood of homosexual relationships, adulthood became a menace that required postponement. Fawcus suggests using the modern, cellular juvenile ward (a rudimentary reformatory) to extend sexual immaturity and innocence even after the body has matured, in a limbo of arrested development. Institutionalization thus generated the problem, the solution, and also the specimen, or the child who had been rendered as an object of study because his adulthood had been warded (or walled) off.

By the 1870s, homosexuality had been firmly established within the reformatory as a sign of premature adulthood. The Heeley-Mackenzie-Lambert report, which Richard Temple commissioned in 1874, constructed homosexual activity in juvenile wards as the abuse of younger boys, or 'real' children, by older boys who had already reached an unnoticed adulthood that did not correspond to their age. The opposite view, that older boys were seduced by the 'immoral propensities of some of the smaller boys' also surfaced on occasion.[80] It indicated a contradictory perception that the homosexual menace was imbedded in childhood itself and specifically in the childhood of the native, arising from the combined androgyny of an immature 'soft' sexuality and an inescapable civilizational stain. It was the adult male that was in danger of having his 'mature' gender destabilized by the proximity of the child — a displacement onto young boys of the homoerotic desire of the older boy as well as the adult observer. The narrative of the seductive child offender parallels the metropolitan Victorian fixation with juvenile temptresses that Pamela Horn has described,[81] feminizing the younger native male in the process. While it might be noted, as Nandy has done, that the colonial encounter was suffused by a concealed panic and desire that white adults might themselves experience such a reversal,[82] it was the native adult and especially the older child who were most 'at risk', because their resistance was undermined by cultural flaws and the softness of youth.

Nevertheless, the discourse of homosexuality in the reformatory highlighted the threat posed by older children who were not really children at all. The authors of the 1874 report recommended greater watchfulness by jailors, so that the secret adults could be identified and segregated.[83] By the time the first RS Act was passed, that watchfulness had been projected extramurally, in an attempt to detect and exclude children with homosexual tendencies from the reforming institution. The Northwest Provinces and Oudh administration drew up provincial regulations that sought to make the new law more perfect in its application: 'No boy should be sent to a Reformatory who has been convicted of an unnatural offence, or of gross indecency indicative of habitual immorality'.[84] In the same paragraph of the rules, children from various CTs were also excluded from the reformatory.

These regulations carry more than one set of anxieties about institutionalized Indian children. Sexual experimentation by boys in the reformatory constituted an unacceptable practice of autonomy over bodies, habits and categories in a laboratory where the right to experiment had already been claimed. The desire to screen out homosexuals reflects not only the sense that any kind of sexual impulse (which in a homosocial setting would typically manifest itself as homosexual or autosexual) is antithetical to childlike innocence and hence perverse when exhibited by those whose ages indicated childhood, but also a specific horror of homosexuality. It further implies a belief that only those children whose natures are relatively intact, innocent and hetero-celibate can be 'reached' and reformed through correct nurturing. The homosexual child in the reformatory is thus not only constructed as a moral contaminant, he is also rendered as an interloper in a particular ideological and political space — precocious in his 'predatory' presence in a juvenile geography, and a competitor of the reforming experts whose ages and status as adults coincide unproblematically.

The lumping together of homosexuals, the 'habitually' immoral and CT children is not insignificant. By the mid-1870s, homosexuals in the incarcerated population were treated as a subspecies of habitual criminal, or as a conceptual criminal tribe in their own right. Well before habituality became generally grounded in the body of the offender, the homosexuality of children had been cast in the mold of an embodied and identifying habit. This construction would gain strength in the mid-1890s, when it became common practice for reformatory administrators to pride themselves on their vigilant exclusion of boys with a recorded habit of criminal behaviour, including homosexuality.[85] Since 'habit' was understood as a congealing of the nature of the child, reformatory administrators sought children without habits, whose nature was still fluid, innocent and thus, genuinely childlike. That finding such children was a perpetual struggle indicated the challenge of the field and revealed — as homosexuals, as records, as disgust — the peculiarity of childhood in the periphery.

In the 1920s, predictably, we find a shift in the discourse. The discussion of sexually aware girlhoods in 1872 had sought to identity two distinct populations of girl children — genuine children, who were sexually innocent, and what might be described as underage adults or young girls rendered adult by their association with prostitutes. In 1928, Indian legislators also focused on childhood in the brothel, which they presented as a counter-reformatory. With its middle-class/masculine assumptions about gender, class and childhood, Act X of the Central Provinces declared that children between the ages of four and sixteen could not live in, or visit, brothels.[86] Instead of identifying separate groups of sexual and asexual children, they constructed distinct phases in the lives of a single set of children — some sexually unformed and thus so childlike that they were safe in the brothel, others in jeopardy both because they were children and because they were sexually/morally impressionable. The differentiation between sexual and pre-sexual (rather than asexual) children was not new, but experts of the pre-war years typically drew the line in the middle teens. In the Indian-dominated legislative chamber, the distinction was made much earlier in the life of the child. Even the childhood of the inmates of the brothel could be 'saved', the legislators implied, provided it was retrieved early. It would not be marked by habit, either of the parent or of the child itself. It would not be retrieved for the society of elite legislators, but for the imagined community that they were engaged in retrieving from the colonial state.

Adolescence

The older children that preoccupied the forebears of the legislators of the 1920s were a productive lot — they had been the first Indian adolescents, rendering visible the metaphor of savagery that G Stanley Hall had associated with the teenage years.[87] Kakar has identified in Indian epic literature an 'adolescence' based on the affirmation of sexual desire,[88] but colonial administrators who deployed the word were informed not so much by the *Mahabharat* as by the experience of punishing natives. In the Indian penal institution, the upper edge of childhood had been established as a problem by the end of the 1870s; the anxiety surfaces in the reformatory archive immediately after the passage of the first RS Act. Kirschner wrote from Alipore about inmates who gave him the most trouble, 'They are all big boys from fifteen to seventeen years of age, and are looked up to by the younger boys who have never been to jail as heroes worthy of imitation.'[89] Three years later, he wrote, 'The discipline among the boys was much improved….by the release of some of the biggest boys who were incorrigible, and by their bad example…corrupted the others.'[90] Kirschner also transferred some of the boys from the juvenile reformatory to the adult jail (also in Alipore); being resistant both to authority and to reform, the teenagers had revealed their candidacy for an early and punishing adulthood.

By setting the age of sixteen as the upper limit of admission to the reformatory, the RS Act had itself underlined the adolescent problem that Kirschner and his colleagues confronted. The liminality of this particular variant of the incarcerated juvenile — its difficulty of precise definition and treatment — was central to its menace and to its status as an 'offender'. There is only a faint line between adolescence and delinquency in the Indian reformatory: each is made up of a set of tendencies, constituting an imprecise zone between criminality and innocence. Not coincidentally, the two concepts emerged simultaneously and in the same institutional settings, feeding off each other. When the first RS Bill was being debated, there was no consensus among colonial administrators about the content of native adolescence, or its place in the reformatory. While some wanted a relatively high age limit of sixteen years for admission into the reformatory, others preferred the lower ceiling of fourteen. The Inspector General of Prisons in Bengal argued for the lower number, declaring that sixteen year olds were 'old in vice and in no way amenable to reforming influence'.[91] In the governor's office, Temple disagreed, and his administration notified the central legislature:

> In England, it is believed that sixteen years is the maximum age up to which boys can be sent to a reformatory, and [Temple] sees no reason to believe that boys in this country up to sixteen years of age are not as amenable to discipline and reformation as they are in England; or…that a boy after fourteen years is irreclaimable, and not likely to be hardened and confirmed in crime if incarcerated with older and adult offenders [in jail]. While…a boy of sixteen years, released from the reformatory, would be too old to be subservient to the discipline and control of his parents, he would…be too young to start on any profession, or to undertake any settled occupation as a means of livelihood.[92]

We have here two views of the plasticity of sixteen year olds. The dim view of the Inspector General is at odds with that of his boss (Temple) and his predecessor (Mouat), and with the modern perspective on adolescence that would later inform the Borstal schools. In his relatively conservative vision, the Indian adolescent is practically an adult and too precocious for Temple's English reference to be applicable. Temple holds the progressive view, which is based not only on the plasticity of the adolescent (who might be molded for good by the state in the reformatory, or for bad by adult criminals in jail), but also on the universality of that plasticity. The latter view lends itself to an expansive concept of delinquency as well as of childhood, whereas the former serves to restrict both.

Temple did not see adolescence as a period of unqualified plasticity. He was convinced that adolescents could not be reformed effectively at home. The position that he put forward was that as a zone of questionable impressionability, adolescence could exist only in the institutional and discursive spaces of colonialism, where the economic dependence of the juvenile could combine productively with the contingent plasticity of the near-adult. Both positions survived the amendment of the RS Act in 1897, which continued to limit the presence of adolescents in the reformatory (by lowering the maximum age of admission to fifteen years) even as reformatory administrators wrote voluminously about the adolescents they had discovered in their institutions.

The 1890s also saw the conflation of the adolescent with the sexually dangerous quasi-adult, and investigations of adolescence in this period cannot be separated from the project of articulating the question of whether a sexually mature teenager is a child. Most Indian reformatories adopted a policy of segregating boys who had reached puberty from the prepubescent.[93] The attempt to locate adolescence in the body of the inmate, and its partial detachment from a specific age, marked the abiding suspicion of experts that age was an unreliable indicator of childhood in the periphery. Inspections of the body, however, did not prove to be a failsafe means of detecting adolescence, and in the post-war years, there was a renewed reliance on age parameters in determining which children might be recognized as adolescents, with the United Provinces administration telling the Home Department, 'The existing criterion of puberty is an uncertain one and not entirely satisfactory and it is preferable to fix a maximum age'.[94]

Much had changed between the 1890s and the 1920s that would make an age-based, legally produced adolescence more tenable in the later period. There was a greatly increased specialization within the infrastructure of child correction, and the emerging network of Borstal schools and Borstal Acts required that adolescents be mass produced with a certain bureaucratic predictability, rather than in fits and starts through the work of experts in dispersed reformatories. Certainly, the 1920s witnessed a dramatic extension of adolescence, not so much at the expense of childhood as of adulthood. The Jails Committee of 1922 noted:

> Adolescent criminals, i.e. prisoners who are sixteen years of age but ordinarily not more than twenty one years old (the maximum limit being extensible to twenty three years) should not be sent to ordinary jails but should be treated specially on the lines of the English Prevention of Crime Act, 1908 and should be confined in separate jails or institutions to which no adult prisoners are sent. Adolescents guilty of grave crime such as murder, dacoity, rape, etc. would be sent to juvenile prisons and other adolescents would be sent to Special Adolescent Institutions. The latter institutions would be reformatory in character and all details would be arranged to that end, the adolescents being termed 'inmates' and prison terminology being avoided as far as possible. It is recommended that…detention should vary from a minimum of three years to a maximum

of five years, followed by a further period of supervision. The Committee also recommend the adoption of the English system of release on license but no adolescent would be so released until work has been found for him. The Borstal Institutions and Juvenile Jails which have come into existence in the various provinces in India in recent years would facilitate the execution of the Committee's recommendations although a great deal would have to be done in various ways.[95] [Parentheses in original]

On the surface of this proliferation of childhoods, the adult/child segregation was maintained at all times, protecting the large category of the child even as its internal complications of age, delinquency, criminality and relative potential for redemption were identified and addressed institutionally. Below the surface was a protraction of adolescence. The ceiling of 'childhood' had risen by three to five years since 1897, even as discretion over the edge of childhood had shifted away from the expert in the reformatory to the bureaucrat and the Indian legislator. A twenty-three year old had been categorized as potentially adolescent, to be kept apart from 'real' children as well as 'real' adults. What had been extended was his plasticity, or the period when he might be reached by either the state or the adult criminal.

This postponement of adulthood was hardly unprecedented in the history of colonial interventions, but the Indian support was something new. In 1875, when the Legislative Council was drafting the first RS Act, another colonial law — the Indian Majority Act, which set twenty-one years as the age of majority in matters of inheritance — had come under fierce attack in the Indian press, which saw it as an unacceptable attempt to extend the subservience of fatherless natives to the colonial Court of Wards.[96] In the 1920s, however, the extension of native childhood through a long adolescence was broadly acceptable, not least because the production of children had become subject to monitoring, debate and alteration on political stages that were undeniably colonial, but partially in Indian hands. Indian legislators such as J A Saldanha (Madras) showed no hesitation in denouncing Borstal regimes as oppressive, but did not criticize them for prolonging childhood; rather, they attacked the adolescent institutions of the 1920s for treating their inmates like adults, and implied that the childhood of the adolescent would be better served in a decolonized reformatory.[97]

The reference to English precedent in the Jails Committee's report is not insignificant either. It implied the closing of a political distance, manifested in a universality of modern child correction and childhood that was attractive to 'native opinion'. Even in the 1920s, there were penal regimes in British India that resisted any attempt to construct the adolescent as a special category of juvenile offender, seeing it as a misguided, sentimental and potentially seditious attempt to shield native criminals by invoking metropolitan models. The Burma administration, for example, dismissed the Jails Committee's recommendations by retorting, 'At eighteen a boy [in Burma] is ordinarily well beyond a period of adolescence and has become a man'.[98] In marked contrast is the outlook of S C Contractor (IMS), the Chief Inspector of Certified Schools in Madras in the 1930s and early 1940s. In 1940, Contractor wrote:

> The so-called criminal tendencies in the adolescents are more to be considered as badly developed habits which react towards society at large. No amount of punishment will set right their undesirable habits if we do not find out and eradicate the causative factors for the delinquents' misbehaviour. We must find out whether it is due to mere poverty, ignorance and want of proper control; or to mental defect and easy suggestibility; or to emotional conflict and misdirected outlet or energy; or to bad company and example, either at home or outside. This should be ascertained first by careful investigation and study, as it is an important preventive work in cutting at the root of any antisocial tendency at an early stage. If we [then] apply remedial measures to rectify the defect found out, we may be confident that we have done what was in our power to turn out the individual to be a useful and honest citizen. Hence...the presence of a consulting staff is essential. After an investigation of the social, educational, physical, psychological and psychiatric conditions, recommendations best suited for the individual cases [should be] made for the acceptance of the magistrates.[99]

Contractor's vision of adolescence as a psychologically informed, expertly supervised phase in the life of the child is derived from metropolitan discourse,[100] but it produces the adolescent as an innovation — and a modern Indian — in the colonial reformatory. As an expert, Contractor was a true heir of Mouat and Napier, but as an Indian professional, he was engaged in usurping the reformatory, not to mention the IMS. His narrative is squarely positioned within the post-war trend of individualizing the juvenile delinquent and it shows a corresponding medicalization of the language of reform — the biology and psychology of delinquency and 'habit' are increasingly seen as individual aberrations, responsive to an individualized treatment that the colonial state had not provided. Purnima Bose has observed that individualism in colonial societies generally posits the individual in opposition to the state.[101] In the specific context of punishment, this is substantially because the instruments of the state worked to avert individualization, not impart it as Garland has argued about late Victorian British prisons.[102] As the Burmese government acknowledged, this medicalized individualization had already transformed white delinquents in the metropole, creating a powerful model of the modern. Whereas colonial experts of the nineteenth century had often sought to distance themselves from the metropolitan model, seeing the periphery as the key to their own authority, native experts in a colonized society were impatient with their status as peripheral professionals and sought affiliation with the progressive west.

In the process, the colonial reformatory became more of a laboratory than ever, but the native child acquired new ideological dimensions, including those of the 'citizen'. This ought not to be taken literally; as Chatterjee points out, Indian elites writing about their 'own' society were unable to detach themselves from colonial (and colonizing) procedures and relations of knowledge creation, even when their objective was to impart sovereignty to the specimen.[103] Middle-class Indians who designed the new reformatory regimes were certainly ready to use Borstals to police the boundaries of class, by linking class-appropriate behaviour with normative childhood in a manner that would have been quite familiar to the experts of the 1870s.[104] Nevertheless, as a shadow self of the native expert, the native adolescent had been brought in from the periphery of punishment and modernity and released into a national space.

Nature, Nurture and Inheritance

Due to the fact that the reformatory undertook investigations of the adult native as well as of the child, the link between the criminalities of the adult and the child became a major subject of speculation. The broad questions of nature/nurture were not extraordinary, but the answers were informed by the peculiarities of the periphery, where native bodies and societies, along with colonial relationships, supplied variables that were simultaneously frustrating and rewarding for the child-correction expert. A discourse of genetically transmitted nature was present from the outset, but it was not hegemonic. Much of the time, colonial experts perceived that the nature of the juvenile delinquent was itself formed by nurture, i.e. environmental and associational influences; they believed that socially acquired nature could be dented, although not undone, in the reformatory. The depth of the impression made would depend upon the age of the child, his location in class, caste and the penal-bureaucratic grid, the duration of his stay in the institution and his segregation from other natives; it would reveal, moreover, the limits of his limited plasticity.

In the final decade of the nineteenth century, the 'genetic' and the 'environmental' understandings of the transmission of delinquency both came to emphasize the body as the site of nature. The biological and the genetic were, therefore, not inseparable in the colonial reformatory. The idea of a bullet-proof heredity was conspicuous by its restriction to relatively small numbers of children. The strong environmental emphasis reflected the wider phenomena of colonialism — the contest between administrators and native parents, and eventually a re-evaluation of the relationship between state and society in the era of the Indian expert.

In her insightful study of the CT phenomenon, Radhakrishna dismisses the possibility that colonial perceptions of hereditary criminality were biologically informed; such a preoccupation, she argues, would have undermined any administrative agenda of control.[105] Nevertheless, the idea that the criminality of the native child offender might be hardwired in nature surfaced early in the discourse of the reformatory. In 1863, C Hervey in the Department of Thuggee and Dacoity told the government that unless it paid more attention to the reformation of the children of Thugs, a latent criminal inclination would reassert itself and the good work of Sleeman would be wasted.[106] Later in the decade, Lynch utilized a modification of the same idea to suggest that the reformatory must expose incarcerated children to graded levels of pain, depending on the extent to which their inherent delinquency had become manifest. The child who is inclined towards depravity, Lynch argued, will become more depraved as his nature is progressively colonized by criminality, which could be either inborn or environmentally induced. The treatment or counter-colonization must depend upon the stage of the progress.[107]

Before the end of the century, further refinements had been made in the knowledge about the child that had inherited its delinquency. In a series of judgments, the Calcutta High Court linked the delinquent children of 'respectable' parents with the children of the habitually criminal. Both were 'casual' offenders, but whereas the casualty of the former indicated impulse, or the superficiality of delinquency, that of the latter indicated exactly the opposite — a deep-rooted delinquency in which crime became casual, or natural.[108] While this represented the common emphasis on a delinquency that the colonial reformatory must reveal, confront and manage, an alternative perspective on inherited nature was put forward in Madras by Duncan, who wrote, 'The sole object of a reformatory school is to reform the character of the youthful offender by awakening the intelligence [and] training the conscience'.[109] The institution was expected to 'awaken' a dormant nature that was actually benign, that had been rendered comatose by depraved parents. Duncan assumed that this innocent nature was universal in children and implicitly denied that the criminality of institutionalized children in India was driven by the peculiarities of native biology, even as he, like many of his colleagues, embraced the work of scraping off nurture to reveal what lay beneath.

Madras, in particular the Chingleput reformatory, was at the forefront of explorations of the nature of the delinquent child, and a perspective on inherited nature that was related to Duncan's (but hardly identical) emerged from Chingleput in the early 1890s when H A F Nailer was the deputy superintendent. Nailer wrote about the growing number of inmates who came to the reformatory from Madras city:

> They do not think it wrong to steal if they could escape detection, being guided solely by animal instincts. They come devoid of any religious or moral principles and with their better instincts underdeveloped. Moral principles have to be instilled into them by means of moral lessons, advice, etc. and their better instincts have to be developed by means of a firm and rational discipline and a careful training.[110]

In this construction, 'animal instinct' — or nature — is a universally shared 'hardware'. It is quite negative and not unrelated to original sin. 'Better instinct' is also a part of the nature of the child, but it is subordinate to animal nature, or dormant. Moral training functions as the software that activates this nature. The reformatory does not so much change the 'bad' child (bad because he is a criminal, a native and a child), as bring out what is already there, and change the balance between his two 'natures'.

In 1895, Nailer — now Superintendent of Chingleput — returned to the subject of urban children, but he was careful to ground animal instinct and moral failure more securely in the body of the child, showing a partial absorption of an older moral discourse of nature into an increasingly medicalized vision. He wrote:

> The majority of the boys possess marked facial peculiarities which point to strong animal instincts and to low mental and moral qualities. These characteristics account for their presence at the school. It is only by a long course of training with a view to suppress the one, and to improve the other, that the reformation of the pupils in this school is mainly sought. It is evident that in the majority of cases the juvenile delinquents inherited a more or less absolute want of moral sense which was aggravated by poverty, wicked associates and other disadvantages which the lowest classes of people are subjected to.[111]

The mutation or damage perceived is in keeping with the contemporary emphasis on racial-criminal 'measuring' and late-Victorian anxieties about a pathological urbanity.[112] Nailer does not explicitly phrase the abnormality of the boys in terms of a racial norm. He is aligned with the scientists of racial typology (especially Risley), but there is also a tension, based on Nailer's inclination to see deviance as an individual development (rather than a trait of the racial collective), that might generate its own medical and pathological classifications.

The medical basis of this reformulated nature is also evident in the idea that reform is a cure, or a physiological adjustment in the nature of the individual child. We can see here the beginnings of the individualization of the delinquent that becomes dominant in the 1920s; Nailer and Duncan provide a schematic that would be invaluable to the ideologues of the interwar years, Indian as well as European. In its rebuttal of the report of the Jails Committee of 1922, the Burma administration argued that the delinquency of native children was substantially rooted in 'mental defect' and that 'arrested mental development' was not an 'inherent...tendency'.[113] In the process, while the criminal nature of the child became more grounded in his physical pathology, it became detached from the parental tie. What was natural, the Burma penologists argued, could also be abnormal.

The individualization of the delinquent in the form of the patient does not mean that the idea of inherited defect was discarded. In 1928, when the Bengal Legislative Council was debating the provincial Borstal Bill, J Campbell Forrester of the Tanjore Borstal Association made a dramatic speech in defence of inherited nature as the defining feature of the habitual criminal. Forrester said:

> One has only to spend a little time in our Police Courts or assizes to watch the prisoners as they are put in the dock for trial; every now and then interspersed among the trivial and accidental cases appears one whom an expert criminologist condemns by his face, for there you will find written in his face the human jackal, fox, tiger, the ape or compound of them all; some story of robbery or violence is told, the evidence is incontrovertible, and the accused is found guilty. Then...up gets an official and...reads a long list of previous convictions. When he is turned loose again, it must follow as the night the day, he will return to his only business, that of preying on society, and the training and breeding of other like unto himself. One must recognize that there are types of men who ought no more to be let loose on society than should a wolf or a rattlesnake. It is the born neurotic among whom the sub-class of habitual criminal is found, the man or woman who...occasionally robs, swindles or murders for gain, in whom the ape or tiger nature is unquenched or unquenchable, who goes astray from his mother's womb, that is a distinct species or subspecies of the order, and all criminologists, Governors of Prisons and others who have to do with criminals recognize this type,

and many consider that like wild savage animals when once captured they should not be turned loose on society. Kindness, discipline, nothing will alter this type. They have inherited this terrible disease; nothing on earth will cure it.[114]

Other criminals were different, however, and for them Forrester recommended Borstal regimes:

But when we come to the ordinary criminal, then it has been clearly proved that mercy and charity, tempered with firmness, produce better effects on the government of men than any amount of anger or vindictive cruelty, and nature answers the voice more readily than the spur. Make a healthy man of your criminal or prospective criminal, give him a sound well-developed brain to think with, and rich cleaned blood to feed it upon, and an opportunity to earn an honest living — then preach to him if you like.[115]

In Forrester's self-consciously scientific view, nurture is nearly irrelevant to delinquency, either as cause or as correction. He is not necessarily describing a native biology; he envisions a criminal biology that cuts across race and culture because nurture is inconsequential. Nevertheless, as Dirks, Bates and others have pointed out, the early twentieth-century science of behavioural physiology was driven by colonial race science, and Risley is present as a ghost in Forrester's identification of animal traits in human faces and natures.[116]

Forrester was by no means alone or innovative in seeing child offenders in this light. At the turn of the century, G G Giffard, the Superintendent of Chingleput reformatory (and an IMS man) had not concealed his pleasure at discovering an inmate with a 'Jack Sheppard-like head'. Giffard had been certain that the head shape reflected the boy's crime (murder), even as he noted that the child was actually quite well-behaved.[117] The 'recognition' of the head shape of an early eighteenth-century English thief (and folk mythology figure reinterpreted by metropolitan criminology) in an Indian juvenile delinquent had excited Giffard, just as the animal faces excited Forrester. The former had noted his inability to match the boy's crime with those of Sheppard, and the boy's good behaviour with Sheppard's reputation for stubborn resistance, but such problems only made the reformatory a worthwhile experiment.

It is important to note that neither Giffard nor Forrester saw inherited nature as the key to the delinquency of all, or even most, children in the Indian reformatory. They sought, instead, to articulate a separation between the deviant (biologically flawed, no reform possible) and the delinquent (socially damaged, reform imaginable) as sub-categories of the juvenile offender. Forrester, in particular, identified the former category with the habitual criminal. Nailer, like Giffard, had fantasized about reforming physiological deviants by curing them, but he had seen his craniological curiosities as precisely that — curiosities in the midst of a larger population of delinquent children. They had thus imposed a fairly consistent set of restrictions on the scope of natural deviance in the Indian reformatory.

At the outset of the colonial project of reforming native children, nurture — the transmission of delinquency by the social environment of family, caste, peer culture and the institution itself — had been the dominant discourse. Plans for the reclamation of the children of dacoits, for instance, had eschewed references to 'dacoit children', implied a capability on the part of administrators in overcoming any residual inherited criminality through expert nurturing and allowed the children of criminals to mingle with the children of relatively respectable peasants.[118] Even the children of habitual criminals, who were most frequently viewed as having inherited their parents' delinquency, were just as often seen as socially habituated delinquents. (In either case, they were consistently distinguished from children who had 'fallen' into habit, acquiring criminal habits relatively late in childhood.[119]) It was not uncommon for reformatory administrators to assume that if such children could be institutionalized while they were still very young, then environmentally acquired habits could be eradicated before they congealed into a physiologically imbedded nature.[120]

In the new century, while some scrutinizers like Forrester looked for inherited traits, most experts were more interested in identifying and confronting the effects of the environment upon embodied nature. They were, in other words, doctors but not geneticists. The reports from Chingleput in the early 1900s show a perception that although criminal tendencies were rooted in the body like diseases, the plasticity of the child combined with the social environment of the city or the reformatory itself to produce the disease.[121] After the Great War, certainly, it was the discourse of the environmentally acquired but physically manifested disease that predominated in the Indian reformatory, and I use the word 'Indian' deliberately to indicate a political shift. When Forrester made his remarks in the Bengal legislature, Bhupendra Narayan Sinha retorted:

> In the West where the science of criminology is fast crystallizing into an accurate and reasoned course of things, the criminal is treated as one curable, crime being regarded as one of the pathological states of the human mind. I know that such a daring statement will not commend itself to some of the older members present in this House, but a perusal of some of the best works of psychologists, men who have made this

branch their special study, will find this startling revelation enumerated. Crime is curable, and if curable, why not cured?[122]

Sinha's comments reflect a reluctance to accept the static 'specimen status' to which Forrester consigned native juvenile delinquents. Rejecting the marginality of the colonial laboratory as well as the immutability of genetic defect, he demands a more elaborate set of discursive and disciplinary tools, by which practically any child offender can be 'cured' of crime and effectively regenerated. Sinha was quite unexceptional; in Madras, Contractor wrote:

> The view that criminals are born and not made is no longer held by modern thinkers. Hence misbehaviour cannot be attributed to some innate wickedness but only as a symptom to show that the offender is maladjusted to his environment. Mental analysis…is essential, for misconduct, like other forms of conduct, results from mental causes and therefore the intensive investigation of the individual is the only way to the solution of the baffling problems of criminality and nowhere will this result be more fruitful as in the proper and thorough investigation of the young delinquent, for the deciding factors of a delinquent's career are found amongst the conditions of the offender's early life.[123]

He added, 'It is absolutely essential to provide recreation to the children apart from the games and other educational entertainments' and recommended more trips to the beach and the cinema.[124] Whereas Forrester had constructed the colonial reformatory as a zoo filled with tropical animals for metropolitan experts to visit, Contractor sought to take the inmate to the real zoo, i.e. to a signifier of modern childhood.

Contractor provides a more elaborate breakdown of nurture than his European predecessors, and a very different vision of the relationship between nature and criminality than what Forrester had offered. While biology is privileged in his analysis, he is clear that biology reflects an environment that is both flawed and marginal, and also that biological defects are amenable to correction. This is related to earlier assumptions about the gelling of habit into nature, but whereas in the past, that gelled nature was seen as perverse, i.e. morally and politically menacing, Contractor sees it as merely defective. The response, not surprisingly, shifts from an emphasis on policing and controlling, to studying, detecting and curing. By portraying the delinquent as a marginal representative of a marginalized population, Contractor is able to marginalize the problem itself, even as he works to recover the individual defective child from this periphery. This does not mean that he represents the problem as insignificant. He implies, rather, that the defect is restricted to the margins of Indian society, that it is not reflective of a larger social/racial/national flaw and that it can be corrected by confident, if undervalued, experts like himself.

Scrutinizing the education of Maori, white and 'mixed race' children in early twentieth-century New Zealand, Sue Middleton has observed that the burgeoning interpenetrations of race and mental defect (or health) were premised on the potential 'equality' and assimilability of the natives.[125] Even if her reading is accurate, white reformatory administrators in India were not burdened by a similar vision of assimilation. This is what set H A F Nailer apart from Contractor, who otherwise shared his white predecessor's assumptions about the individuality of the defective child. The attention that an 'assimilator' like Contractor paid to 'mental analysis' was closely aligned with both his interest in correcting defects and his anticolonial assertiveness. Kakar's work suggests that psychological studies of cultural phenomena — such as crime, or childhood itself — modernize the analyst as well as the analyzed; quite apart from being self-evidently scientific, such studies are nationally oriented, with a 'national psyche' as an implicit or explicit frame of reference.[126] Also, as Hartnack has noted, colonial psychoanalysis developed as a sub-plot within a discernible political conflict of the early twentieth century, with Indian and British analysts seeking to use the discipline as a metaphor of conquest, resistance and competition.[127] Contractor's vision of the juvenile mind is similar to that of Girindrasekhar Bose, who approached the troubled child as an engineering problem rather than a problem of excavation, not least because the latter technique was inseparable from Freudian-European hegemony within the field.[128] It is not, however, an identical strategy. Unlike Bose and other Indian psychoanalysts, Contractor and his colleagues in the reformatory sought a close affiliation with the metropole, consigning their European colleagues to the inferiority of a peripheral practice.

Shortly before Indian independence, S Rangnekar, the President of the Bombay Aftercare Association, wrote that while reformation must continue to outweigh retribution in juvenile punishment, particularly if Indian penal practice was to be aligned with 'modern social thought', it was also important to emphasize pre-emption, since prevention was 'better than cure'.[129] Rangnekar made the remarks in the context of his efforts to persuade mill owners to hire formal Borstal inmates. On the surface, this was the completion of a circle that began with the apprenticeship schemes of 1850 and the licensing provisions of Sassoon. Rangnekar, however, was engaged in a different project. He was occupied in a search for moral, modern and civilized mantles, but from inside the system as the colonial state came to an end. The persuasion-over-cure outlook that he advanced is based on the old idea of an essential innocence which is liable to be damaged by a flawed environment, but like Contractor's prescription of trips to the zoo, it is a scientific recasting of the idea and an assertion of ownership over the environment as well as the child. Rangnekar did not write from a position of overwhelming confidence; reformatory reports in the 1940s are full of chagrin about released inmates who had 'reverted' to crime. Even as the state had become less sanguine about its efforts at repairing the damage done to children, however, it had also become more willing to intervene aggressively in the damaging environment.

Conclusion: The Nature of the Native

The colonial reformatory produced a body of knowledge about the nature of the native, in addition to knowledge about the child and the juvenile delinquent. The process of production was not unidirectional; rather, the native, the child and the juvenile delinquent were generated through a process of constant cross-referencing. The native that entered or emerged from the reformatory was not consistently a distinct racial entity. For professionals who were particularly invested in metropolitan credentials, such as Mouat, the racial peculiarity of the native could be nearly submerged within the universal modernity of the institution. Even for these experts, however, peculiarity could not be made to vanish entirely. Napier, who was Mouat's ideological ally in almost every way, based his call for a modern institutional regime in an assertion of racial difference, writing that 'a particular consideration of the physiognomy and history of crime in India may induce Government to modify their objections to the institution of Reformatories'.[130]

The European, Napier argued, was not so much representative of the universal as a normative model in an experimental site where levels of difference might be tested and compensated for. Conservatives who resisted the applicability of reformatory regimes in India were even more insistent on the peculiarity of native nature. On occasion, they envisioned the native as innocent and the European as corrupt, with Howell writing, 'The lowest classes in this country are probably very superior in the scale of humanity to the similar classes in England'.[131] In this rather romantic view, the moral and the civilized were distinct and existed in an inverse relationship, not unlike innocence and age; the modern reformatory could only be corrupting of native innocence.

The more common view, by far, was that native nature was marked by incorrigibility and precocity, or the combination of limited plasticity and an equally limited innocence. The tendency of reformatory administrators to be 'defeated' by boys who refused to be reformed and who had to be sent to jail, reinforced this perception of an unchildlike lack of plasticity. When D W D

Comins, the Inspector General of Prisons in Bengal, complained about the early age at which native children became hardened in 'habits of depravity', he linked his complaint to the 'precocity of lads in this country'.[132] Comins' perspective on native precocity was rooted in a particular view of native nature, which emphasized a natural absence (rather than loss) of innocence. This absence of innocence was not tied to any specific criminal act; Comins used the word 'habit' to describe this natural 'depravity', indicating that it is delinquency that is natural in the native. A D Larymore went a step further than Comins and located depraved 'habit' in the native environment, in multiple senses of the word 'environment'.[133] Delinquency was thus equated with a natural precocity, shaped by the nature of the land but more directly by social influence, determining not only the apparent difference from Europeans but the specifics of punishment and reform.

Not surprisingly, the institutional vision of the colonial reformatory was geared towards evaluating levels of plasticity and capacity for reform, which in turn indicated racial characteristics, which indicated what could and could not be achieved in a specific colonial setting. The reformatory supplied the statistics that appeared to 'prove' the racial basis of precocity. The 1898 report from Chingleput points out that whereas fifty percent of boys admitted to British reformatories in 1897 were under the age of fourteen and twelve percent under twelve, the corresponding numbers for Chingleput were eighty and twenty-three percent. The superintendent comments in the margins, 'This would imply that a criminal tendency in youth shows itself at an earlier stage of life in India than in Great Britain.'[134] The Burmese penal record states, while noting a sharp rise in the population of incarcerated habitual criminals, 'The habitual starts his career of crime early in life; about thirty per cent commit their first offence before they are twenty one years of age.'[135] Here, the process by which juvenile delinquency was informed by the discourse of habitual crime was reversed, and the larger category of the habitually delinquent native constructed with reference to juvenile delinquency.

The simultaneous narratives of innocence, incorrigibility and precocity appear to leave the colonial expert with a set of unanswered questions, the most basic of which is whether the native could actually have a childhood. The ambiguity fuelled the reformatory, and it is actually somewhat deceptive. Innocence, incorrigibility and precocity were all components of childhood in the periphery and reflections of a larger relationship between the colonizer and the colonized. The incorrigible and the precocious were not childlike, and in that sense, they were adults disguised by age. The perverse discrepancy between what might be considered moral age and biological age, however, deprived their adulthood of political value, and consigned them to the ranks of the childish. By constricting the 'childlike' status of its inmates and calling into question the validity of a line between the child and the adult in India, the colonial reformatory expanded the 'childish' status of a much wider population of natives. When Indian experts moved to create an unambiguous and fully articulated native child, they also moved to delineate an unambiguous, fully articulated native state of adulthood.

3

EXPERIMENTAL CHILDHOODS: PAIN AND THE REFORMATORY

In 1853, Charles Hathaway, Inspector General of Prisons in Punjab, wrote a memo to the provincial government outlining the problems posed by juvenile offenders. The system in place for the punishment of children, Hathaway wrote, was a dismal failure. Young vagrants and thieves drifted in and out of British-Indian jails, returning often and becoming progressively delinquent with each visit. Under such circumstances, the Inspector General asked, 'how is his chance of reformation bettered?'[1]

Hathaway's alarm illuminates an ideological and administrative crisis within the colonial reformatory, shortly after the passage of Act XIX of 1850 and long before the RS Acts and the Bayley-Napier debates. Due to the work of Arnold and Ernst[2], we are as familiar with the shortcomings of colonial modernity as Hathaway appears to have been. The colonial prison was not Bentham's Panopticon or even Ignatieff's Pentonville, and it would be unreasonable to expect the child inmate to become 'a hostage in his own hands'.[3] Nevertheless, taking their cue from Foucault, scholars of disciplining institutions have generally made two related points. One is that nineteenth-century modernity was optimistic about the possibility of managing disorderly populations by subjecting the individual offender to measured doses of discomfort. The other is that this modernity was marked by a steady, albeit incomplete, withdrawal from the deliberate infliction of physical injury.[4]

Both assumptions, while reasonably correct in some institutional settings, must be treated with caution. Early Victorians tended to view flogging as preferable to the penal transportation of child criminals, and corporal punishment remained a feature of metropolitan pedagogy long after Arnoldian 'moral influence' had become commonplace.[5] Even 'cruelty men' like Benjamin Waugh and the NSPCC supported the flogging of juvenile offenders, although they did it to attack existing prisons (and in the process, exposed themselves to charges of 'cruel, barbarous and retrogressive' thinking).[6] In British India, the modernity of the juvenile institution failed to generate conviction even as it generated buildings, cells and classrooms. Moreover, it did not necessarily move in a direction that might signal an ideological shift away from physically painful punishment. In fact, the punishment of children in the colony ran counter to the expectations that usually accompany the new prison — here, the use of 'pre-modern' punishments, especially flogging, actually expanded alongside modern infrastructure. A rough periodization illustrates the problem. Before the 1860s, children convicted by British-Indian courts were typically incarcerated with adult prisoners in wards without cells. This led some observers to call for entirely separate reformatories. While a patchwork of laws and reformatories began to take shape in the 1870s, a larger apparatus of special courts, probation and age graded institutions for juvenile offenders had to wait until after the World War. The interim years were marked by calls for reform, unsatisfying experiments with cellular prisons and children's wards, and an increasing reliance on the whip.

Modern punitive techniques, particularly cellular confinement, were not consistently utilized in India because they were incompatible with British assumptions about the nature of Indian children, including the suspicion that delinquent habits were so pervasive in India that the reformatory could neither hope to accommodate the problem infrastructurally nor identify a normatively moral society against which delinquents could be identified, judged and rehabilitated. Prospects for recognizably modern reformatories in India were further undermined by fluctuating contests involving British prison administrators, Indian jail employees, unofficial observers and of course, children. While nearly all British administrators engaged with juvenile delinquency in India were convinced that the reform and rehabilitation of 'bad' children were desirable, only a few retained the hope that reform — the conversion of idle, disorderly and disobedient children into productive and disciplined native subordinates — could be effected under Indian conditions.

It was generally agreed that reform required a triple segregation : the separation of child criminals from their families, from adult convicts and from each other. Yet this consensus was superficial, and below the surface, there were serious disagreements about the degrees and conditions of what was to be a separate punishment. Under the circumstances, those officials who saw a modern reformatory regime as the solution to the problem of child offenders became despondent about their ability to sustain multiple segregations over the duration of an extended institutionalization. This eroded their faith not only in the broad principle of locking up children, but also in the efficacy of reforming institutions. What developed in consequence was an enduring reluctance on the part of the government to incarcerate children and an increasing reliance on corporal punishment. The Whipping Act, which in 1864 was greeted by colonial administrators and jailors (including Hathaway) as an attractive alternative to reformatories,[7] retained its relevance even as juvenile delinquency became more complex and internally differentiated, and after the creation of laws and institutions geared for young criminals.

The Troubled Regime: Segregation, Education and Prison Labor

An obsession with segregation — the separation of the child from the adult, the redeemable from the incorrigible and the reformed from the corrupting — drove the reformatory as it developed in the nineteenth century. Not surprisingly, when British observers declared that colonial reformatories were failing to reform their inmates, their observations were underpinned by a perception that it was segregation that had substantially failed. In British India, as in French Indochina, there was a stutter between the fantasies of progressive experts and actual bureaucratic practice. Zinoman has shown, in Indochina, the coexistence of bold plans for agricultural communes for child offenders and the disheartening reality of juveniles imprisoned with adults in common jails.[8] In India, the RS Acts were only partially implemented — there were not enough children serving long sentences in existing reformatories to justify the expense of new institutions.[9] Also, while colonial administrators from the 1860s onwards were willing to accept a limited quasi-parental responsibility for native children, they shied from any state activism that might be construed as charity.[10] The numbers of children convicted for long sentences remained low because there were few specialized reformatories to receive them. In the 1890s, when the Legislative Department began its deliberations on amending the RS Act, the original law had not been implemented at all in Punjab. Here, as in much of British India, the envisioned institutions had simply not been created. What had been built instead were halfway measures in the form of juvenile wards attached to large prisons, which were not significantly different from the juvenile wards of the 1850s and 1860s.

These were significant setbacks, especially since the case for a comprehensive reformatory regime in India had been made as early as 1853. Hathaway, who proposed the idea, had put forward a detailed plan that combined vocational training and finely judged levels of punishment and reward within the institution, with elaborate schemes for the probation, rehabilitation and long term control of prisoners released from the reformatory. For repeat offenders, Hathaway had recommended a program of solitary confinement, silence and general deprivation — a vision of correction that is easily recognized as the Pentonville model. Even as he echoed the enthusiasm of his metropolitan colleagues, however, Hathaway had anticipated failure, admitting that his plans 'may…appear Utopian' in the Indian context.[11] This was an accurate forecast. The methodical classification upon which Hathaway's scheme was based was never systematically attempted, because most convicts on the Indian mainland, children included, served sentences that ranged from a few days to a few months.[12] When they arrived at institutions with significant juvenile populations, such as jails in Gurdaspur, Lahore and Calcutta, it made no sense to separate them into distinct classes, because the reforming movement from class to class was not feasible in the short period of their incarceration. Some juvenile prisons, like Gurdaspur, made an effort to separate younger children from adolescents, but that was the extent of the classification.[13]

To understand the difficulties of enforcing a comprehensive segregation within the institutions that developed between the 1850s and the 1870s, it is useful to look briefly at Gurdaspur. This reformatory had originated as the children's wing of the Sialkot jail in 1862.[14] Taking on an institutional identity of its own, the wing had relocated to Gurdaspur. Typically, it had the largest population of juvenile offenders of any prison in Punjab, averaging between forty and ninety boys. Gurdaspur's inmates were not local youths, but came from all over the province. Also, they stayed longer than juveniles in other jails — only boys with sentences of six months or more were sent to Gurdaspur. The reformatory shared a compound with a prison for adult convicts, but a measure of segregation was nevertheless maintained. The boys worked in their own manufactory yard, attended classes separately from adults in the daytime, and slept in their own barracks at night.[15] To prevent sexual contact, boys under the age of twelve (there were twenty-two of these in 1870) were required to sleep in a separate barrack from the older children.[16]

In some ways, the arrangement worked. A M Dallas — very much an enthusiast of modern penology — noted approvingly in 1867 that the children 'appeared clean and quiet, and orderly in their conduct'.[17] At the same time, frustrations developed that never quite faded. Early in his tenure as Inspector General of Prisons, Dallas expressed his discomfort with the fact that the reformatory was part of a prison compound. 'I do not think that a reformatory of this kind should be placed in a jail occupied by adult prisoners,' he wrote in 1863. 'The great object is to remove the boys from all influences of a criminal character; if they be in the same jail as adult criminals, it will be found impossible to isolate them.'[18] This sense of a compromised segregation remained a recurring theme in Dallas' reports about Gurdaspur. In 1870, he noted that the older boys had been compelled to labor in the adult work yard, and complained that the juvenile dormitories were too close to the adult barracks.[19] The situation had not improved two years later, when he discovered that boys as young as thirteen were working with adult prisoners.[20]

The failures were all the more demoralizing to prison administrators because the larger reformatories were intended to function as the sites of an inland penal transportation for children. This intent was not universal; some administrators, such as Bayley and Lord Lawrence, believed that native children were biologically incapable of surviving relocation to an unfamiliar soil and climate even within their natal province.²¹ Their anxiety was outweighed by the determination of others (like Napier and Dallas) to remove children from the social environment of their crimes. The Gurdaspur institution was looked upon favourably by British penal professionals because of its isolated location and the railway line that facilitated the importation of child convicts.²² It is not coincidental that in 1866, a ten year old, sentenced to penal transportation for life, was initially sent to Gurdaspur. Dallas forwarded him to the Andaman Islands, 'to give him a chance there of leading a useful life'.²³ Like transportation to the Andamans, incarceration in a remote reformatory (as opposed to a local jail) made sense in the context of a delinquency generated by social associations. It promised to disrupt those ties and discourage the re-emergence within the prison of the associations of the outside. Since it isolated the convict from the comforting and corrupting company of his peers, it was simultaneously punitive and reforming.

That this plan for isolating children was floundering in Punjab was acknowledged by Hathaway, who was appalled by what he saw in the prisons under his jurisdiction. He complained to the provincial government:

> What character *but* a 'bad character' *can* remain to a boy of fourteen or fifteen, who has been first corrupted by the scenes he witnesses during his period of Barrack servitude, and the crimes of lying and thieving he is forced to commit, for the hard taskmasters his lot has placed him under? When committed to Prison, he associates with grown-up criminals seven times more wicked than himself. He goes in a vagrant, he comes out a thief; when released, what is he to do? He has no home, no means of subsistence. If he migrates to another station, he is a vagabond. If he stays where he is, he is a Jail Bird.²⁴ [Emphases in original.]

Hathaway's remarks show a sympathetic understanding of how prisons produced delinquents in the discursive sense as well as in the practical senses of corruption.²⁵

While adult-child contact in the wards triggered the most visceral reactions from critics of the colonial prison, it was also recognized that child offenders had to be separated from their families, including their parents. Yet this was precisely what the early Indian reformatory, with its constant ingress and egress of delinquents and its inability to maintain an exclusive authority over the released, failed to deliver. Faced with an institutional environment that rendered extended segregation exceptional rather than normal, officials like

Dallas became skeptical not only about the possibility of reform, but also about the effectiveness in India of reforming techniques such as prison education and supervised labor. They made compromises that only added to their sense of failure, because a prisoner who left the prison with no recognizable skills could not be given a ticket of leave, which was critical to the colonial regime's attempt to control former prisoners.[26] A released delinquent without a state-approved job might return to his delinquent family and occupations, erasing the beneficial effects of his erstwhile isolation.

In its content as well as in its essential rituals, prison education promised multiple benefits to British penal professionals who worked with children in India. It was seen as a source of moral inspiration and an aid in the Victorian project of 'character building',[27] which in this context meant overwriting the natural unreason of the native with the ability to control unreasonable impulses. It was also the means of inculcating the ethos and skills of labor, training in the discipline and the hierarchy of the classroom, and a practical punishment for a population that, with some exceptions, found schooling 'extremely distasteful'.[28] A morally charged education had already been tested as a colonizing strategy for the native elites, and it is not unreasonable to follow Foucault in observing that a different curriculum, utilizing not Shakespeare but work, docility and subordination, was deployed in those sites of power where the poor and marginal were concentrated.[29] In spite of an apparent consensus on the desirability of these ends, however, tensions developed within prison schools about the specifics of what children were taught, and a conflict between education and labor was evident well before Indians like Mukerji and Gidumal entered the fray of reformatory administration.[30]

The basic structure of prison education in Punjab, especially for child convicts, was developed in the early 1860s; Hathaway had taken the lead in pushing the provincial government in this direction.[31] Schooling in jails and reformatories was placed under the supervision of the Department of Public Instruction (DPI) and the curricula brought in line with those already in use in district schools. Teachers and inspectors were to be provided by the DPI, and prisons were required to conduct daily classes in reading, writing, arithmetic and geography. While most of this instruction was in Urdu and Hindi, Dallas reported in 1867 that several of the inmates of Gurdaspur had 'made progress in English'.[32] Typically for a regime which was uneasy about its ability to impress any but a limited segment of criminalized children, prisoners whose sentences were shorter than six months, and those who were determined to be physically, mentally, or temperamentally 'incapable of learning', were excluded from classes.[33]

This education, however, was not all that juvenile convicts were expected to absorb. 'Book learning' took a back seat to vocational training, which was frequently a euphemism for labor that generated revenue for the prison. Boys at Gurdaspur were put to work on spinning twine, weaving, carpet manufacture, pottery and — playing havoc with gender — knitting.[34] Prison administrators saw this as essential for the boys' reform, not only because it trained them for 'honest' occupations, but also because it might impart a tolerance for the idea of regular, repetitive work. Even observers who conceded that spinning twine in prison did not constitute vocational training accepted the labor regime as educational. Dallas pointed out that 'it is work that can be easily learnt, and performed profitably by boys'. The profits, he made clear, should accrue to the institution, and not the children.[35]

The problem, however, was that labor and education in the reformatory did not always reinforce each other. Since work took time away from reading and writing, classes were irregular and brief. This was true of nearly every juvenile prison in India — in Calcutta's Presidency Jail, children were made to labor for ten hours every day, and studied only at night and when they were allowed to take a break from work.[36] In Punjab, even Dallas, who was typically upbeat in his assessment of progress in the classroom, noted that some prison administrators were 'disposed to view the education of prisoners as a waste of time'.[37] Textbooks were non-existent. Conceding that education in the conventional sense had not 'taken the position it ought', Dallas explained that the reason was the overwhelming emphasis placed on 'teaching trades'.[38] British readings of Indian culture, including a sympathetic adoption by prison administrators of the prejudices of elite Indians, also undermined the education of delinquent children. Dallas cited the example of one boy who had been excused from school 'because he was a sweeper' and another because he was 'employed on a certain kind of work in the manufactory'.[39] Here, the defining occupations of Indian children — decided by jailors with reference to caste, social status and appropriate work — determined their position within the reformatory, and made some inmates appear unsuited for 'book learning'.

An unreservedly critical appraisal of prison education came from R Grey, who temporarily replaced Dallas as Inspector General of Prisons in 1869. Grey declared that prison schools had failed altogether, and that students had made minimal progress. He blamed overcrowded classrooms and a general paucity of the 'right sort' of teachers.[40] Some British observers — notably Carpenter — wanted Indian reformatories to employ European instructors, who might forcefully impress their moral-racial selves upon material that was still soft.[41] More typically, colonial jailors and bureaucrats recognized that respectable whites would demand respectable white salaries, and generate peculiar ideological problems as surrogate parents for poor native children. They preferred elite, but adequately subordinated Indians who might provide a model of respectable native adulthood that did not encroach upon British cultural and political prerogatives.[42] The racial identity and social location of the teachers mattered because prison education was itself a process of segregation, or a technique of isolating juvenile delinquents from the society of criminals in the present and in the future. It was important, therefore, that the teachers be sufficiently distant from the delinquents and the British themselves in terms of their place in the colonial order.

What Grey saw in several Punjab prisons was child convicts being instructed by elderly *burkundazes* (guards) who doubled as teachers in exchange for two or three extra rupees every month. Jail inspectors in Bengal and Mysore noted that convicts themselves were frequently employed as teachers of imprisoned children.[43] In other jails, the teachers came from outside the prison, but their positions were neither stable nor remunerative. They tended to resign and move on, bringing classes to a standstill. Their salaries were pitiful — between seven and fifteen rupees monthly. Such instructors could hardly be expected to function as effective agents of social relocation. With some exceptions, British observers had scant respect for the men who taught child convicts in Indian jails, seeing them as underqualified and indifferent.[44] Dallas remarked upon the disorder he saw in the classroom at the Sirsa prison, and added that the teacher 'had little influence to keep [the students] quiet'.[45]

The advanced age of *burkundaz* teachers was a ubiquitous phenomenon. It may be surmised that in a social relationship that required close contact between juveniles and low-status native men, the arrangement was calculated to reduce the chances of sexual abuse. Age would also have widened the generational distance between teachers and students, allowing teachers to function, theoretically, as surrogate grandfathers. This was very much an innovation of the periphery — the juvenile delinquency establishment in England showed an explicit preference for younger supervisors, believing them to be best suited to understand the needs of the child.[46] In India, where the British had convinced themselves about the Oriental reverence for age, older men were the more suitable guardians.

Solitary Childhoods

Disappointment with existing juvenile institutions led colonial administrators to evaluate two options that were seemingly located on opposite poles of the discourse of modern punishment. One — flogging — was emblematic of the physical torture and limited ambitions that Foucault has indicated are jettisoned on the road to modernity.[47] The other — solitary confinement — is the quintessentially modern punishment, in which the criminal is deprived of society and left to reflect endlessly, so that he might be tormented internally by his own demons and reformed in the process. Corporal punishment and solitary confinement co-existed in the colonial prison as two parts of a single, albeit not seamless, punitive strategy. The ideological tensions between the two approaches to punishment, which are not irreconcilable to begin with,[48] were partially muted here in a pragmatic search for short term control. This allowed for simultaneous experiments with cells and the flogging post, and for the hope that either could solve the problems that plagued juvenile institutions.

The reformative effect of isolation in cells has impeccable Benthamite credentials; the idea is at the heart of the English penitentiary and its various institutional cousins.[49] In India, the architecture of solitary confinement was a relative latecomer. Although proponents of cellular jails, like Mouat, sought to bolster their case by pointing out that Macaulay had called for such prisons as early as 1838,[50] the first full-scale cellular institutions began to appear in India only at the end of the 1800's, half a century after the building of Pentonville. Nevertheless, colonial administrators who encountered juvenile convicts called early for a system of solitary incarceration. Hathaway included it in his plans for repeat offenders.[51]

In the mid-1860s, quite soon after the passage of the Whipping Act, solitary confinement emerged as the great white hope of professionals who wanted a modern reformatory regime in India, and who saw the project foundering on the rocks of apathy, resistance and culture. Mouat, in particular, saw the associated (non-cellular) carceral institution in India as the sign of a regrettable distance between metropolitan and colonial penology, declaring that such buildings were 'antiquated in form, defective in construction, and unsuited to the present advanced state of public opinion'.[52] Asserting his own affiliation with metropolitan prison reformers like Mirabeau in France, Mouat called for the conversion of a wing of the Presidency Jail into a cellular prison for children. Within the larger project of the reformatory, the cell was a primary experimental space, enabling certain schemes — such as the institutionalization of girls and the children of respectable parents — precisely because it was conceived in opposition to corporal punishment.[53] At a very basic level, the infrastructure of separate confinement reified delinquency as a problem, and as a legitimate area of state action and professional expertise. Not long after the passage of the RS Act of 1876, one hundred and fourteen new cells were added to the reformatory in Hazaribagh, formerly a mental asylum for Europeans.[54] When the additions were under consideration, a trio of enthusiastic jailors and policemen reported to Richard Temple:

> We would begin by providing accommodation for two hundred boys. On the institution of a reformatory, many boys now sentenced to flogging or to short terms would no doubt be sent to it; and in very short time the number would probably rise to two hundred, at which we would propose to keep it till the institution should have justified itself by its results.[55]

Heeley, Mackenzie and Lambert were optimistic that the cellular reformatory would allow for subtle gradations of delinquency and correction, and allow them to establish and protect the 'juvenile' within the 'juvenile offender', with the school and the family — the definitive children's institutions of late-Victorian England — mitigating the prison. In the process, the punishing 'governor' would be transformed into the *pater familias* and headmaster, not altogether unlike the image that O B C St. John and Chester Macnaghten were creating for themselves in the Chiefs' Colleges in the same period.[56] The three men wrote Temple (who forwarded their report to Howell):

> The boys are to be kept under strict discipline, but otherwise treated as little like prisoners as possible. A cheerful spirit is to be encouraged, and no harshness of any sort will be allowed on the part of the officers. The punishments should, except in the case of extremely bad behaviour or incorrigible idleness, resemble school punishments rather than jail punishments, and only in the last instance should flogging and solitary confinement be resorted to — the former to be confined to five strokes, and the latter to six hours' confinement in a cell, except with the sanction of the Inspector General or two official visitors. No jail officer except the governor will be allowed to punish any boy.[57]

That the cellular reformatory might facilitate the categorization of disorder was obvious to bureaucrats who began to implement the RS Act. The Northwest Provinces administration told the Government of India that in the new buildings that were expected to materialize, the children of habitual criminals, children criminalized by poverty and the offspring of the respectable could be punished separately.[58] The cell thus promised to broaden the scope of the reformatory, by providing experts with a way around the political and ideological difficulties of whipping particular categories of native children. S Lynch, Superintendent of Calcutta's Presidency Jail before Mackenzie, envisioned the cell as an instrument that would allow adult monitors not only to intercept mutual influence among incarcerated juveniles, but to detect the nature of the child and of delinquency itself:

> The difficulties of dealing with remanded, convicted, and reconvicted boys disappear when cell accommodation is provided. With separate cell accommodation, one yard, one teacher, and one work overseer and guard, will suffice for remands, vagrants, mendicants, petty offenders, felons, the recommitted, and the specially depraved children, each of which classes may be represented by a single individual on their first admission. The strictest seclusion would be advisable until the characters of the children disclosed themselves.[59]

Nature, once discovered in the cell, could also be manipulated within the cell. Lynch was ready to interpret separate confinement as a triumph of institutional discipline over the indiscipline of childhood, but he also saw a more facilitating relationship between the cell, the colonial state and the native child. In his vision, the cell — used as a site of education and profitless labor — allowed the jailor to nurture the nature of the native in ways that were conducive, rather than obstructive, to reform. Lynch described a night-time scene in which boys studied in their cells by candlelight while the teacher walked past each cell, instructing the children through the grating in the locked doors. He wrote:

> It is a fact, characteristic of the disposition of Native children that this arrangement for learning seemed to displace and provide an efficient substitute for the spirit of mischief and the natural love of play, which one is accustomed to expect in children. The order and quiet which prevail now in this juvenile yard is remarkable, and more especially after lock-up, a time which formerly was devoted to attempts to communicate with adjoining cells, to singing and noises of all kinds.[60]

Lynch had thus developed a comprehensive ideology of solitary confinement for juvenile offenders, and was able to tell the provincial government that because cells 'diminished [the] temptation to do wrong', they also reduced the 'necessity for punishment'.[61] By 'punishment' he meant crude interventions in the body of the inmate, especially flogging. Even jailors who insisted upon an overtly punitive process of correction were able to see the cell as a vital asset. Fawcus, who was Lynch's counterpart in Alipore Jail, wrote in an oblique critique of the juvenile regime in Calcutta's other major prison:

> Their sojourn in jail should be made more disagreeable than it is at present, in order that imprisonment may have a deterring and reforming effect. All these objects can be attained only by means of cellular imprisonment, which will also render instruction easier, for the boys, prevented from passing their time in idle conversation with their comrades, will be only too glad to relieve the monotony of their life in a cell by a little study. All [work should] be done in the cells, and should consist in picking oakum, knotting towels, spinning, weaving, etc., as it is almost impossible to teach a trade…without the disadvantages of association.[62]

Fawcus and Lynch represent a broadly shared enthusiasm for solitary confinement in spite of their different visions of the correction that might take place within the cell. There was a practical side to their enthusiasm — it was understood that the central government might refuse to sanction reformatories that were fully separate from jails (and hence expensive), and that it would be cheaper to place children in cells within existing prisons like the Presidency Jail.[63] The cell could, in fact, forestall certain kinds of institutional and ideological revision— a function that was attractive to conservative administrators like R S Ellis, John Strachey and Arthur Howell, and even to Hathaway, the early Mouat, and J P Walker (the former Superintendent of the Andaman Islands penal colony[64]). All noted, at various points in the 1860s, that ongoing efforts to provide cells for jailed children had rendered the building of reformatories redundant.[65] For innovative jailors like Lynch and Mouat, the solitary confinement of children was an important compromise with the obstructionists, allowing them to retain the identity of the modern professional.

Solitary confinement was seen by some officials as a practical method of isolating boys from sexual contact with adult prisoners and with each other. By the 1860s, the cell had become a site where the sexualized native and native adolescence might be recovered for childhood.[66] (Stone observes that flogging — the major alternative to the cell — generated its own possibilities of sexual pleasure, which contributed to its growing disrepute, but that was largely a metropolitan concern.[67]) Mouat believed that sexual 'contagion' was endemic within all incarcerated populations of male criminals and — again identifying himself with French penology — referred to the non-cellular Bicetre prison as an universal example of a contaminating space,[68] but he was also convinced that Indians were naturally precocious and incapable of self-restraint, and that cells were an essential device of containment.[69] The sole juvenile inmate of Gujranwala jail was rarely allowed to leave his cubicle.[70] R Montgomery, the Judicial Commissioner of Punjab, sought to describe a scene in which cells were unavailable:

> The ribaldry, obscenity, and the gross wickedness which goes on among masses of oriental criminals so congregated, can be better imagined than described. They forget for the time their punishment; they harden each other in sin and vice.[71]

Montgomery believed that all prisoners who had been sentenced to rigorous imprisonment, including juveniles, should spend some time alone. He saw solitary confinement as a viable alternative to long prison terms, substituting a brief, intense period of isolation for an extended and unreliable segregation.[72] He found support in the office of the Lieutenant Governor of Punjab, which agreed that all new jails should have cells for at least fifty per cent of its inmates, and declared that 'there is no description of punishment whatever, that can compete in effectiveness with [solitary confinement] in the case of the boys of the [professionally criminal] classes'.[73] In 1871, the Punjab government noted that forty new cells had been built in the province's jails over the past year, and another one hundred had been commissioned. In the same breath, the government conceded that the numbers were 'far below the requirements of several jails'.[74]

On the surface, all this would seem to be an endorsement of the utility of cells. It is, however, clear that existing cells were underutilized when it came to incarcerated children. In the 1850s, when the reformatory was still in its infancy, Hathaway observed that 'solitary cells are in nearly every Jail kept empty, or used only for those awaiting to take their trial for murder, and other heinous offences'.[75] Half a century later, with the construction of specialized infrastructure relatively far advanced, the Punjab government observed that magistrates were not using the buildings to their full capacity, and were sending children to jail instead of the reformatory.[76] The problem, therefore, was not simply one of unavailable architecture; it was also a fundamental ambivalence on the part of colonial jailors and bureaucrats about the appropriateness of solitary confinement for Indian criminals, especially children. A significant section of the penal administration had refused to distinguish consistently between native children and adults when it came to incarceration, and some native children had not become convincingly childlike.

To some extent, this antipathy to solitary confinement reflected a conservative resistance to the universalizing tendencies of experts like Mouat. Bayley, who typically opposed Mouat's proposals for an expanded cellular regime, saw in the cell a necessary gap between the metropolitan and the colonial.[77] Indian criminals were too different from their European counterparts, he felt, to warrant a common set of institutional approaches. Also, because solitary confinement individualized delinquency, it generated skepticism in colonial jailors accustomed to thinking in terms of a culturally determined criminality. The problem was not, however, simply a matter of 'old fashioned' administrators refusing to use a 'modern' method of punishment. Dallas, who was in many ways a modernizer, was a determined opponent of placing children in solitary cells.[78] The skeptics often articulated their resistance to cellular confinement in terms of their own modern credentials, arguing that some, possibly all, children were unsuited to the cell. F F Handley, an active participant in the planning of the Alipore reformatory, referred not only to the culturally acquired unmanliness of Bengali boys,[79] but also to their physiological development while expressing his reservations:

> I doubt the advisability of [cellular confinement] for youthful offenders. If it be used at all, it should be for only short periods…never exceeding one week at a time. Bearing in mind the timid and superstitious nature of the people of this part of the country, I doubt if boys who are not

accustomed to sleep alone could be safely left alone, without possible injury to their health.[80]

Even Montgomery, a believer in solitary confinement, conceded that the cells might be better suited to England, Ireland and America than to India. His pessimism stemmed partially from his doubts about the racially determined capacity for reform in 'oriental criminals', but there were additional and equally powerful reasons to be skeptical about cellular reformatories in India. There was the north Indian climate — many jailors worried that cells became too hot in the summer and cold in the winter.[81] This was not frustration with the weather, or simply another manifestation of what Harrison and Redfield have identified as the intersecting discourses of climates and racialized bodies within colonial institutions.[82] It was implicitly related to the politics of the colonial prison, because although it was understood that cells could be heated in the winter, it was also recognized that the expense could not be justified in the context of 'native institutions' where the actual reform of the inmates was doubtful.

Montgomery understood that his arguments in favour of cells would be weighed against this pervasive skepticism. As he outlined his plans for a more perfect solitary regime, he conceded that 'such a system can only be carried out with a very superior and trustworthy Jail establishment, such we cannot command at present'.[83] Solitary confinement was not simply leaving the prisoner to rot in a cell; it was an elaborate tactic of isolation, surveillance, persuasion and calibrated deprivation. It required not only a modern jailor, but modern prison staff that would not allow the prisoner to leave his cell, to have visitors, to enjoy his confinement, to waste his time, to feign sickness, to become sick, or to die. None of this could be taken for granted in India, because as Arnold has noted, even the most energetic administrator had to contend with subordinates who did not fully share the reforming agenda of their supervisor, and whose participation in the prison regime was sporadic and perfunctory.[84]

Other prison administrators emphasized problems that had to do with the children themselves. Inmates of cellular prisons sometimes coopted the infrastructure of punishment and thus diluted its punitive content. Hathaway, a strong proponent of solitary confinement, noted with chagrin that Indian juveniles desired rather than dreaded the solitary cell, as a result of which 'our system of solitary confinement does not seem to have that wholesome effect which is contemplated'.[85] He shared the opinion of jailors who were convinced that Indians were a little too comfortable with the idea of a cell of their own, where they might escape the rigors of 'rigorous imprisonment'. J S F Mackenzie, Assistant Superintendent of the jail in Coorg, explained, 'Solitary confinement

[is] more suitable to the European than the Native, whose natural disposition prevents his feeling the full force of the intended punishment.'[86]

Quite separate from the revelation of native perversity was the issue of whether solitary punishment was actually helpful in the treatment of juvenile offenders. Dallas was convinced that it was not. Yet Dallas was not opposed to the basic principle of solitary confinement — he supported its use with adult convicts. In his mind, there were two objections to locking up juveniles in solitary cells, both of which derived from the universalistic conviction that children were more amenable to reform than adult criminals. Dallas believed that placing children in cells wasted an infrastructural resource that was better reserved for adults; he believed also that the best way to reform juveniles was through selective contact, not complete isolation. From his perspective, it made no sense to lock children away in cells, where they would have little communication with those who might mold them morally.[87] Dallas was hardly a maverick; his thinking was aligned with the 'visitation' schemes that were central to Victorian campaigns aimed at the dangerous classes, and which Carpenter tried (unsuccessfully) to encourage in India. Even Pentonville, for all its emphasis on isolation, encouraged contact between convicts and those who might exert a reforming influence.[88] Given these various concerns, solitary confinement remained underdeveloped as a punitive technique in the colonial arsenal.

Corporal Punishment and the Reformatory

Rattan and birch, on the other hand, were used often and with gusto. As a policeman in Burma in the 1920s, George Orwell could caricature the British nostalgia for the days when disobedient servants were sent to the station house with a note saying, 'Please give the bearer fifty lashes'.[89] Orwell's implication that flogging was a momentary assertion of dominance in a political environment devoid of hegemony was anticipated by the colonial government during the Rebellion of 1857, when the Governor General in Council observed that corporal punishment would be used 'in lieu of imprisonment…until order is completely re-established throughout the country'.[90] As Rudrangshu Mukherjee has pointed out, the Rebellion was a time when colonial society lost much of its modern skin and the establishment of political authority became reliant on spectacular displays of violence.[91] After the war and following the implementation of the Indian Penal Code in 1860, some of this reliance not only persisted, but became enmeshed in the fabric of the law and institutional practice. In this context, innovations like modern imprisonment were actually dissonant, and the dissonance registered within administrative circles as support for corporal punishment. Flogging remained a central feature of colonial penal practice, and many prison administrators remained convinced that it was the one punishment that Indian criminals, including children, truly dreaded.[92]

The concern with violence and authority was itself a mechanism of producing childhood, differentiating between adult and juvenile offenders, and of merging them when necessary. The Whipping Act of 1864 explicitly defined a child as a person under the age of eighteen.[93] The intent behind the drawing of this line was not to shield children from the whip, but to keep them from the adult space of the jail by facilitating the use of flogging as a substitute for incarceration.[94] In the final years of the century, the Whipping Act was seen by administrators in Madras as the ideal means of dealing with juvenile offenders who were fit for neither the reformatory nor the jail, and thus were neither children nor adults. But whereas the violence of the beating could be utilized to make gradations in the juvenility and criminality of the individual offender, a concern with authority was not far below the surface. J W F Dumerge, the Chief Secretary to the Government of Madras, wrote that the parents of punished children should be 'allowed' to watch the flogging.[95] The parent was simultaneously to be given a demonstration of the colonial state's authority over the native child, and displayed as a colonized native.

As late as 1932, the Whipping Act remained a semi-transparent instrument of the authority of the paternal state. The Delhi and Bombay administrations used the law to punish children arrested in connection with the civil disobedience movement.[96] One boy in Bombay was given twelve strokes of the rattan on his buttocks; the magistrate told the fourteen year old that the beating was intended to 'teach you a lesson'.[97] Clearly, the 'lesson' was intended to be retributive and perhaps deterrent, but not reforming. Colonial captors regarded the nationalist political offender as a variation on the habitual criminal; each was incorrigible, and political offence was a 'habit' in its own right.[98] With juveniles in 1930, the contagion of a modern political ideology without the redeeming oversight of British adults had eliminated romantic innocence as well as the plasticity of native childhood. After the incident in Bombay was reported in the Indian press, the Home Department decided that recourse to the nearly seventy-year-old law was likely to 'outrage public opinion both in India and in England' and ordered magistrates to desist.[99] The colonial state had reached the limits of the Whipping Act, and with it, an impasse in dealing with the native juvenile delinquent.

Between the 1860s and the 1930s in British India, the flogging of juvenile offenders was both widespread and contentious. Many in the government and within prison administrations saw the cane as an indiscriminate approach to punishment, and echoing their metropolitan counterparts, as useless. As one police officer wrote in his diary, 'These juvenile offenders are getting rather numerous, and a few stripes do not seem to deter them much.'[100] In 1864, the office of the Lieutenant Governor of Punjab took the position that 'as regards boys of the classes professionally engaged in the commission of crime, [flogging] is almost wholly inoperative'. The memory of the pain faded too quickly, and the ritual gave the boys an opportunity to defy the state physically before the admiring eyes of their peers. In fact, the memo continued, to punish such boys with flogging (instead of imprisonment) would be to 'afford a premium on crime'.[101] As early as the 1860s, some prisons, like Sialkot, did not use the cane at all on juvenile inmates, instead dressing them in special uniforms and putting them to work in the jail garden, the idea being that cultivation was both morally and occupationally rehabilitating.[102] In 1882, a discussion of the demerits of corporal punishment directly led the Government of India to order the Northwest Provinces and Oudh to establish a reformatory, or an alternative to flogging, for its juvenile offenders.[103]

By the early 1920s, every province of British India, including Burma, took the official position that whipping was an effective punishment only in a small minority of cases, and that repeated whippings were not effective at all.[104] This should not be read as an indication of inexorable progress towards the rejection of corporal punishment, but it does indicate the permeation into the colony of an evolving metropolitan discourse of juvenile correction, and also the feminization of Indian child-saving.[105] That such similar positions were voiced by administrators over a period of sixty years indicates a persistent ambivalence towards the efficacy of whipping children who, because of their peculiar criminological location, were not considered especially responsive to reformatory regimes. The flogging of child offenders persisted in spite of these reservations, indicating the retributive/deterrent and particularistic orientation of much of colonial penology.

An early and forceful attack on the corporal punishment of juvenile offenders came in the mid-1860s from Napier, who made several closely related points. He declared that whipping was a 'transitory and brutal punishment' and as such, both ineffective and morally indefensible. It was regressive, since it defeated the 'humane and enlightened intentions of the authors of the [Criminal Procedure] Code'. It literally marked boys as criminals and rendered correction impossible, Napier pointed out, and cited Captain Drever, a Madras police officer 'of high experience and ability', to support his case:

> I do not think whipping is a correct punishment for juveniles, and it is probably resorted to only because the Judges do not know otherwise how to deal with them. When a boy is flogged he is branded for years, if not for life; and certainly in all the large towns these boys grow into adult criminals, and these in turn breed juvenile offenders; so the supply is constant, and nothing but Reformatories will stop it.[106]

Conscious of his own image in the eyes of other officials, Napier reassured his audience that even in the absence of flogging, 'the Reformatory...must have its own features of severity'.[107] He found it necessary to make the point because the colonial punishment of children was a highly gendered exercise of authority not only over natives and native criminals, but also over the effeminate (and female) advocates of a less violent child correction.[108] Also, in an environment in which supervisors of juvenile punishment were typically ambivalent about just how childlike the offender actually was, there was a corresponding ambivalence about how severe, or lenient, the punishment ought to be. Napier argued, however, that whipping had damaged the wider project of the colonial reformatory by distracting the colonial government from the need to build infrastructure that was conducive to 'suitable discipline and training'. Without such infrastructure, by which Napier meant cellular reformatories, the administrators of juvenile punishment were notoriously inclined to fall back on whipping. One-third of the convicted juveniles in Bombay (186 out of 567) had been flogged and released in 1866, he noted, and pointed out that this had resulted in a relatively small institutionalized population that gave the misleading impression of a small financial obligation on the part of the government.[109]

The problem that Napier perceived was not limited to Bombay or any one province. A J Arbuthnot, Napier's colleague on the Sassoon board who also took a broad interest in juvenile punishment, provided statistics indicating that not only was the flogging and releasing of convicted juveniles endemic in Madras, the administrative logistics of flog-and-release obscured the age of the offender.[110] Flog-and-release, for Arbuthnot, violated childhood not only because it prevented the proper institutionalization of the child, but also because it prevented the recognition of the juvenile offender as a child by submerging him in a general pool of punished natives.

In most prisons in Punjab, the cane was used simply because other methods of punishing children had not been developed adequately. In Montgomery Jail, Dallas noted, 'There were no special arrangements for boys in the Jail; when juvenile criminals are committed, the Deputy Commissioner states that they are almost always sentenced to whipping.'[111] The use of flogging to compensate for infrastructural shortcomings became more regularized in the late 1860s and 1870s, because the Punjab government found it cheaper than sanctioning the construction of new cellular facilities. In 1870, for instance, the provincial administration declined to make available the funds for a new, improved, reformatory in Gurdaspur, and instructed magistrates to sentence children to whipping whenever they could. This policy was justified with the observation that flogging was 'a more appropriate punishment than imprisonment in jails with no special accommodation, and where children cannot be altogether removed from contaminating influences'.[112] Since flogging substituted for imprisonment, it allowed the Punjab administration to claim a measure of success in the campaign against child criminals. Between 1870 and 1871, the number of child convicts in three prisons — Delhi, Lahore and Amritsar — fell by nearly fifty percent.[113] This fall in numbers allowed the government to defend its decision not to fund the new building in Gurdaspur. A disappointed Dallas, who had pushed hard for the new institution, was convinced that it was because increasing numbers of children were simply being caned and released.[114]

Napier, Arbuthnot and Dallas were thus able to point not only to an ideological dilemma for the self-identified 'modern' penal professional, but also to a cyclical relationship between flogging, insufficient funding, inadequate infrastructure and the underdevelopment of juvenile delinquency as a social problem and a penological reality. The whip and the cell each 'produced' colonial criminals, but the products were different : whereas cellular confinement in the reformatory could produce the juvenile delinquent, flogging produced (through discourse, penal record, enforced habit and 'breeding') the undifferentiated phenomenon of the native criminal. Napier concluded:

> One of the best results of the successful prosecution of the reformatory system would, in my opinion, be the mitigation of 'the present system of whipping such offenders'. I would institute Reformatory and defer the lash, instead of deferring the Reformatory because the lash is at work.[115]

In spite of such concerns, the benefits of corporal punishment were self-evident to bureaucrats like Bayley and Howell, who were instrumental in overruling Carpenter, Napier and others who called for whip and cane to be replaced by fully segregated reformatories. In their debate with Napier the late 1860s, Bayley and Howell made two related arguments that might be considered the 'conservative' position against new-fangled experiments with juvenile institutions. The first was that juvenile delinquency — understood as a set of deviations from a broadly recognized societal norm that might be corrected through institutionalization — did not exist in India, where either individual offenders were normative within their societies, or entire societies were protected by romantic assumptions of uncorrupted innocence. Indian children, parents and societies were thus fundamentally different from their European counterparts, the conservatives implied, and reformatory enthusiasts who prescribed universal punitive strategies were mistaken. Howell wrote in 1868:

> India is not yet sufficiently civilized to breed up the large vagrant population, the offspring and heirs of poverty and crime, that...infest most of the large cities of Europe. An ignorance of these facts has induced

philanthropic persons, fresh from the experience of Mettray and similar institutions in Great Britain, to advocate the introduction by Government of measures almost as unsuited to the circumstances of this country as a thuggee school of industry or a *zenana* mission would be in England.[116]

The second argument, made forcefully by Bayley, derived from the conviction that since most juveniles convicted by Indian courts were not moral deviants, it was better to flog them and return them to their parents than to introduce them to the moral cesspool of a penal institution. Support for whipping could be merged with a discourse of parental privilege, because flog-and-release provided an alternative to removing children from their parents and placing them in reformatories. The point was reiterated nearly thirty years later by Duncan in Madras.[117] Duncan and Bayley did not, however, present identical readings of the intersection of parenting and flogging. For Duncan, at the end of the century, an active parental role or the normative dependence of the child mitigated criminality. He was therefore reluctant to disrupt this role by institutionalizing the child. For Bayley, in the heat of his argument with Napier, the major benefit of corporal punishment was that it allowed the state to differentiate between the children of the essentially decent and the offspring of absent or habitually criminal parents. When he rejected the Madras government's plea for a reformatory, Bayley wrote:

> The proper object of Reformatories…is rather to save, from growing up in a course of crime, children who, from vicious disposition and teaching, or from gross and palpable neglect, are in danger of becoming habitual criminals. Thus, a Magistrate might send to a Reformatory a ragged boy caught picking pockets, and shown to have been abandoned by his parents, or to have become an inmate of a notorious thieves' resort; but he certainly would not so treat a boy, the son of honest or respectable parents, if brought before him for some trifling offence committed, perhaps more out of frolic than wickedness."[118]

Yet there were serious political problems with whipping the frolicsome children of 'respectable parents'. Even as Bayley and Howell made their remarks, a discussion was underway between the provinces and the central government about the propriety of using the Whipping Act against people whose class prerogatives had recovered from the vengeful aftermath of 1857, and whose buttocks were partially covered by British class sensibilities.[119] The government of the Northwest Provinces noted:

> The object of the [Whipping Act] was to enable [judges] to deal effectually with reckless offenders or persons belonging to the habitually

criminal classes, who are not deterred from crime by a short imprisonment, and who therefore needlessly crowded the jails, and...it was not intended to supply the means of inflicting a specially degrading penalty on [those] whose case is sufficiently met by...imprisonment."[120]

The implication was that penal institutions were for the relatively decent, and the whip for the truly delinquent. While this is the opposite of Bayley's expressed desire to flog the respectable, there was agreement that some children must be flogged in order to keep them apart from those who must be locked up. In 1864, the Punjab government had expressed its preference for an approach that distinguished between the offspring of 'hereditary criminals' and the children of 'respectable' peasants.[121] By the end of the decade, it had become clearer which were to be whipped and which institutionalized. What emerges is a bifurcated and hierarchical vision of juvenile delinquency and punishment that reproduced the colonial encounter with adult criminals — prolonged confinement, redemption and rehabilitation for one set of boys; incorrigibility, flogging and short sentences for another. It was decided to turn away the novices as well as the most disorderly (habitually criminal) boys, after imprinting upon them — albeit temporarily — the marks and sensations of the state's authority.

For those boys who were institutionalized instead of being flogged and released, the prospect of corporal punishment did not fade discernibly. The use of the whip within the institution must be understood in the context of the disorder of the colonial reformatory, where a direct relationship can be identified between the inmates' resistance and the administrators' recourse to corporal punishment. In its second year of operation in 1879, the Alipore reformatory had only ninety-six inmates, but administrative records indicate five hundred and three instances of flogging, and only twenty-six allocations of solitary confinement.[122] Kirschner, the Superintendent, called this a 'melancholy' record, but he also provided a wider picture of a new carceral institution, marked by open violence and competition between administrators and the older children for moral and political leadership of the inmate population. One flogged boy had solicited the admiration of his peers by trying to brain Kirschner with a rock (but missed and hit the Indian clerk instead).[123]

The use of corporal punishment in Alipore seemed to fall sharply in 1880, with only two hundred and forty-one whippings inflicted. The appearance is misleading, because Kirschner had decided to concentrate the floggings upon 6.7 percent of the boys (as opposed to 12 percent in 1879), focusing his attack against the leaders of inmate resistance.[124] The pattern visible in Alipore can be seen again in Hazaribagh in 1891, where the Deputy Superintendent, J Hill, was assaulted by several 'big boys' led by a adult convict named Naboo, who had come from Bhagalpur Jail to teach the boys basket-weaving and apparently acquired a following among the juveniles with promises of tobacco. The boys were flogged.[125] In Chingleput in 1895, the official pride in a carceral institution with 'no wall, bolts, nor bars' was undermined by the frequency with which corporal punishment was used against boys who took advantage of the laxity of visible restraints.[126] While the no-walls discourse evident in Chingleput indicates a conscious search for a penal architecture (literal and metaphorical) that was manifestly modern, humane, and non-reliant on force, the problems with 'conduct and discipline' and 'insubordination' led administrators to fall back, at first quietly and then more dramatically, on the established means of maintaining the order of the colonial prison.[127] There was much flogging of intramural offenders in the Jubbulpore reformatory in 1901, to combat the prevalence of fighting and vandalism in decrepit old buildings that had once housed apprehended Thugs.[128]

When using corporal punishment to combat 'indiscipline' inside the reformatory, Kirschner and his colleagues in Hazaribagh and Madras typically blamed habitual offenders.[129] To an extent, the habit of the habitual offender was identified by his challenge to colonial/adult authority, and reified by his flogging. Not surprisingly, when reformatory administrators sought to cast their regimes as mature and successful, they sought to marginalize the habitual offenders in their institutions, as Kirschner did by concentrating his pool of flogged children in the second year of the Alipore reformatory, or by keeping them out altogether through flog-and-release practices. The inclination to keep juvenile 'habituals' out of the reformatory by flogging them instead indicates a reluctance on the part of colonial jailors and bureaucrats to admit the full connotations of delinquency into institutions that were only sporadically under their control. After 1875, when Temple and other Bengal officials 'proved' the existence of native delinquents by drawing explicit parallels between Calcutta and London,[130] Howell and Bayley gave in to the call for separate reformatories, but they did not accept the reformers' demand that first-time offenders and unconvicted children be institutionalized, as they were in England.

With the delinquency of the native child and the modernity of the colonial reformatory thus restricted to a margin, the discomfort of flogging became tolerable. Given the difficulties experienced with cellular confinement and the short sentences that most children actually served, flogging emerged as both an alternative to a long but damaging incarceration, and a way of making brief stints of imprisonment more punishing.[131] Also, while the naked violence of whipping juveniles was appallingly primitive to modernizers like Napier and Carpenter, it was apparent to many reformatory administrators that corporal punishment could itself be modernized or, at any rate, disguised from its critics. It could be merged with punitive labor — in Alipore in the

1880s, intramural offenders were occasionally sentenced to operate the *dhenki*, or heavy rice husker.[132] While conceptually similar to the tread wheel in the repertoire of Victorian punishment, the *dhenki* went beyond meaningless and painful physical activity — it inflicted the rehabilitative promise of rural labor upon the refuse of the colonial city.

Also appealing to modernizing jailors was the reality that practically every kind of corporal punishment could be medically supervised. This was not difficult to organize in an institutional context in which large prisons and reformatories were either headed by doctors like Lynch and Fawcus, or had medical officers who might either support or restrain the punishing arm of the superintendent.[133] In Calcutta in 1867, Lynch began to administer penal diets to offending children, prescribing the pangs of a measured hunger.[134] Colonial jailors engaged in consulting English reformatory procedure in 1880 noted that their metropolitan counterparts had already bureaucratized the process of depriving juveniles of 'that portion of the meal that renders it agreeable'.[135] While they did not slavishly copy European examples, and indeed, were in the vanguard in many respects, they were nevertheless eager not to be left behind. When Kirschner moved to restrict flogging in the Alipore reformatory the same year, he compensated by increasing the infliction of penal diets.[136] The diet was not uncontroversial; Westmacott, who was Kirschner's contemporary in Bengal, saw it as 'a bad form of punishment for growing lads', and expressed a strong preference for the whip.[137] Nevertheless, as a discreet and scientific manifestation of corporal punishment, the penal diet persisted alongside flogging. It was prescribed frequently in Chingleput in the 1890s, and usually as a 'follow-up' punishment to caning.[138]

Caning was itself a significant development within corporal punishment, evolving as administrators tried to develop more subtle, visually acceptable and differentiated methods of inflicting physical pain. The heavy rattan and birch, applied spectacularly to the back or the buttocks, were supplemented and eventually, largely supplanted, by lighter instruments applied discreetly to the palm of the hand. One of the first administrators to distinguish between 'whipping' and 'caning' within the reformatory was, perhaps predictably, Kirschner. In his report for Alipore in 1882, Kirschner noted 'whipping' as an absence, and 'caning' as a punishment concentrated within a diminishing population of habitual offenders.[139] The following year, Westmacott defended the Hazaribagh reformatory, where ninety cases of 'whipping' had been recorded, by explaining to the Bengal government that most of the cases 'consisted…of only a few cuts on the hand'.[140] In 1906, W Bell — the Director of Public Instruction and Inspector General of Reformatories in Punjab — differentiated between 'birching' and 'caning' when reporting to the provincial government on the reformatory in Delhi.[141]

The more spectacular forms of corporal punishment did not disappear. After a brief suspension in favour of penal diets and canings at the turn of the century, whipping returned to Chingleput with a vengeance, and was defended by T S Ross, the acting Superintendent in 1901, as an 'educational principle...in a school which has to deal with boys, some vilest of the vile and others inured to hardships, fisticuffs and kicks before coming to this school'.[142] Ross clarified that the education was deterrent rather than retributive. Corporal punishment was especially contentious at Chingleput because this was an institution that tried hard to claim the status of a reformed reformatory. Giffard, the Superintendent in 1899, raised the old specter of the habitual offender when he complained about the inefficacy of using penal diet on impertinent adolescents who 'had been beggars and outcasts all their lives and were very undesirable persons to keep in this school'.[143] Even caning, Giffard wrote, 'is practically a farce as a punishment to a set of horny-handed young scamps who spend half a day in gardening, carpentry and the blacksmith's shop'.[144] As a 'mild' form of corporal punishment, caning was a contest of authority in which the victory of the adult colonizer was not assured. This made it essential, for Giffard, that the more impressive tactic of a whipping on the buttocks be revived. Also, Giffard obviously believed that the reformatory regime itself had literally produced the thick skin that allowed the inmate to defy the cane. Such usurpation of the disciplinary mechanism represented a form of insubordination, which had to be countered with the overt violence of a public flogging.

The variations of corporal punishment that developed in the late nineteenth century in response to the quest for an acceptable punishment found secure niches in institutional practice for decades. Physical pain continued to acquire gradations and specifications that differentiated between adults and children, between adolescents and younger children, between children of different classes, and between children showing unequal levels of political deference. The site of the punishment itself became ideologically meaningful as punishers differentiated between buttocks, backs and hands, and between the courtroom and jail, jail and reformatory, open yard and closed room. The Madras Children Act of 1920 mandated that boys sentenced to corporal punishment be whipped in court rather than in prison — a provision that the Indian Jails Committee of 1922 approvingly recommended for all-India use.[145] The Inspectors General of Prison who sat on the committee approved of the Madras law not only because they felt it 'embodied' the best features of the English Children's Act of 1908,[146] but because flogging children in court was an attempt, however awkward, to find a compromise between the need to retain flogging in the 'primitive' environment of colonial political confrontations, and the 'modern' desire to distance the child from the geography of adult punishment.

Similarly, the advocates of palm caning saw it as a hallmark of their own modernity. When the Central Provinces legislature passed Act IX in 1928, allowing for the establishment of a Borstal school and borrowing heavily from legislation already enacted in Bengal, it went to some pains to distinguish between whipping and palm caning, and to abolish the former.[147] Indian legislators were heavily involved in the drafting of a law that might be seen as the reclamation of authority by racially and nationally legitimate adults over the body of the native child. But it also marked a continuing refinement of corporal punishment in a partially decolonized reformatory. Through the 1930s, palm caning was consistently distinguished from whipping, and inflicted more frequently.[148]

The flogging of juvenile offenders could therefore be brought, however unconvincingly, into the circle of the modernity that penal experts in British India felt compelled to observe and negotiate. Demetz and Mettray, Mouat and Carpenter, had left their mark on even those jailors and bureaucrats who sought to leave their marks on the child, in the sense that the discourse of the school (especially the vocational school) continued to encroach upon the prison. Flogging survived, and even thrived, because by the 1860s, the reformatory had been cast as an institutional and ideological middle ground between the habitual/serious juvenile offender and his casual/respectable counterpart. This peculiarly colonial location meant that other institutions for dealing with offending children — jails, whipping posts, CT camps — could not be done away with; they continued to develop alongside the reformatories. The Bombay government noted when the first RS Act went into effect:

> The present juvenile prison at Poona could be converted into an excellent reformatory school as far as education is concerned, but being part of and within the walls of a district jail it cannot be utilized for such a purpose within the meaning of the Act, besides such a prison will still be necessary for boys convicted of serious crimes, whom it would not be desirable to send to a reformatory.[149]

The 'separateness' of the prison did not, of course, mean that children in the reformatory were safe from flogging. In Madras in 1939, two hundred and sixty-eight boys had been caned on the hand, and six boys had been whipped for insubordination.[150] Palm canings and whippings reflected a fundamentally colonial relationship between the generations, classes and races that could not be jettisoned without simultaneously re-imagining the political rights of the modern citizen and the modern child. Alongside the school, the jail — and adulthood — also encroached constantly upon institutions for children.

Conclusion

The colonial state's initial experience with juvenile delinquency is very much a part of the larger history of British-Indian prisons and punishment, and it is not surprising that similar problems afflicted the two projects. In both cases, the modern expectation of 'self-command and self-discipline' for convicts as well as prison employees was incompatible with a political system in which the colonized were to be commanded by colonizers. Nevertheless, in both cases, certain gestures of modernity were made, complete with terms like 'juvenile delinquency', 'reformatory' and 'solitary confinement'. These gestures had real consequences for thousands of Britain's colonial subjects, but the consequences were not quite what the colonizer had intended. When Indians gestured back, through disorder, escape, indifference, or even cooperation, there was a perceptible dissonance between call and response. Since the native would always remain external to the political self of the reformatory administrator, a certain kind of resistance could never be eliminated, and could only be tackled with physical violence. Under the circumstances, the pervasive reliance on the cane becomes quite comprehensible. In spite of its unreliability as an instrument of reform, the physical pain of flogging was a brief moment of truth, when the criminal responded to punishment much as he was expected to respond. In a political relationship where long term control and transparency were uncertain, these moments were the best that colonial administrators could hope for.

4

GENDERING THE REFORMATORY

While the second RS Act allowed for girls to be included in the category of the 'juvenile offender', neither of the RS Acts provided for the incarceration of female children in reformatories. The 1897 legislation might be seen as a tentative half-measure, but the extension of the infrastructure of juvenile punishment to girls was explicitly discouraged by both laws, and it was not until the 1920s that systematic efforts were made to import native girls into the penal archipelago. Nevertheless, like the child of the Criminal Tribe, the girl child was a persistent shadow within the reformatory, rendered marginal but all the more interesting by the ideological and political dimensions of her exclusion. There was, in fact, a substantial body of opinion in colonial child-correction circles that held female children to be especially delinquent and endangered in the native context. That girls were not 'reformed' on a larger scale reflects the peculiar place of females and families in an evolving vision of Indian society. The delinquency of native girls was perceived by experts as too great a problem for the reformatory to manage. Furthermore, administrators overwhelmingly believed that locking up girls would destabilize the native family, and thus create more disorder than order. In the process, they aligned themselves with Indian men who, in Partha Chatterjee's well-known phrase, sought to implement a 'nationalist resolution' of the problem of women and the colonial state.[1]

The alignment, however, was chimerical. Although Indians were reluctant to allow white experts to define the biological and moral content of the girl child, they were not especially opposed to an institutional practice that might locate them in a desirable social and civilizational niche. Delinquent girls and reformatories (imagined and extant) were powerful instruments of cultural and racial critique that could be used against other Indians and against the other sex, not to mention foreigners of either sex. Since colonial administrators usually constructed the delinquency of girls as sexual in its content, a highly charged ideological and professional space was generated within the reformatory where Indians, especially Indian women, might project themselves as uniquely qualified experts on the basis of race and gender. Child-saving could, in the process, be represented not only as women's work, but as a national service.

The simultaneous production of child and parent in the reformatory was inevitably a gendered project. When punishment is merged with reform and civilizational criticism, and meted out by a sternly and often violently paternal state, conflict between parent figures is a also clash between 'rational' and 'disciplined' male administrators and 'superstitious' or 'helpless' native mothers, and between male professionals and women interlopers. These are conflicts within a broader set of transformations in the power structure of Victorian and Progressive-era families.[2] Nevertheless, the metropolitan context in which elite women had already acquired a certain hegemony over the domestic was complicated in the colony by the restricted political roles accorded to women by colonial and nationalist discourses. The mother, therefore, was a peculiarly problematic figure within colonial child-saving: a mistrusted but grudgingly acknowledged and even accepted presence.

By the turn of the century, feminine/maternal agency was occasionally seen in the colonial reformatory as preferable to masculine/paternal instruments of inculcating delinquent children with the virtues of order and deference, particularly when the children were female. There was, however, a major caveat: such women were expected to be white. The qualification provided child correctors with a way of reconciling the middle-class cult of moral maternity with their horror of the *zenana* and its population of native mothers. In the 1920s, this formulation was usurped, rather than overturned, by Indian women, particularly Cornelia Sorabji, who saw in her own 'English living' and feminine identities an ideal set of child-saving credentials — a strategic civilizational distance from children, Indian women, and men of all races. The development provided the colonial reformatory with a limited rhetorical space into which it could expand, and where females could be accommodated among the damned/natives, the salvageable/children and the modern/saviours.

Delinquent Girls and the Colonial Institution

Female children were no strangers to colonial carceral institutions. They were routinely sent to the women's wards of jails, and the Female Penitentiary in Lahore was, in 1894, home to a seven-year-old girl sentenced to ten years of rigorous imprisonment for 'complicity in a murder'.[3] Except in Madras, however, there were no specialized reformatories for girls in nineteenth-century India. Yet the case for including girls in the Indian reformatory had been made well before the first RS Act was passed. Not surprisingly, the most eloquent advocate of the institutionalization of female children was Mouat, who wrote simply that 'the abominations of my female wards I cannot venture to unveil' and that such unspeakable delinquency could be effectively dealt with only if the children were segregated from the adult women.[4] By referring to a horror that could be imagined because it could not be seen, Mouat implied that a natural and contagious hypersexuality was the basis of the delinquency of the native female. Simultaneously, he equated the unreformed prison ward, with its hidden spaces and its indiscriminate association (and confusion) of children and adults, with another moral black hole of the colonial imagination: the *zenana*.[5] These rhetorical manoeuvres would enjoy a long life in the Indian reformatory.

Indian men did not disagree with Mouat. Gurdyal Singh Man, a judge in Ferozepur, wrote to the Chief Court of Punjab:

> Can there be any improvement in any form of civilization without improving the condition of women? The influence of woman is very strong both for evil and for good. Juvenile persons more than any others fall victims to the influence of their elders, and are more apt under proper supervision to be educated out of a bad course of life. This applies to males and females alike, and both should be treated alike by the State. It would be downright negligence of moral duty if a civilized Government neglected the reformatory education of girls. In India women are more dependent on men than in other civilized countries... If they can be taught an honest means of earning their livelihood, they would be less liable to fall victims to the evil influence of a criminal relative.[6]

By issuing a subtle critique of a hesitant colonial regime, the native Man reached for a modern civilizational mantle, but he went about the process on ideological grounds that cast the Indian woman in a particular light. She was both ultra-child and ultra-adult, the dependent and influenced victim, but also the criminal hand that rocks the cradle. In each case, Man implied, the state had a role to play in her punishment and reform, which could be merged not only in the rights of Indians, but also in the rights of women.

There was, in fact, no shortage of officials, especially Europeans, who agreed that the nature of the Indian female was particularly well-suited to correction by colonial agents. Also using the language of equal rights to punishment, Greeven wrote in the Northwest Provinces:

> Few Magistrates have not experienced a feeling of regret in sentencing little girls to imprisonment for petty offences, when...the power to order detention in the Reformatory School would have removed the dilemma. It cannot be asserted that the female Reformatory, regarded purely as an educational and civilizing instrument, has not been conducted with success; I would invite attention to the history of the female section of the Sansiah Reformatory at Fatehgarh. In the present [1897 RS] Bill the

exclusion of females is specially unjust. I strongly contend that girls are equally entitled to the benefits of this provision if retained, and that… they are even fitter subjects for it.[7]

A generation before Greeven and Man, Napier had ventured that religious instruction would work wonders 'especially where girls are concerned', although he had hastened to add that the missionary-run orphanage, and not the government-run reformatory, might be called upon to undertake such politically sensitive work.[8] Napier had assumed a universal docility and religious inclination in the female child that made her receptive to reforming influence, even as he acknowledged that the colonial environment imposed peculiar institutional needs. Convinced that delinquent girls required stricter segregation from adults, males and other children than did boys, Napier had tried to devise a way to locate this isolated childhood outside both the penal institution and the natal family.

The reformatory regimes that Napier hesitated to endorse (but that Greeven and Man called for) began to take shape in Madras in the 1890s, albeit more frequently in the imagination than in brick and mortar. These were built upon an ideological bias among provincial officials that had its origins in Napier's tenure as governor, and in a conviction that the large Christian population of the south would not object to the institutionalization of girls.[9] The provincial administration was said to be 'entirely in favour' of including girls under the terms of the new RS Bill, so that when a physical infrastructure of reformatories and industrial schools emerged, the legal machinery would already be in place.[10] Bengal, somewhat reluctantly, drew up plans for a gendered regime of rehabilitative labour for girl inmates, noting that if the new law did sanction female reformatories, then 'the best training would be that which would qualify the girls for domestic service and hospital nursing'.[11] Punjab, which also witnessed early experiments in the incarceration of females,[12] likewise initiated a process of planning, although not much came of this until the 1920s.

The plans in Punjab also reveal the complexity of imagining a reformatory for female children. J R Drummond, the Deputy Commissioner of Gujranwala, wrote that there was a need for 'an asylum or house (home?)' for young girls. [Emphasis and parentheses in original] He suggested establishing one or two large institutions, adding:

Separate accommodation might be gradually provided for those inmates that have actively displayed a criminal taint or belong to tribes hereditarily criminal by instinct and profession. No practical difficulty need arise…in combining the reformatory with the home, because the waifs, though not through their own fault possibly, have usually passed through experiences while in the hands of kidnappers, or women stealers, which would render their promiscuous association with other children a peculiarly responsible experiment.[13]

Drummond's ambivalence is close to the surface: he is reluctant to use the word 'reformatory' in the context of female offenders, and shows a corresponding preference for the domestic/rescuing connotations of 'asylum' and 'home.' He anticipates that the domesticity of a 'home', coupled with the fallen ('experienced') nature of the girls, will eliminate or minimize public disapproval. At the same time, he is excited by the possibilities of the 'experiment'. The criminality of the girls he envisions is mitigated by the circumstances of individual misfortune, but not entirely — something remains rooted in heredity, nature ('instinct') and early nurture ('profession'). The idea that fallen girls should be associated with other, presumably less damaged children is very unusual. It resembles the good-influence schemes of Victorian punishment, but those schemes usually involved adult influences.[14] The metropolitan child was too well protected to warrant such experiments, but in the colonial periphery, experimentation is imaginable, not least because of the scarcity of suitable adult influence.

The case for the institutionalization of delinquent girls had been strengthened as well as undermined by other encounters between female children and the colonial penal system — encounters that were apparently located outside the reformatory, and articulated in terms of protection and rescue rather than criminalization and punishment. These had to do with the age at which prostitutes might have sex. Unlike those 'consent controversies' that focused on the wives of respectable Indians,[15] the 1872 debate over Section 373 of the Penal Code (which prohibited trafficking in minors and required a precise definition of 'minor' females) was about a native female who was definitively a delinquent even when she was not a criminal. (That latter status went to her client, when the female was judged to be a minor.) Philippa Levine has observed that prostitution in the nineteenth-century empire generated a potent investigative modality that further produced the degeneracy of a wide section of the colonized.[16] Bringing together the variables of age, sexual behaviour and a delinquency that bordered on savagery for the child as well as her adult parent and client, the question of minor prostitutes constituted an extension of the debate about girls in the reformatory, creating a small but significant body of knowledge about the social, biological and penological circumstances under which an Indian female might be considered a child.

The 1872 debate undoubtedly provided a forum for officials who saw the penal system as an instrument that might identify and enforce a childhood for

Indian girls. P S Melville, a judge in Punjab, argued that the age of sixteen was the appropriate line between adulthood and childhood, and that native habits that encouraged sexual transgressions across that line should be criminalized without hesitation:

> As to the 'social custom of natives of this country' I think that in a matter of this kind it should not be treated with any great tenderness. When it is remembered that the efforts of the Hindu population have been directed for centuries towards hastening the marriage of their daughters, that this resulted in a considerable amount of physical degeneration, that mechanical means are...resorted to by even respectable persons so as to render girls of immature age capable of having sexual intercourse with men (Chever's Medical Jurisprudence, edition of 1870, page 6891), there would appear to be good reason for putting obstacles in the way of prostitution of girls under the age of sixteen rather than for promoting it.[17] [Parentheses in original]

Melville thus constructed childhood as an antithesis of native savagery, which was itself constructed as sexual activity involving young girls.

In Bengal, however, the provincial government argued that while sixteen years should be the age of consent for females who were not prostitutes, the age of thirteen should be the cut-off point for the girl 'who is by habit and repute a professional prostitute'.[18] In the process, the Bengal administration articulated three categories of native girls, with different boundaries and components of childhood: the prostitute, whose sexual/juvenile identity was determined by social identity and who became an adult very early; the wife, whose status as a child or an adult was determined substantially by her husband, who 'possessed' her identity in that regard; and the ephemeral female who was neither a wife nor a prostitute, for whom individual consent actually had some meaning. It was only for the last that the state conceded some obligation and ability to step in as the guardian of sexual availability, or of a childhood that was independent of physical development and social location.

The debate over Section 373 thus strengthened conservative officials who were convinced of the peculiarity of native childhoods and impatient with the progressive desire to replicate metropolitan experiments in India. In the mid-1860s, George Couper in Oudh had argued that the perversely young age at which an Indian prostitute ('a girl of that caste') entered 'the full swing of her trade' rendered her unlike English girls of her age and the protection of her childhood irrelevant.[19] Couper's memo was widely circulated and cited during the 1872 controversy. As with boys, social location could nullify or at least qualify childhood in girls. With girls, however, the connection between sex and delinquency was closer than it was with boys, being imbedded more deeply in the body of the child and the nature of the land. Various district level and provincial administrators advised the government that native girls who had reached puberty could not be considered minors, and that climatic conditions predisposed Indian females to become sexually mature by the time they were twelve years old.[20] In the process, they established that whereas the sexual precocity that constituted delinquency was inseparable from puberty in native girls, boys who reached puberty were not necessarily precocious even when they were incarcerated.

This made every female from the marginal sections of native society a delinquent as soon as she became ten, eleven or twelve years old, unless she was married. Her sexual delinquency was constructed as a 'habit' much like the habits of male property criminals, but whereas there was considerable disagreement about whether the delinquency of habitual offenders was rooted in the body and treatable, there was no denying that puberty was embodied, ubiquitous and not especially responsive to 'treatment'. The problem of female juvenile delinquency was thus magnified to a level that colonial experts could hardly fail to acknowledge, and that clearly had much to offer the reformatory. The dismissive observation of J Woodburn in the Home Department that the 'real reason against girl reformatories is that (fortunately) habitual girl criminals are few'[21] [parentheses in original], is therefore superficial. The real question was whether the reformatory, as a political, ideological and physical space, was large enough to accommodate the problem.

The Case for Exclusion

Official policy tended to answer the question in the negative before the 1920s. Colonial administrators commonly pointed to the political difficulty of institutionalizing native females of any age, and female children amplified the problem because they seemed to represent the continuity of culture. After the Mutiny, the argument went, locking up girls would constitute an unacceptable and inflammatory 'interference' in Indian society. The 1864 Committee on Jails and Jails Discipline, which included conservative bureaucrats like John Strachey but also progressive jailors like Mouat and Walker (who had experimented with innovative rehabilitation schemes involving the wives of convicts in the Andaman Islands[22]), had expressed the fear that any expanded plan for the institutionalization of girls would lead to 'suspicion and disgrace'.[23] The suspicion and disgrace, it was clear, would adhere as much to the state and its agents as to the females.

Related anxieties had surfaced during the Napier-Bayley debates. H D Phillips, a member of the board of the Sassoon reformatory, had criticized Napier's fantasy of turning over delinquent girls to church-run institutions on precisely such grounds.[24] Phillips, it should be noted, had found the state-run reformatory an acceptable alternative for native girls, focusing his objections on the idea of church homes.[25] By the mid-1870s, however, the 'suspicion and disgrace' objection had been fixed more firmly on the government's own reformatories, which were a more distinct and fully articulated possibility than they had been in 1864. Temple took the position that female reformatories were politically impossible in India, and his stance substantially carried over into the first RS Act.[26] The assumption appeared nearly axiomatic when the time came to amend the law, with Woodburn remarking that 'the seclusion of girls for a period of years might be regarded with much mistrust and suspicion'.[27]

The appearance of conviction is somewhat misleading. Woodburn, like many senior bureaucrats, was very vague about just who might be mistrustful and suspicious were the government to place girls in reformatories. 'Native opinion' was remarkably diverse and contradictory on the issue, and district-level colonial administrators in the 1890s were aware of it. In Rohilkhand, J Hooper informed his superiors about interviews he had conducted with the mofussil elite: 'The doubts of the Government of India that such a measure would be looked upon with suspicion by the native population were scouted by these gentlemen, one of whom said frankly that he considered that Government was being unduly timorous.'[28] J G Silcock, Hooper's counterpart in Jhelum district, wrote to the Chief Court of Punjab that in his experience, girls did not require reformatory regimes; he added, however, that the government's concern about a public outcry was also uncalled for, because 'for girls of the classes who would come under the operation of the rules there is very little regard, and I do not think any one in India would go to the trouble of forming an opinion on the matter one way or the other'.[29]

These conversations about the native family and the colonial state between native elites and junior administrators, and junior administrators and their parent bureaucracies, indicate, firstly, that the issue of the delinquent girl was gendered in more than one way. Hooper saw it as a test of the masculine determination and courage of the colonial state, and a ground upon which the state risked being seen as weak or effeminate. This highlights the 'conquest and control' aspect of colonial juvenile delinquency — its value as a demonstration of the retributive power of the regime, as well as its function as a means of invading uncolonized spaces.[30] Secondly, he understood, as did Silcock, that elite natives were indifferent or supportive towards state intervention in the lives of marginal natives. The 'nationalist resolution' was limited by class, context and the native elite's desire to selectively appropriate the ideological benefits of a modern penological enterprise. The apparent indifference to criminalized girls generated a political space within which the masculine-adult state might operate as an actively colonizing/punishing force. Senior bureaucrats, however, remained doubtful about whether this space beyond the limits of the nationalist resolution actually existed, and about how much room it actually gave the colonial expert. Since the reformatory for girls was necessarily located in this doubtful space, it remained restricted.

It might be argued that this restriction was undergirded by a significant degree of sympathy, amounting to collusion, on the part of colonial administrators for the 'intelligent native opinion' that constituted the nationalist resolution. In the 1890s, certainly, protecting the officially recognized structures of patriarchy and caste within the native family emerged as a major priority of colonial administrators who contemplated placing girls in the reformatory, and who ultimately decided that the two objectives were incompatible. After its consultations with provincial governments and district-level administrators had been exhausted, the Home Department concluded:

> The main reasons…in support of the view that separate Reformatory Schools for girls are not needed are:
>
> (1) that they would have to be detained beyond the marriageable age, and would therefore rarely be able to marry upon release, and thus would be drawn into a life of immorality
> (2) that they would be discarded by their relatives on release, and being unable to secure employment with respectable families, would be reduced to destitution
> (3) that there would be a risk of contamination and corruption, in an institution where a large number of girls of different castes and characters are kept together
> (4) that native opinion would be opposed to the establishment of these institutions especially on account of the custom of early marriage.
>
> These objections have considerable force, and perhaps the view of the majority of Local Governments and Administrations that Reformatory Schools for girls are unnecessary may be accepted in this Department. Cases of offences committed by female juveniles could best be met by a reprimand or (where the offenders are not unmarried orphans) by making the person in whose tutelage the girl is, responsible for her future good behaviour. [Parentheses in original]

At the heart of the objections was the assumption that placing girls in reformatories damaged their marriageability, i.e. their future respectability and adulthood, and thus pushed them irretrievably into a set of social and conceptual margins. Respectability was constructed as dependence upon male relatives, which would have nullified the adulthood of males; females, however, were adult precisely when they embraced this dependence. Not having recourse to this dependent respectability would leave 'reformed' girls in a limbo — since they would presumably be unable to marry or find respectable work, they would not become adult, and since they would be consigned to prostitution, they could not be children either.

Whether or not incarceration actually rendered women unmarriageable is beyond the scope of this study; the answers inevitably depend upon the circumstances of the individual family, class, community and society, including the society of the prison itself.[31] The government's qualms were probably accurate for the relatively 'respectable' sections of peasant society, which is precisely the social model that the reformatory aimed to propagate in the margins. The reformatory, in this anxious vision, would make it nearly impossible for the paternal state to promote and protect models of gender, labour, class and caste relations based on stable hierarchies and paternal authority.

This perception of the reformatory and the girl child was not limited to conservatives closeted in the Home and Legislative Departments. It was shared by a number of officials who were self-conscious and proud of their claim to expertise in reformatory administration. In Madras, where the provincial government had successfully argued that Christians did not share the marriageability concerns of Hindus and Muslims,[32] Duncan wrote:

> If there were in India as in England independent careers open for women as well as for men, a strong reason could be urged in favour of giving youthful female offenders the same opportunities for reformation as are given to boys. But in this country the youthful female offender would ordinarily at the end of the period of detention be handed over to the custody of her parents or guardians; and...she would seldom be in a position to carry on in after-life any industry, such as needlework or lace making. No doubt, girls in a reformatory school who are the children of depraved parents would gain from being separated for a few years from their home surroundings and kept under the strict discipline of a school, where they would receive intellectual and moral training similar to that which is given to boys, but the difficulty of dealing with them on their discharge would be much greater than in the case of boys.[33]

Duncan's enthusiasm for universal mechanisms of social engineering was not incompatible with his vision of an environment of rehabilitation and release that was depraved in an exotic and very specific sense. The Orientalist model of the defining inequality of native women[34] made the female reformatory a cultural misfit and a signifier of civilizational difference and hierarchy.

Duncan's is a deeply pessimistic take on the reforming project, because it concedes that there is no place for the reformed girl child in colonial society.

In spite of the dissenting voices at the lower levels of the administration, the discussions of the 1890s led to a broad conclusion that while orphaned and unmarried females might occasionally be managed by the state, girls with husbands or families were best left to the control of male relatives. The delinquent boy, being less subject to patriarchal ownership, could go directly to the state and its institutions. Under the RS Act as it was passed in 1897, a girl offender was to be 'delivered' by the court to a parent, guardian or adult relative who could post a bond; the bond did not require the relative to pay money, but it did require him to assume legal responsibility for the girl's 'good behaviour' for up to a year.[35] Husbands and fathers were thus cast in the roles of alternative (and preferred) managers of disorderly girls, and a collusive ideological relationship was established between the patriarchy of colonial punishment and that of nationalist resolve.

It was a misplaced and frustrating collusion, because British administrators had extended their acceptance of the hierarchy of the elite family to children that existed on the periphery of respectable India. This was not so much an accident or a mistake as a pitfall of the modernizing project, and it is not a coincidence that when dealing with girls, administrators remained as pessimistic about the reforming capabilities of the native family as they were about the effectiveness of the reformatory. While they hesitated to intervene with girls even in marginal families, they were unable to find within those families the redeeming and autonomously reforming qualities that respectable Indians might bring to bear upon 'their' girls. By the 1890s, the masculine agency of colonialism was increasingly a handicap in the feminized social-political contexts within which family, childhood and Indian girls were located, and the child-saving project had reached an ideological bottleneck.

Cornelia Sorabji and the Feminization of Reform

A potential solution to the problem was the recruitment of women into the project. While the 1860s generation of experts had occasionally imagined that European women (missionary wives, nurses, 'matrons' and 'spinsters' with the appropriate combination of dour authority over children and natives, subordination to white male superiors and asexual religiosity) might be involved in the Indian reformatory, such women proved hard to find. In any case, the encounter with Carpenter indicated an acute discomfort on the part of administrators when the metropolitan woman with professional credentials of her own actually entered the Indian theatre. Moreover, by the 1890s, the ideological obstacle that white male experts faced when dealing with Indian girls also applied to white women. The wives of reformatory superintendents did, on occasion, supervise the dietary and nursing needs of incarcerated boys,[36] but such informal arrangements lacked the authority of expertise and were not widespread. It was evident that an expanded feminization of the field would necessarily have to involve Indian women, and Man called in 1896 for the recruitment of 'suitable female matrons' to staff any institutions for girls that might emerge from the amended RS Act.[37]

Such matrons were both promising and unacceptable. At the time, a broad spectrum of native women had been consigned discursively to the recesses of the home, by white as well as elite Indian men in the colony.[38] Those recesses had been imagined either as morally perverse or as shelters from the colonial world, but the 'recessed' nature of the native female also promised to make her useful as an agent of the reformatory. The experimental use of Indian women as agents of the colonial regime, deployed within the criminalized native family, had been tried out in the context of female infanticide. The Prevention of Female Infanticide Act of 1870 had encouraged local administrations to recruit village midwives as improvised policewomen and place them under the supervision of (female) European nurses and (male) IMS doctors. Colonial officials engaged in outlining female infanticide as a problem had hoped that state affiliated native women could keep an eye on adults of both sexes in Rajput homes where newborn girls might be at risk.[39] The midwife-as-policewoman proved to be an unsatisfactory solution, because the moral and political loyalty of marginal women could not be taken for granted — it was feared that midwives were as likely to protect the 'infanticidal' elites with whom they had established ties of deference and patronage, as they were to serve the colonial state.[40] Reliable agents, who shared the ideological vision of the child-saving state, would have to come from locations that were less peripheral.

The period following the World War, Geraldine Forbes has noted, was a historical moment when upper-class Indian women and their organizations became increasingly engaged in 'social work', bringing the domestic credentials of the modern housewife — updated from Victorian discourses of the 'angel of the house' and the *grihalakshmi* — into the public sphere.[41] The world and the nation could be reconstructed as extensions of the home, to be ordered, cleansed and saved by professional wives and mothers. This was hardly a new or unusual development; it had predecessors in a host of Victorian social campaigns and a highly visible contemporary in American Progressivism,[42] and its engagement with juvenile delinquency might be seen as a rudimentary form of what David Garland has called 'penal welfare'.[43] It was, however, of particular significance in India, where the expert consensus that Garland takes for granted was severely complicated by the politics of colonialism. The emergence in the public sphere of upper-class women who had already been enshrined as representatives of a national morality could serve to articulate anticolonial agendas, erode the moral credentials of an alien regime, and further the 'colonization' of the colonial state by Indian elites. It is in this context that we might locate Cornelia Sorabji's involvement in a host of issues surrounding children, including prostitution, the age of consent and reformatory procedure.

Sorabji has been the subject of much scholarly interest in recent years,[44] and I need reproduce only the barest skeleton of her biography. The daughter of Anglican missionaries, she was a pioneering female student at Oxford in the early 1890s, a barrister and Lady Assistant to the Court of Wards in India and, Antoinette Burton has indicated, a watchful agent of the colonial state inside an 'orthodox' native home that she herself helped to construct.[45] There can be little doubt that she existed on the periphery of colony and nation, although, like other elite figures on the margins, she also inhabited 'the heart of the empire'.[46] She was self-consciously a professional who shared much with her predecessors in the Indian reformatory, including not only Carpenter, but also Hathaway, Mouat, Napier and Duncan. She was also quite unlike any of them. She was grounded in modern academic and occupational credentials rather than in the church or the civil service, and her qualifying 'experience' was less dependent upon improvisation. As an Indian, a Parsi, a Christian, a loyalist, an unapologetic elitist, an imperial cosmopolitan and a woman, she was well-placed to launch unpredictable critiques of natives as well as Europeans, colonialism as well as the colony, women as well as men.

Burton, who has been the most insightful among recent scholars of Sorabji, has identified her as a self-promoted '*zenana* expert', who not only took metropolitan consumers on carefully guided tours of the Oriental home, but also worked to stabilize and insulate that home in a defensive reaction against the politics of nationalist feminist 'progress'.[47] While the suggestion is not without merit, Burton overstates Sorabji's fondness for the 'old fashioned' women she encountered and revealed. Sorabji encountered such women in at least two modes: as a worker in the Court of Wards and subsequently, as an activist in the reformatory. In each case, she experienced the women as children; the Court of Wards and the juvenile courts both rendered their 'wards' as juveniles. Aware of her status as the cultural and authoritative adult in these encounters, Sorabji demonstrated an interest in correction that is not consistent with a desire to stabilize the exotic. In her perception, these child-women (and their children) had to be saved not only from the contamination of modernity and modern Indians, but also from themselves and from the colonial state.

As a consultant to the Bengal government during the legislative initiatives of the 1920s, and as an activist for a reformatory that was sensitive to the modern needs of the child (particularly the girl child), Sorabji embraced the concept of child-saving as woman's work. She embraced it, however, for a particular kind of woman who represented the racial, moral, political and professional niches that she herself inhabited, within which the childhood and femininity of delinquent girls might be recuperated. Cox has noted that in the female missionary circles of India in the late nineteenth century, a rhetoric of professional expertise gradually displaced the older ethos of 'amateur' work by mission wives. Cox places the new 'heroic professional' women, some of whom were Indian, chronologically ahead of the 'true' (white) professionals of the twentieth century.[48] 'Heroism' — self-conscious struggle against the perceived adversities of religion and gender — qualified professionalism, but was compatible with expertise. Sorabji might be located in the grey area between the two categories of professional women; indeed, she might be seen as emblematic of a third category.

Sorabji illuminated two peripheries in the colony — one enlightened, 'English living', modern and rescuing, the other primitive, in need of punishment and rescue, and overlapping with something that she called the 'orthodox'. She was more critical of male control in the reformatory than she was of natives of either sex and any age. She accepted the peculiarity of Indian children, childhoods and juvenile institutions, but maintained that this was a reversible peculiarity, and sought to implement the reversal. While she could utilize the juvenile delinquent to articulate a strategic distance from native society for herself, she was also able to articulate a distance from Britain and claim a dissenting space within an Indian nation. She was thus able to claim the Indian child offender for the nation's women (provided that the women were not quite natives), illuminating a way of bypassing the bottleneck that the reformatory had reached in the late nineteenth century.

The Critique of the Native/Female

Sorabji held herself politically and culturally apart from other Indians of nearly all classes. She remained stubbornly hostile to nationalist political organizations throughout her adult life, preferring to align herself instead with a Cannadinean empire that contained an elaborate fantasy of elite cosmopolitanism.[49] This distance generated an undeniable affinity with colonial criminology. In her conversations with the government and the press about juvenile delinquency, female infanticide and the age of consent, she positioned herself as a crusader for girls victimized by cultural perversity, and told the Bengal government, 'I wish that early marriage were for the orthodox only a bad habit and on a par with too many cigarettes or whisky pegs, or too much cocaine. How easy the solution would be!'[50] The implication that native culture was an addiction and a failure of self-moderation was ideologically consistent with long-standing colonial understandings of delinquent 'habits'.[51]

Sorabji's participation in discussions of the Children Protection (Amendment) Bill of 1928, which would have raised the 'protected age' for unmarried girls from fourteen to sixteen, and that for married girls from under twelve years to thirteen or fourteen, allowed her to spell out her location *vis-à-vis* native parents and natives generally. She wrote to the Bengal government, 'It should be remembered...that all progressive measures are of necessity initiated and supported by the communities who are themselves not in any way likely to be affected by the proposed changes.'[52] She thus located herself in a community of reformers that was not itself in need of reform. In a separate memo to the Judicial Department on the subject of medical examinations of girls in juvenile court, she provided names for this community, 'twelve to fourteen is the age at which girls of the educated English living and emancipated Communities attain puberty in Bengal'.[53] Englishness, in other words, was not necessarily a race or a nationality, but a lifestyle, a moral habit, and a limited biological condition (puberty at a certain age) for people who she felt were like herself. Their marginality within native society, backed up by the discourses of medical morality and moral medicine, was transformed into a position of authority.

From this position, she was able to describe the relationship between native society and the criminalized or sexually implicated girl child. Much of that society was summarized by the term 'orthodox' — a category produced tautologically by the positions that her Indian adversaries adopted on issues of female children. On the age of protection issue, she wrote:

> It matters nothing from the point of view of the Orthodox whether you raise it to twelve or fourteen. Conversion from orthodoxy when it comes will mean entire conversion *to the principle*: and therefore to the higher age – straight away. [Emphases in original][54]

Clearly, Sorabji saw child-saving as a pedagogical forum in which the child was not so much the object to be educated, as an educational text for its orthodox adult relatives. Within the fantasy of 'converting' the orthodox, there is an echo of Carpenter's evangelism. While Sorabji did not pursue religious conversions, religion featured prominently in her vision of orthodoxy. She was, she wrote, sensitive to the difficulties of saving children 'when religious sanction...is behind the practice sought to be "reformed"'.[55] Equating child marriage and the abuse of child prostitutes, she observed: 'The victims of this obnoxious practice will be found mainly in ignorant and orthodox Hindu houses — children whose parents believe that religion commands that a child should be married...and that the benefit accruing to the parent of the child, is in inverse ratio to the age of the child when married?'.[56] She drew attention to the collusion of husbands, priests, parents, in-laws and illiterate women in concealing sexually victimized girls, their ages and the abuse, and explained this collusion with reference to '*Shastric* sanction'. That turned out to be the kind of improvised scripture that Orientalists abroad had long relied upon:

> As to the superstitions referred to above, they are still slated in the form —
>
> 'A girl child may not be married the first three years of her life.
>
> If married between her fourth and her sixth years, her Parents attain the highest heaven.
>
> Between her sixth and eighth years, the next highest.
>
> Between her ninth and eleventh years the one below that.
>
> After the age of twelfth if she is still unmarried, there remains for the parents destruction alone.'
>
> When to the supposed scripture is added the fact that a child is reckoned to be as of a year old on the day of its birth – the situation is seem [sic] to be rather serious. The only remedy is to get the women of Orthodox Hindu houses on the side of reform. But this cannot be done without house to house propaganda.[57]

In an anthropological exercise reminiscent of the work of nineteenth-century scholar-administrators, she kept meticulous notes on 'orthodox' life cycle rituals such as naming, head shaving, investiture of the thread, adoption and marriage, and festivals — *Diwali, Shivratri, sankrant*.[58] She noted disdainfully that orthodox parents submitted horoscopes to the government when asked to register the births of children.[59] Orthodoxy could thus signify a rift between Indian racial and moral identities, within which the properly qualified child-saver might be located. It might be argued, furthermore, that her use of phrases like 'the orthodox and illiterate classes'[60] and call for state intervention against these classes was a refashioning of the old idea of criminal collectives, utilized to produce strategic distances within Indian society.

Orthodoxy was, however, also a gendered construct — it signified the peculiar obduracy of the native woman. Even as Sorabji urged the Bengal legislature to pass the Children Protection Bill, she remarked pessimistically that 'the law is like [sic] to be for some time a dead letter — since it is impossible to police the Indian *zenana* or to obtain reliable information about the age of a girl child'.[61] A familiar frustration with the imprecise ages of Indian children is wedded here to the colonial suspicion of the domain of native women,⁶² which is rendered as a cultural space that obscures the knowledge that might facilitate the capture of native childhood within a modern state and imagination.⁶³ The law had to be passed anyway; the work of the expert activist and legislator was heroic and morally significant precisely because it was not easy. It was a heroism that Indian men, who were inheriting the organs of the colonial state but were too weak to resist their wives, were apparently incapable of:

> Since marriage is essentially the business of the women of a household…they would be obstructive here as elsewhere. However enlightened a man may be, he must in all orthodox Hindu houses eventually yield to the wishes and *superstitions* of his womenkind, e.g. the Minister of a Provincial Government has lately been unable to prevent in his Family the marriage of a child of eight: and not only her marriage but the exodus at this early age to the house of her husband.⁶⁴ [Emphasis in original]

The discourses of native effeminacy and the perverse/ignorant/powerful *zenana* are thus linked by the issue of child protection. While Indian men, Hindus and conservative women are all 'othered' by Sorabji's rhetoric of orthodoxy, the last are cast in the role of Sorabji's nemeses, and as the carriers of a competing feminine/native moral authority. Women in the orthodox home are not naturally the child's allies and affines, she implies, and the failure is made worse by upper-class expectations of domesticity and feminine nature.

The Critique of the Colonial/Male

Due to her self-location within the civilizing mission and her hostility to women's suffrage in India, it is easy to dismiss Sorabji as a reactionary with a disingenuous veneer of radicalism. It is a deceptive ease. Sorabji's defence of the child against its orthodox relatives is comparable to Pandita Ramabai's defence of Rukhmabai, the *cause celebrée* who went to court in 1887 to nullify a marriage arranged in childhood. Sudhir Chandra has pointed out that the radical potential of Ramabai's activism lay in her linking the patriarchy of colonial law with the patriarchy of Indian orthodoxy; to a degree, this can be argued of Sorabji also. Chandra notes, also, that Ramabai's radicalism was undercut by her acceptance of a hegemonic equation of law and justice.⁶⁵ The same might be said of Sorabji, who spent much of her life working in the colonial courts. While this is stronger evidence of her 'reactionary' bent, it is a reaction that is necessarily tied up with the modern native's investment in the inherited apparatus of modernity. Within the limits imposed by that investment, Sorabji articulated a critique of masculine agency in child-saving that was no less corrosive than the subversion of European expertise by nationalist legislators and reformatory inspectors.

While colonial administrators were typically suspicious or contemptuous of Indians with pretensions to Englishness, Sorabji was substantially exempted from the charge of mimicry and invited to participate in debates about native children. Her Parsi-Christian background (which she wore on her sleeve, if only to demonstrate that she was neither Hindu nor Muslim), combined with the years at Oxford and the loyalist politics, allowed her to 'pass' in limited contexts, child-saving being one of them. Most importantly, because she articulated the cracks within Indian civilization that European observers themselves perceived, it was useful to colonial administrators to accept her as an honorary Englishwoman, and to invite her to present her views on Indian society and its children. It was useful, furthermore, not only because she was a woman, but also because they believed her to be an Indian in the final analysis — the views of white/male experts like Forrester did not carry nearly the same weight. Also, at a time when the day to day workings of colonial child-saving were passing into the hands of Indians, consulting Sorabji gave the regime a way of retaining some initiative and control over the agenda, the pace and the methods of the reformatory.

It is evident however, that Sorabji's gender and race were unstable assets for her sponsors in the government. Her contempt for 'orthodox' women, for instance, was undercut by the strains of sympathy that Burton has highlighted. Burton does not suggest that Sorabji may have sought to protect the orthodox from her own British patrons, but that appears occasionally to have been the case.[66] While on a tour of princely states where the rulers were minors under the dual influence of the *zenana* and the British political officer, she remarked:

> In some states [the mother regent] undoes all that is done in other directions, by her influence in the *zenana*. In other states[67] she...was the wisest person in her son's entourage: and the Administrator might consult with her with profit on matters political as well as domestic.[68]

Since maternal influence could vary in its moral, political and cultural content even in the *zenana*, Sorabji implied, the government could not legitimately adopt a uniform policy of ignoring or suppressing the mothers of princely children, and turn minority administrations into *de facto* exercises in direct rule. Sympathy for the native mother could thus conceal an oblique critique of colonial policy, aligning Sorabji with the princely families that hosted her during her tour, and whose relationships with the British-Indian government and its political agents were often contentious.[69]

A more subtle 'taking of sides' in the politics of colonial children might be discerned in Sorabji's views on the policing of female infanticide. Writing to the Bengal government, she began predictably, differentiating the Indian problem and its punishment from what was practiced and practicable in Europe. Indian infanticide was driven by religion and male-enforced codes of wifely obedience, she wrote, and Indian women sometimes killed illegitimate children out of vindictiveness, to propitiate a deity (on the advice of a priest), or under economic duress. Under the circumstances, the law had to be 'both educative and deterrent'.[70] However, she added, the Female Infanticide Act did not anticipate cases in which the mother might be mentally deranged after giving birth. To deal with this possibility, she called for 'the medical examination of the accused mother in all cases, and the application of leniency if she is proved to be, however temporarily, a mental patient'.[71] Alongside and just underneath the usual attack on orthodox parenting, there is a perceptible sympathy for what is constructed (expertly, scientifically) as a woman's problem. There is an echo here of an old colonial sympathy for infanticidal women who ended up in court, jail and the penal colony,[72] but Sorabji roots the crime in a treatable and temporary psychiatric condition, rather than in culture alone.

The stance (sympathy for the native mother) and the discursive means (neonatal science) are both significant. Sorabji's inclination to support state intervention in the lives of female children, even as she stressed the difficulty of such intervention, highlighted and facilitated her position as an Indian who had made the moral choice to step outside, carrying with her the insider's knowledge (of orthodoxy, the *zenana*, scripture, etc.). She was able to advise the Bengal government that 'work among Orthodox Hindu women should be undertaken as soon as possible, on a scheme approved by those who have experience of the orthodox Hindu *zenana*'.[73] In a rhetorical manoeuvre that was beyond her predecessors in the field of Indian child-saving and child-correction, Sorabji was thus able to claim that her experience came from a carefully managed position within native society, and not from institutions located in the periphery of that society. The dual location within and without 'India' also distinguished Sorabji from Carpenter, although both women claimed the moral credentials of femininity.

When the colonial state was no longer unambiguously foreign, the loyalties of such an 'inside agent' could not be straightforward. Sorabji shared much of the nationalist animus of her male colleagues within Indian child-saving bureaucracies and legislatures of the interwar years. Like Contractor and Rangnekar, she was inclined to point out the membership of the Indian child in a universal childhood. In her suggestions to the government for amending the Bengal Children Act of 1922, Sorabji explicitly drew from the 'English plan' of 1908, which excluded the public from the juvenile courtroom. She recommended that as in England (where the child-saving state was recast as 'friends of the family'[74]), Indian court procedure should be not so much a trial as 'a friendly family enquiry'.[75] In England in the late nineteenth century, Behlmer has noted, child-savers who interfered with parental rights defended their work as an attempt to save parents, no less than children, from the outrages of child abuse.[76] In salvaging 'universal' children, Sorabji was similarly engaged in recuperating a nation of parents who actually possessed rights, although in the colonial context, this was a nation of surrogate or 'representative' parents — 'unorthodox' (preferably 'English living') adults who might represent politically those Indians whose children actually came before the juvenile courts.

In 1929, Sorabji wrote in *The Statesman* of her 'delight' at the amendment of the Bengal Children Act, establishing a central court for juvenile offenders under a stipendiary magistrate in Calcutta.[77] This marked a departure from the existing practice of *ad hoc* trials before a floating bench (and sometimes in adult court, especially when there were adult co-defendants), inconsistent rules and lack of professional guidance. She publicized her case studies of unsatisfactory probation: the parents of a thirteen-year-old boy accused of selling alcohol had not been properly interviewed, and the (male) probation officer of a ten-year-old convicted of theft had not cared that the boy was chained for two months by his father to keep him from running away. Such episodes would have been impossible in England, Sorabji wrote, because in the metropole, probation was 'a Reformatory without walls' and 'the cornerstone of redemption'. She called for 'a suitable House of Detention' in India, and hoped that donors would step forward, like the Cadbury family had in England, to fund an infrastructure of juvenile reform. A specialized system was made all the more urgent by India's 'differences of race, its lack of institutional provision for the care of children, its habit of juvenile migration from Province to Province, and its absence of [administrative] precedent'.[78] She expressed high hopes for 'a Children's Court which is a friendly enquiry, almost as if it were a domestic enquiry by a head of a family with the assistance when possible of members of that family — and for result not a sentence, but a family programme for betterment, and for a fresh chance'.[79]

The concerns about migratory juvenile delinquents reflects an anxiety about disrupted villages that was by the 1920s a fixture of the colonial reformatory, while the complaint about children being tried in the manner and institutions of adults was likewise a permanent component of reformatory discourse in India. In voicing these, Sorabji is unremarkable. The insistence upon emulating post-1908 England, however, is a symptom of the universalism driving Indian institutional enthusiasts in the 1920s. When she criticized existing probation regimes, Sorabji was engaged in marking out probation as a location of professional-scientific expertise and a civilizational model. While this model illustrated the difference between England and India, it was also intended to be imitable, or a blueprint for the erasure of difference. Like her male Indian colleagues, Sorabji subscribed to a model of treatment that was applicable anywhere in the world, although she did not hesitate to refer to the peculiarities of native children who might reach puberty at an age determined by race and medical expertise. The paradox is deeply rooted in what Greenfeld, adapting Nietzsche, calls *ressentiment* nationalism, or the nationalism of existential envy.[80] Since the individual marked by *ressentiment* presupposes the existence of a particular community as well as its externally enforced inferiority, she must insist simultaneously upon uniqueness and universality.

There are obvious problems with ascribing *ressentiment* to a 'loyalist' such as Sorabji unless the ascription is qualified. Sorabji was not a nationalist in the sense in which the next generation of Oxbridge educated, 'anglicized' Indians were nationalists. Her political outlook was closer to that of Ranjitsinhji, Dadabhai Naoroji and even the early Gandhi. While these individuals represent a diverse ideological spread, they shared to various extents a cosmopolitanism based on mobility within the empire — the assumption that if they made certain cultural, geographic and discursive adjustments, their 'Indian' national identity could be accommodated within an imperial state, on universal and thus equal political terms with identities that were 'English', 'Australian' or 'Canadian'. While this political stance had never been uncontested, by the interwar years, it had become untenable. This generated frustration even when it did not produce outright rejection of the imperial tie, and those who had hoped to be central in an inclusive imperial fantasy attempted to carve their niches on the margins of a colonized nationhood.[81]

In a memo to the Age of Consent Committee during the Sarda Bill[82] deliberations, Sorabji claimed to speak on behalf of disaffected 'Indians of all races' — Arya Samajis, Brahmos, Hindus who had given up purdah and caste, literate Muslims, 'all' Christians, and women.[83] The last, especially, had been 'stirred emotionally' by the publication of Katherine Mayo's *Mother India*, and wanted to show themselves and their country 'to be on a par in all things with the enlightened countries of the world'. It is apparent that the emotional stirring to which Sorabji alluded was not inspiration alone, but also a galvanizing embarrassment. She was anxious not to lose this emotional momentum, because 'history teaches us that revulsions of feeling and relapses into conservatism often follow sudden departures from ancient usage — unless such departures are recognized and helped'.[84] Sorabji's response to *Mother India*, it seems, was more complex than a straightforward identification with Mayo.[85] Native agency at the intersection of childhood and femininity was driven by a nationalism that competed with 'orthodox' Indians as well as with non-Indians; this double-edged national agenda allowed Sorabji, like the framers of the Children Act of 1928, to imagine their work as the 'conservation of the child as a valuable asset of the community'.[86] Obviously, the nature of the 'asset' needs to be problematized; Sorabji saw it differently from how poor parents and the 'orthodox' may have seen it. The fact that Sorabji was not herself a parent may also have shaped her views on the relationship between child, parent, society and state. Nevertheless, it is apparent that the community that might own the child was Indian and that the asset was to be recovered from the periphery to which it had been consigned by the colonial reformatory.

The Indian child-saver's embarrassment about *Mother India* was shared, to a degree, by the colonial government on the international stage. W D Croft, the 'Indian' delegate at the League of Nations, struggled to formulate a response to the book, seeking an alliance with Indian reformers even as he portrayed child-saving dismissively as a woman's issue.[87] In 1931, the Child Welfare Committee of the League spent much time discussing systems for dealing with juvenile delinquency. India was not specifically mentioned, but the delegation from the British Empire proposed that a resolution be adopted emphasizing the importance of the issue, and urging countries that had no juvenile courts to create them quickly, and to involve women in their functioning.[88] Mayo's attack on the 'condition' of Indian women was unavoidably significant for all child-savers who claimed to represent India, partly because the female child in the tropics was apparently afflicted with the problems of the female adult, and partly because of the increased feminization of childhood as an area of activism. In certain contexts, the colonial state could choose to highlight the achievements of Indians like Sorabji, and to appropriate their modernity for itself — the teacher putting forward his best students as proof of his own enlightenment. Sorabji's activism should, therefore, be seen in the context of this internationally observed, state sponsored, institutional reform, which held up the mechanism of child correction as well as the engaged female activist/expert as hallmarks of civilized government.

Sorabji's critique of colonial juvenile courts and reformatories had three interrelated components. One, noted above, was their reluctance to concede that metropolitan institutional models were necessary in the periphery. Another was their lack of a recognizable expertise. The third was their lack of female agency. The threadbare expertise of the colonial reformatory was noted by more than one Indian contemporary of Sorabji; a judge in Calcutta told the Bengal Presidency Council of Women (BPCW, to which Sorabji belonged, and which functioned as an upper-class, multi-racial advocacy group in discussions of child reform[89]) that in his opinion, juvenile cases 'should be treated, as in England, by men having some knowledge of psychology'.[90] To this, Sorabji added that, 'unlike…in Calcutta, when a child came before a court in the Western countries, reports from a competent doctor, a clinical psychologist, a school teacher, a probation officer…always accompanied the charge sheet.'[91] At another meeting, Sorabji observed that, 'The old way with juvenile delinquency was to protect society from the child by punishing it; the new way is to study the circumstances in which the child had been brought up and to protect it from becoming worse.'[92]

Sorabji and Justice Costello, like Contractor, were engaged in the transformation of childhood into a psychological condition.[93] Even as childhood was separated from adulthood, the child was enmeshed in a network of adults empowered by new languages of authority, such as medicine, pedagogy and psychology. The native elite's desire for a modernity that is similar to the metropolitan was implicitly a critique of the colonial, if not of the colonizer. The charge that the Indian reformatory represented the 'old way' was a damning accusation in the context of a self-consciously modern project, and Sorabji had no hesitation in seeing in the methodological shortcomings the unequal, colonial nature of the child (or adult) that might emerge from such inexpert reform. It is worth noting that she had remarked, while criticizing the difference in salaries for white and Indian officers of the Indian Civil Service, 'You cannot boast of 'equality' and yet make distinctions'.[94]

The failure of equality — a combination of expertise and universality — was, for Sorabji, both a symptom and a cause of the apparent absence of female agency in an apparatus intended for children. Probation, certainly, was one of the 'unequal' areas that she illuminated through her case studies in *The Statesman*.[95] Not surprisingly, it was a profession that Sorabji sought to claim for women in India. 'Philanthropy is doing its best to get into personal touch with the children,' she told the Bengal government, naming the BPCW, the Society for the Protection of Children in India (SPCI) and the Salvation Army as potential sources of recruitment for female probation officers, and adding that the existing cadre of untrained, male probation officers were worse than useless.[96] The suggestion is not without its contradictions; 'philanthropic' organizations like the Salvation Army were unlikely to produce the professional social workers and specialists that Sorabji saw in metropolitan juvenile punishment. Probation, which meant the provision of alternative and temporary parents with a moral vision different from that of natural parents, remained the impossible holy grail of the colonial child-saver. What is significant is that Sorabji believed that it might be attainable, were the agency to be feminized and located in the 'English living'. It was a step that her predecessors, like Duncan in the 1890s, had not imagined, because they had not imagined that the 'right sort' of women might exist in India.

Sorabji also devoted a great deal of attention to medical inspections of children arrested by the police. We find here a more elaborately articulated attempt to engender the colonial reformatory. Unhappy with the common practice in which girls brought into juvenile courts or reformatories were examined by male physicians, she pointed out to the provincial government that the Bengal

Children Act of 1922, which required medical examinations to determine age, virginity and 'specific offenses,' also stipulated that the doctor 'shall when practicable be a Woman'. She added that girl children might not 'consent' to examination by male doctors, and that forced examination by men 'may have such dire consequences'.[97] On behalf of the BPCW, and supported by the Salvation Army, the YWCA, the Calcutta Vigilance Association and the SPCI, she wrote, 'Our objection is to a man *as such*, being employed for the examination of minor girls.'[98] [Emphasis in original]

The horror at the male doctor's presence is reminiscent of Carpenter's reaction to the presence of male teachers in schools for young Indian women.[99] Even in 1928, child-saving had placed Sorabji at the head of a motley collection of the moral and the modern. Her own discomfort was not explicitly based on moral concerns, but rather on the psychological impact on the child of a medical procedure, and upon what might be described as professional propriety. She placed herself in the role of the witness to a rape, with the child-saving state as rapist. The juvenile court was thus cast in a highly ambiguous role — it was the protector turned violator. The violation was inextricably linked to male agency; if this was replaced by female agency, then the protective function would be restored.

Sorabji did not reject the medical procedure; she rejected only the gender of the doctors. The authority of modern medicine, which might reveal childhood in the body, was a critical part of the expertise that she sought to implant in the Indian reformatory. The strategy had metropolitan precedents, but there were also significant departures: whereas medical activism in English child-saving: was typically opposed by the champions of 'the liberty of the individual' (parent),[100] in India, the doctors and their allies were the proponents of individuality (located in the child) and the implicit right to liberty. Key decisions in the punishment of girls must be made 'by Doctors alone', Sorabji wrote, adding that the doctors should be women, assisted by female social workers.[101] She brought the idea of consent into the reformatory, but also implied that consent to inspection was a non-issue when the doctor was female. The attempt to capture childhood in the name of femininity was also an attempt to capture the masculine professions that must surround the child in a universally modern society. Writing in *The Statesman*, she complained about 'pleaders who came to court with the idea that it was a professional opportunity, whereas in England counsel did not seek to display their legal skill, but were simply one of the family inquiry'.[102] Since Sorabji's own credentials as a child-saver were supported in part by her legal training, the attack on lawyers who saw juvenile trials as professional opportunities is ironic. It was feasible because she was herself redeemed by her claim to feminine/professional familiality (and by the fact that unlike the common Indian-educated pleader, she had studied law in England).

Sorabji's stance is consistent with Cox's description of a clash between professional women and self-consciously masculine bureaucrats in colonial India,[103] but her demand for female agency had its limits. Some were practical compromises while others reflected the limits of her own radicalism, imposed by class and the same peripheral location in empire and nation that enabled her critiques of male-run child-saving projects. She wanted women social workers in the juvenile courts, and women jurors ('most useful in England') to decide age-of-consent cases, but she was comfortable with the idea of a male judge presiding over the 'family' of the court; in her descriptions of the model juvenile court, the judge is always 'he'.[104] She rejected the idea of using policewomen for 'the invasion of homes', indicating a preference for 'the voluntary help of trained but non-Police women.'[105] While police work offended the elite woman's sense of appropriate femininity and required the recruitment of unreliable lower-class women for invasions of the 'home' (which, through a slippage common to colonial reformatory activists, could be a nationally central concept even when it belonged to the marginal), social work was acceptable in the upper-class Indian context of the 1920s.[106]

In spite of its limits, Sorabji's ideological approach to the colonial reformatory broke through some of the barriers that had stymied the experts of the 1890s, not to mention those of the Napier-Mouat generation. When she accused the state of rape in the guise of medical inspections, she graphically described the trembling, weeping collapse of a sixteen-year-old girl 'rescued' from a brothel, brought into court, and confronted by a male doctor accompanied by Sorabji herself. Prostitutes were not immune to feelings of 'repugnance' at such inspections, she observed.[107] By doing so, she took the novel position that Indian prostitutes could in fact feel shame, that sexualized females could also be children, and that child prostitutes possessed a streak of innocence that made repugnance — and thus reform — imaginable. While she was not above equating and condemning public women of particular kinds (she dismissed women who participated in Gandhian politics as 'prostitutes', in a decidedly unsympathetic use of the term[108]), she nevertheless retrieved a specific form of female delinquency from its gendered marginality within the reformatory.

She was also able to suggest new ways of imagining the Indian family, the Indian woman, the colonial state and the reformatory itself, so that her mostly male colleagues could extend the institution to a wider circle of Indian society, including females. Her call for a dramatically expanded network of reformatories that might encircle prostitutes as well as 'beggars and petty offenders'[109] provided for an expansion of delinquency that Bayley had been unable to contemplate except in irony, but it was consistent with the Indian elite's desire for a modernity that moved beyond the colonial and into the national. Her impatience with incrementalist approaches to reform[110] — the adoption of the posture of a heroic bulldozer that would clear colonial and 'orthodox' obstacles simultaneously — was politically practical largely because she asserted herself as an Indian (albeit English living) and a woman. While the child and the reformatory enabled a powerful convergence of professional expertise, the intrusive state and femininity, the last also enabled a colonial reformatory that was considerably less peripheral in its potential than its nineteenth-century predecessor.

Conclusion

The marginalization of female children within the Indian reformatory is inseparable from the perception among some colonial administrators that the hypersexual nature of the native female was not only unmanageable, but also corrosive of childhood. Thus, girls stopped being redeemable much earlier than did boys. This curtailing of childhood combined with other ideological and political projects — reinforcing a domestic patriarchal order in Indian society by preserving the marriageability of female delinquents, and maintaining an exaggerated and misplaced regard for the 'nationalist resolution'.

It is not as if elite Indians in the period separating the two RS Acts did not care if girls were sent to the reformatory. Their contradictory responses to the idea are exemplified in Man's memo to the Punjab High Court:

> I do not see how we can shut the doors of the reformatory schools and refuse the advantages of this kind of education to them when we freely confer these on boys. They must share the advantages and disadvantages of prison life with their brothers. The only reason perhaps for leaving the girls out would be a hesitation on behalf of the British Government in meddling too much with the religious and social institutions of the people in India. No doubt the Government must maintain *perfect* neutrality in religious matters and should not interfere as far as practicable in the social matters, for these are closely connected with religion in all Eastern countries. If this is neglected, the measure will be extremely unpopular amongst the people.[111] [Emphasis in original]

By merging the 'religious' and the 'social' in 'Eastern countries', Man followed the Orientalist separation between a West in which the Enlightenment has generated a secular social/public realm, and an East in which there is no differentiation between public and private, society and religion, reason and faith/superstition. He thus appropriated a major strand of the colonial critique of Indian civilization, and used it defensively, seeking to minimize or ward off the impact of colonial institutions on Indian religious/national identities. It is a sophisticated strategy that simultaneously invites and obstructs British intervention in Indian 'society'. By saying yes to the female reformatory, he set himself up as a modern Man and an ideological ally of the modern colonizer. At the same time, he sacrificed a particular set of females (children, poor, criminalized, uneducated) to the reformatory, in order to draw the line of 'religion' more sharply and to warn the British not to cross it.

The intertwined lines of nationality, femininity, sexuality and pseudo-childhood could be crossed only when a particular model of the Indian woman became available to work in the reformatory. The emergence of Cornelia Sorabji as a voice in 'children's issues' was, however, also deeply subversive of the colonial reformatory, because in the process of claiming the field for women, demanding a regime that resembled metropolitan child correction, and including girls in the ranks of the childlike and the redeemable, she dislocated the institution from the juvenile periphery. There can be little doubt that the simultaneous feminization, Indianization and modernization of the reformatory were at least somewhat successful. Inmates in Chingleput in the 1930s celebrated 'Health and Baby Week'; Indians predominated among official visitors, and there were more female visitors than males among the Indians.[112] Where female staff was unavailable to the reformatory, as in Burma, embarrassed male administrators referred to the absence as 'a marked defect'.[113]

5

MASTERS AND SERVANTS: SCHOOL, HOME AND ARISTOCRATIC CHILDHOOD

In the early 1860s, with the Mutiny still fresh in memory, British officers serving in the west and the centre of the subcontinent rediscovered princely India as a colonial frontier. This was, in fact, the discovery of overlapping frontiers — a geographic periphery, a cultural backwater and a political area of darkness. Each was remarked for conquest, and the instruments and sites of confrontation evolved over the following decades. Alongside the post-1858 durbar that McLeod, Ramusack and others have characterized as a new boundary between princely and British India,[1] colonial administrators oversaw a network of educational institutions for the children of the princes. These schools — the Chiefs' Colleges, the Imperial Cadet Corps, relatively modest institutions for modest relatives, experiments in guardianship and tutoring — highlighted childhood itself as a live border in colonial India. The male child at the centre of these institutions was the point of entry into the adult world of political calculations, through which British viceroys, political agents and principals sought to bring about a more reassuring and pleasing colonial order.

The aristocratic native child did not enter these schools fully formed; his childhood, aristocracy and nature were all revealed by the school. This revelation could take place only within a set of experiments in institutional, political and racial order. The very act of revelation, therefore, indicated conquest and order, including possible and even impossible orders. Even when the content of the revelation was cause for anxiety, the larger pedagogical exercise would carry the colonial expert into uncharted societies, families, bodies and minds, where he might find exciting insights about race, environment, and the ability to learn, or the ability to transcend nature — of the individual, of the race, or of the 'soil' — by adaptation.

The focus of this chapter is on the four Chiefs' Colleges: Rajkot and Mayo (Ajmere), which emerged in the 1870s, and Daly (Indore) and Aitchison (Lahore), which were established later in the century.[2] The Chiefs' College was a model institution in more than one sense and the models were not always complementary. The romantic and the utilitarian were both accommodated uneasily within the schools. On the one hand, the colleges manifested a near-parody of bureaucratic modernity, producing confusion and paralysis as often as they produced knowledge. Curzon's secretary reported to him in 1901:

> At Lahore, as at the Mayo College in Ajmere, there is the dual control of a military officer as Governor and of an Educational officer as Principal, and in 1889 a further subdivision of authority was effected by making the Native Headmaster Superintendent of Boarding Houses. [The principal] Mr. Godley considers...that the College has at all times suffered from over control and divided authority. There is an annual report on each boy, forwarded by the Assistant Masters to the Headmaster. The Headmaster forwards them to the Principal, with a report of his own. The Principal compiles another report and forwards it to the Governor, and the Governor adds a general report and forwards it to the Committee. Then there is the Inspector's Report, which is forwarded to the Director of Public Instruction. This is very different from the system at Rajkot, where Mr. Chester Macnaghten was given plenary powers, and did not submit an annual report on the working of his school.[3]

On the other hand, the colleges were the architectural and institutional representations of an imagined despotism, in which principals like Macnaghten made up the rules as they proceeded. The contradiction between the two models was essentially a chronic uncertainty about whether to 'reform', and in what image to reform, the native specimen. The child that entered the Chiefs' College was not so much transformed as paralyzed by this tension.

Superficially, the schools were intended to produce modern/native aristocrats who might participate usefully in the colonial spectacle as loyal and subordinate allies of the British, representatives of an authentic Indian political class, and imperial ornaments and team mates. The surrogate parenting of young Rajputs by white men, fascinated as well as repelled by their own romantic imagination, was an experiment in counter-Macaulayan education; it was intended to produce utility without also producing the political insubordination that was already a hallmark of the urban elites of British India.[4] Yet the 'modern', the 'native' and the 'aristocrat' could not be reconciled within the colonial school any more than 'modern', 'native' and 'delinquent' could be reconciled in the reformatory. Each agenda was so full of internal contradictions that failure was almost inevitable. There is no doubt that by the end of the First World War, the Chiefs' Colleges and the ICC were widely perceived as having failed — they had, in the view of most colonial administrators who took an interest in them, produced an assortment of the foolish, the childish and the apathetic.

The appearance of a failed experiment is misleading. More than the reformatory, which had been founded by Napier and Mouat upon the assumption that metropolitan models might have some universal applicability, the princely schools were based upon the perception of an incompatibility between native material and metropolitan method. They were never intended to be 'public schools', in spite of a significant amount of lip service to 'Eton in India', which some historians have taken at face value.[5] They existed, rather, to outline the English public school and the impossibility of its replication in the colony. Failure was itself a valuable product of the Chiefs' Colleges. By continuously modulating and elaborating upon the distance between Rajput children, English children of various classes, middle-class Indian children and tribal children, they produced a wealth of knowledge about native childhoods and its adult social contexts, including not only the family and the durbar but also the colonial school that was defeated by the perverse strength of native natures and nurtures. Such production was invaluable as a justification of colonialism, as a means of generating children who would never become adults, and as a pleasurable experience of investigative authority and civilizational superiority when political authority seemed uncertain.

The Colonizing Project of Princely Education

The origins of the Chiefs' Colleges go back to the winter of 1862–63, when E I Howard, the Director of Public Education in Bombay, went on a tour of Rajputana. Howard was accompanying the Governor of Bombay; the party included Rao Muhiputram Rupram, principal of the Normal School in Ahmedabad. In the 'memoirs' that Howard submitted to the Government of India, he put forward a compelling vision of the western Indian states as a political and cultural frontier. He wrote:

> The country to the west of the Aravalli range…is wild and jungly, fading into the Great Desert. Yet there is water and an admirable soil. The villages are separated by miles of wilderness, but wherever we saw cultivation the crops were luxuriant. The numerous tombs or rather cenotaphs and other structures of masonry, often adorned with sculpture, indicated a bygone period of prosperity. Ages of anarchy and the ravages of Pindarrees and Marathas have since depopulated the country. The Serohi Durbar has made efforts to attract settlers by liberal offers of land rent free, but no Native Government seems able to inspire confidence, and it was a native who assured me that, without a British

guarantee, they would not be accepted. We saw no traffic between Aboo and Ajmere, save...a train of Commissariat carts laden with porter for the troops at Nusseerabad. Travelling is said by the Natives to be unsafe, from wild beasts and still more dangerous thieves. Dreadful stories were told of a recent robbery and murder by Bheels and Meenas, apparently with impunity, and, it was hinted, for the profit of local Chiefs. Two sons of the Serohi Rajah are living in open outlawry by plunder. Even mails and Government property are not safe. The only roads were tracks through the jungle. In the midst of such barbarism, cities become of great importance, as the only places where trade can be safely carried on and a wealthy man can live unspoiled. It is here evidently that nurseries of education must first be planted.[6]

Howard was able to distinguish between geographies of confidence and anxiety, and to connect those to the states of schooling that he could observe. Jaipur fell in the former category. There he noted 'the opening of an aristocratic school for the sons of Thakoors', with twelve students enrolled and good prospects. He attributed this not only to the enlightened legacy of Jai Singh (who he described as 'an ancient Maharaja'), but also to 'the power for good of an enlightened and energetic Political officer' and the generosity of the Director of Public Education of the Northwest Provinces, who had restored and revitalized Jai Singh's educational edifice.[7] Udaipur was further removed from Jaipur on the political map and correspondingly underdeveloped in its educational infrastructure: here, in 'wild' and 'uncivil' Mewar, the political officer had struggled in isolation to create schools for Rajput children. But all was not lost — Udaipur would soon be connected to Ahmedabad by a new road and children might be taken away from Mewar for schooling in Gujarat. Moreover, Howard mused about Udaipur, 'The Maharajah is a minor, the State being governed by a Council of Regency, and we now have the 'opportunity...for the permanent establishment of education in Mewar.'[8] Minor wards, as a subspecies of the orphan, never failed to excite colonial enthusiasts in native children — they embodied pliability and ease of access.

Howard was cautiously hopeful about the less accessible places that he visited or asked about. Western Rajputana was bereft of 'civilizing influences' due to its 'remote situation' and urgently needed the establishment of new schools under British-Indian supervision. He hoped that the Ajmere College, the forerunner of Mayo College, might do for Jodhpur what Ahmedabad College could do for Udaipur, extricating the children of the elite from their isolation on the map and into British-Indian territory. About Nimach, he observed that the place 'is surrounded by native states, whose unfriendliness is greatly complained of. The people applied to me for a school'.[9]

The educational project is thus founded upon the gaze of the peripatetic colonial official venturing progressively into the darkness of princely India, with Bernard Cohn's 'travel modality' opening the doors for modalities of survey, surveillance and child-saving.[10] Such exploration, Marriott indicates, was essential to the simultaneous creation of race, delinquency and dominance.[11] Indeed, it is difficult to miss the similarities between Howard's penetrating vision of the princely states and Sorabji's interest in 'a hitherto unexplored country' made up of 'the Orthodox Hindu community'.[12] Howard sees a fallen but revivable land, in which British intervention might bring law and order, prosperity, political security and even the restoration of a derelict pre-colonial enlightenment. It is an antirural vision — there is no trace in Howard's narrative of a romantic preference for the countryside — that is closely tied to the discourse of the CT. The thin line between Rajputs and the collectively criminal was not something that Howard imagined into existence; it was present in the emergent model of the 'infanticidal tribe', which criminalized Rajputs at the level of the clan.[13] Howard's description of the moral geography of the princely states and his proposed solutions are rhetorically very similar to contemporary surveys of the tribal geography of Assam and Chittagong.[14] In each case, the society that concealed the child was defined by the limits of colonial penetration into the geographic periphery of empire.

To the knowledge of this frontier that might be opened for (and through) pedagogy, Howard contributed the idea that the delinquency of the Rajput was manifest and correctible in the children of the chiefs, and the corollaries that such children might be herded into new 'nurseries', that the corrective project would constitute a wider colonization of a civilizational periphery, and that educators like himself might accompany governors and military officers in the vanguard of conquest. While he did not deny a role in this educative colonization to natives like Muhiputram and other Indians he had met locally,[15] he was also clear that effective pedagogy was dependent upon the 'weight' of class, race and bureaucratic rank, which together constituted political authority.

Howard had no doubt that this authority was necessary in a colonizing project that was not only geographical-political but also cultural. Everywhere he looked, he found that native moral failures coincided with pedagogical failure and generated backwaters that modern experts might reclaim. He wrote about Burhanpur,

> All the Government schools seem to be of the lowest class, [and] the only inspector is a very old Hindoo from Ahmednugger, from whom it would be unreasonable to look for a new idea. My Department could be usefully employed in organizing the education of this near, but uncivilized province, which till very recently was under the Government of Scindia.[16]

The new schools that Howard imagined were heroic instruments that would prevail over the lack of roads, infrastructure and security, but at a more basic level they would prevail over the indifference and resistance of native adults. In Jodhpur, he discovered that the political agent, Col. French, had established a school — the Vidya Shal — but had not been especially successful in recruiting students. Parents had shown a willingness to send their sons to the school only as long as French provided carriages for their transportation; once the carriage service was discontinued (by French's less imaginative successor), the Vidya Shal promptly closed, and 'is now devoted to some Brahmin priests, who are employed to pray for the Maharajah'. Howard added, 'This story... enforces the lesson that it is a mere waste of money and trouble to set up schools for Natives which, should they want them, they can set up for themselves.'[17]

The school that had reverted to a heathen temple was an apt metaphor of a colonial outpost reclaimed by the savages, and it underlined Howard's perception that a conquest of the cultural frontier of princely children was necessarily a continuing and difficult struggle. Reluctant students and parents would plague his successors among colonial educators: at Aligarh College in the 1870s,[18] at missionary schools[19] and at the Chiefs' Colleges that would follow upon Howard's tour. Howard interpreted this indifference as the natural laziness of natives, but he also saw it as a problem that could be solved morally and practically by clever colonial experiments such as improvised school buses and ultimately the boarding school — the one exotic and entertaining, the other utilitarian. Fantasizing about a future residential school in Jodhpur, he hoped that the students might be vaccinated, even as he mused, 'The people are obstructive, for instance they object to vaccination, though they admit it is a safeguard against smallpox.'[20] As with vaccination, so with education — acquiescence to state medicine could function as a colonial measuring stick of race, civilization and subjugation.[21]

Howard's status as a forefather of the Chiefs' Colleges is not uncomplicated; there are significant differences between his proposals and the institutions that emerged in the 1870s. Howard saw existing schools for elite commoners in the native states as valuable models for educational experiments involving Rajput children. He envisioned local merchants as progressive allies of pedagogical pioneers from British India; Bania fathers and patrons, he wrote, might be counted upon to set an example for the landowning elite.[22] Such mixing of classes and castes would be anathema to the educators and administrators of the 1870s. (Even Howard regarded Banias with ambivalence, and hints of ant-Semitism crept into his rhetoric.[23])

Yet much of Howard's agenda survived, adopted and promoted by obscure political agents like C Walter and not-so-obscure ones like H D Daly, senior bureaucrats like C U Aitchison in the Foreign Department and E C Bayley in the Home Department, and viceroys like Lord Mayo and ultimately Curzon. In 1873, Bayley, fresh from his battles with Napier over reformatories, again found himself embroiled in a debate about the institutionalization of native children. The issue this time was government spending on schools for princely children. Disagreeing vehemently with Temple, who had argued that the colonial government was not required either to invest or to interfere in an internal responsibility of the princely states, Bayley wrote:

> I cannot conceive a reasonable sum being spent in any better way, or more in the direct interests of the taxpayers of British India, than a measure which will conduce materially…to the good government in future of the Native States which surround or are interspersed among our own territories. The influence of the condition of these States over our provinces is so great and so palpable for good or for evil that it is almost unnecessary to allude to it. Not only are the large numbers of our subjects, who either travel in, or hold commercial intercourse with, these States, deeply interested in their good government, but this is essential to Police and to the safety of our own subjects within our own territories. Not an abuse or a crime which has been put down in our territories, but has found a refuge in those of some of our neighbours; suttee, thuggee, dacoity, the receiving of kidnapped children, all have maintained themselves in Native States, and a very slight relaxation of vigilance on our part would very soon bring them back over the frontier. If we could once have the Chiefs and Nobles of Native States well educated, intelligent, and moral, very little interference would be needed on our part. An expenditure on this object [is] as legitimate as any expenditure on external objects can be, quite as much so as Subsidies, Political Agents, or Embassies are.[24]

Bayley declared that the control that came with British-Indian aid was entirely a good thing, and that the colonial government should insist upon the authority to appoint and dismiss the principal and other masters. He added, 'Political Officers [must] be allowed an active share in the management of the institution.'[25] Bayley's call for a link between school governance and a wider political authority was quickly successful. The principals of the Rajkot College and Mayo were both made officers of the Bombay government in 1875–76.[26]

In spite of their differences, Bayley and Temple both saw the Chiefs' College as an imperial embassy in a banana republic, complete with cultural, economic, political and military/policing functions. Bayley was comfortable with the vision, whereas Temple had qualms. For Bayley, as for Howard, the princely states and the moral condition of the princes were signifiers of a civilizational malaise that included sati and thuggee. (Both, it should be noted, reflected a criminality that had been secreted within the intimate recesses of society.) The fear that these might re-infect British India, which had been cleansed by energetic colonialism, turned borders into 'frontiers' at the edges of the princely states, much as it did at the edges of the reformatory. This was also a frontier of the juvenile periphery, because not only were the princes childish, it was their children who were the soft targets that must be colonized and turned into agents of 'good government'.

The concern with political control persisted into the apex years of the educational project for princely children, which might be identified with Curzon's tenure as Viceroy. The idea that schooling facilitated a wider surveillance, allowing British-Indian officials to keep track of the children of the chiefs, surfaces in a report by A P L Tucker, the Commissioner of Ajmere-Merwara in 1902. Tucker noted that it was essential that school authorities not lose sight of children who had gone home for the holidays, and that political agents must be both vigilant and discreet in the matter.[27] He, like Bayley and Temple, understood Howard's implication that the target of conquest was not only the wild countryside where princes and bandits appeared to merge, but the Rajput itself, as an embodied, gendered and acculturated entity.

Aristocrats and Others

The idea that the native aristocracy was gravely flawed acquired critical mass contemporaneously with the consolidation of the Martial Races theory in colonial and nationalist discourse.[28] The coincidence is not merely ironic; it was precisely because certain segments of Indian society were expected to be 'martial', 'manly' and loyal in the post-Mutiny colony that their failures in these regards became glaring to British observers. By the 1870s and 1880s, some officials had identified the educational institution, and consequently, the child, as the location where the flaws within the native aristocrat might be identified, studied, compared and even corrected. Thus, while the Chiefs' Colleges gradually built up towards a Curzonian project of aristocratic solidarity, the schools actually revealed just how unlike proper (English) aristocrats Rajputs were. The production of this distance, rather than its closing, was by far the major goal of those experts who participated in the colonizing of the children of the princes.

The failures of the Rajput child who might be educated were charted on an explicitly racial map by George Campbell, the former governor of Bengal, amateur anthropologist and pedagogical enthusiast. In a pamphlet titled

'On the Races of India as Traced in Existing Tribes and Castes', Campbell provided a map of India marked by ethnic types, and noted that 'Rajpoots must now be considered to be somewhat effete and inferior to the fresher races, especially to the Jats'.[29] Not only did Campbell identify a decayed masculinity as the core of the flaw in the Rajput, he implied that the longer a 'race' stayed in India, the more enervated it became, unless the children of the race were subjected to compensatory educational regimes. Like other colonial schools engaged in masculine political projects, the Chiefs' Colleges staged this encounter with effeteness, which emerged in the late nineteenth century as a ubiquitous curse of the native elites that contended with the British for a share in the colonial state.[30]

The effeteness of Rajput children included the usual complaints about physical weakness, athletic ineptitude and general cowardice,[31] but it extended into flawed relationships with family members and expert assessments of the child's capacity for reform. Effete nature seemed to exist in a state of chronic competition with pedagogical expertise in the very institutions that produced both. Like the 'habit' of the delinquent, it constantly threatened to overwhelm the colonial institution. In a memo on the role of the Chiefs' Colleges in 1900, Curzon wrote,

> Every year there is being turned out an increasing number of young men, who at the very moment when the continued pressure of discipline…is most needed for the strengthening of their character and their conversion into useful members of the body politic, are allowed to drift back into irresponsible lethargy and indolence. More than one promising young life, sapped by indulgence, or dissipated in idleness, points a moral to which no thoughtful person can shut his eyes.[32]

The effete child, in these superficially despairing constructions that were actually satisfying revelations of colonial purpose, was inadequately respectful of proper authority, excessively attached to improper authority, and like the juvenile delinquent, frequently homosexual. Buggery at school was arguably a novel phenomenon produced by a colonial experiment, but it nevertheless revealed the Rajput child as doubly perverse — for engaging in sex, and also for engaging in 'unnatural' sex. It was a ubiquitous concern in discussions of residential schooling and in 1893–94, a 'scandal' at Aitchison College resulted in the expulsion of five students and the resignation of the headmaster.[33] It is unlikely that colonial administrators with public school backgrounds were especially shocked by evidence of sexual experimentation in the dormitories.[34] In India, however, such discoveries reinforced an impression of the unmanly precocity of boys who had emerged not from the properly gendered circle of the elite Victorian family, but from the moral and physical hothouse of the *zenana*.

The idea that Rajput boys were corrupted by their sexual nature must be viewed within the larger context of a British 'discovery' of the sexual nature of native children. Colonial educators in the nineteenth century struggled to come to terms with the reality that their young wards were often married and had children of their own. This was especially true of educators who worked in the boarding schools. As surrogate fathers who sought to colonize a substantial part of the everyday life of the native child, they insisted on supervising the development of 'their' children as sexual-social subjects, denying the possibility that children could be sexual agents even as they produced a stream of evidence that their wards did in fact have sexual desires and 'habits'.[35]

Birth parents were consistently implicated in the effeteness of Rajput children, including their sexuality. Mothers, in particular, were notorious for insisting upon early marriages for young princes, in which case, British intervention was required to temper the effect of wives. Mothers were also held responsible for infantilizing their sons by pampering them, closeting them in secluded indoor worlds, and depriving them of physical exercise, rational nurturing and manly influence.[36] This disdain for mothers is ironic; Stone has pointed out that between the seventeenth and nineteenth centuries, middle-class parenting in England became increasingly permissive, affectionate and 'maternal'.[37] The colony was gendered differently: the indulgence of native women carried no restraining subtext of morality, and the idea of permission was fraught with political menace. While the maternal continued to be equated with the permissive in India, the equation was not given a positive value.

Also, since the sixteenth century and possibly earlier, the relationship between mother and young son, among people who might cautiously be described as Hindus, almost certainly corresponded with narratives of the child Krishna — the sweetly cunning Gopal, uncontrolled, more pampered than punished, with mischief constituting the essence of childhood. This rendered the child godlike even as God became childlike. While the movement was not entirely unfamiliar to European observers in the nineteenth century, it differed from the Victorian cult of infantile divinity. As Kenneth Bryant has noted, the body of the medieval Indian child-god was invested with erotic possibility.[38] Maternal permission in the colony thus produced a native that was perverse not only because he was disobedient and untruthful, but also because he transgressed the basic elite-European assumption about childhood in the period between ubiquitous original sin and ubiquitous Freud.

While some scholars have been skeptical about historicizing parental affection,[39] Stone has argued that the development of 'maternal' parenting in

England was closely tied to a new view of children as individuals.[40] In the colonial context, where individuality barely applied to adult natives, the mother-child relationship could only be imagined as the stifling of individuality and adulthood.[41] (It might be argued that it was the recuperation of individuality by nationalist child-savers in the interwar period that enabled the 'maternal' intervention that Sorabji represented.) In 1875, R J Meade, the political agent and Special Commissioner in Baroda, wrote to C U Aitchison about his plans to intervene in the parenting of the twelve-year-old prince, Syajee Rao:

> He is not of a robust frame, and requires good and nourishing food. He has, however, shown himself to be desirous of practicing native gymnastics, learning to ride, and in other ways of acquiring skill and aptitude in similar matters in which the head of the State should be expert. It is...essential that the Prince shall be separated as much as possible from the palace, where...he is necessarily wholly in the society of the palace females and menial servants. Her Highness has hitherto kept the boy attached to herself and almost always in her sight, but this cannot be continued, and it is most necessary that he shall have a different stamp of companions.[42]

Kakar has described the mother-child relationship in Indian society as a culturally determined prop that serves the psychological needs of parent as well as offspring for a peculiarly extended period in their lives. He has further observed that 'being alone' and 'separation from mother' are peculiarly interrelated in the Indian (he means Hindu) psyche and culture.[43] This dubious speculation was shared by administrators like Meade. Kakar correctly notes that both fears — that of being alone and of leaving mother — are unmanly and childish in the rational-masculine discourse of modern adulthood.[44] Neither the mother nor the colonial surrogate father wanted Syajee Rao to 'grow up'. Each sought to infantilize him, but the queen's 'infant', being effeminate, was further from manhood than Meade's.

It is substantially because the Rajput child was effete that the mission of princely education was internally as well as externally conflicted. The effete boy was subject to persistent uncertainties about whether he could change — whereas the inability to change cast doubt upon his plasticity and childhood, exhibiting change could bring on accusations of mimicry. OBC St. John, the principal of Mayo College in its early years, told the school's executive council (including both princes and British administrators) that his objective was 'not merely the acquisition of book learning, but the stimulation of that energy of mind and body which the nobility of Rajasthan so warmly admire in English gentlemen, and for the attainment of which themselves are so peculiarly fitted'.[45]

St. John's implication is that there was an extant gap between the 'fitness' and the reality of the Rajput child — a decline that the British educator could point out, if not correct. His is the rhetoric of a universally applicable transformation. The Rajput child can be like the English child, he says, asserting and qualifying racial peculiarity simultaneously. He depicts the Rajput as a dormant or potential Englishman, as well as a native who wants to be English. Considering how ambivalent the princes were about the project of 'becoming Englishmen',[46] St. John was being disingenuous. It was, however, a calculated disingenuity. His remarks were not so much descriptive as didactic: he was telling the assembled princes how they should regard the English and what they should desire to become. There is also a concealing flattery in the speech, because by holding out the image of shared aristocratic virtues, St. John just barely hid the racial line that structured practically every aspect of the college.

St. John, like Meade, was an early articulator of what is sometimes mistakenly seen as a Curzonian agenda of restructuring the relationship between class, race and the colonial state.[47] The educators and administrators of the 1870s anticipated by a generation Curzon's interest in infusing the native aristocratic child with selected characteristics of middle-class and English children, while preventing the newly educated princeling from becoming either English or middle-class. Since such precise transformation was both necessitated and impeded by juvenile natures that might be construed as effete, the middle-class child emerged quickly as a primary Other of the child that might be rehabilitated in the Chiefs' College. Also, because the idea of the effete aristocrat had a certain home-grown currency in Victorian England,[48] the project of re-educating the children of Indian princes had an additional experimental value. It could potentially retrieve the aristocrat from the discourse of an obsolete, unmanly and useless decadence. The princely child was therefore to be saved from a double effeteness — that of the middle-class Indian who had been produced by the earlier, Macaulayan experiment in colonial pedagogy, and that of the aristocrat in a modern empire.

Not surprisingly, transparent allusions to middle-class children are ubiquitous in discussions of the shape that education at the Chiefs' Colleges might and must not take. When the Mayo College was being readied in the early 1870s, Col. Brooke, the senior political agent for Rajputana, wrote:

> The object will be to give the boys a liberal education, and more to instruct their minds and give them a moral culture, encouraging them at the same time in manly sports and pastimes than bringing them up as bookworms and cramming them. It is hoped they will afterwards take their position as a liberal minded landed aristocracy.[49]

While there is something of Cornwallis and the Permanent Settlement in this educational agenda, it is also an attempt to 'do Macaulay right'. It constitutes a critique of the competitive, meritocratic, examination oriented, middle-class schoolboy, especially in India but to some extent in England as well. Thus, its anti-intellectualism is both a white critique of uppity racial inferiors and a broader aristocratic critique of the middle class.

The hostility towards middle-class priorities in childrearing should not be seen as a blanket refusal to entertain social inferiors at the new educational institutions, or even as a consistent anti-intellectualism. The issue of class in the Chiefs' College was not a simple matter of finding the poor unsuitable. While there was an overt insistence that plebeian natures cannot be corrected by nurture, there was also a mumbled acknowledgment that boys from relatively humble backgrounds were often more promising human material than aristocratic children. H D Daly, the political agent for the Central Indian States, remarked in 1875 about the presence at the Bundelkhand Chiefs' College of children from relatively modest families, including distant relatives of the ruling princes. This school, like most Chiefs' Colleges at some time or another, was in danger of 'failing'; the princes did not send their children in appreciable numbers, and those children that had enrolled were disappointing to colonial educators as scholars, moral subjects and physical specimens. Daly noted, however, that the children from less prestigious families did better academically than the offspring of the chiefs. He did not express alarm, hoping instead that the presence of book-smart near-commoners might introduce 'an element of stimulation and competition' into the wider student body. If the school was to survive, he implied, the children of the wealthier Rajputs must emulate their more humble classmates.[50] For those that were capable of emulation, academic competition could thus be not only a marker of manly striving, but a leveller within an institution with elite-generated norms.

Daly had earlier solicited the support of commoners for his plans for a Chiefs' College at Indore (which would bear his name), and written of Mir Shahamut Khan, an administrator in Rutlam: 'An accomplished native: gentleman...is ardent in the practicality of the scheme, he is possessed of great influence, and is a scholar and a man of the world — he knows his countrymen thoroughly and their wants.'[51] Like Howard before him, Daly was engaged in a process of identifying allies and informants in the ranks of 'native gentlemen', or the non-princely elites of the princely states, whose political bonds and cultural inclinations might be more fluid than those of the princes themselves. In 1870, Aitchison had appeared to second the sentiment, writing that 'Nothing will revolutionize Native States like the education of Chiefs as ordinary gentlemen'.[52]

Aitchison, however, had raised a canard. By 'ordinary gentlemen', he meant a very specific English class identity: aristocrats and elite commoners who studied and played together as equals in public schools and Oxbridge, and who shared a composite cultural identity that existed in very limited contexts, such as the upper levels of the colonial government. Aitchison suggested that childhood — as a state of innocence — facilitates such interaction, but he and his colleagues remained uncertain that an appropriate set of ordinary gentlemen was available to the children of the princes. Daly rejected any model of education that was geared towards academic achievement, writing, 'We must look to forming men with manly feelings and purposes, and not fly at high scholarship.'[53] It is clear that what princely children were intended to learn through this exercise in emulation was a lesson in emulation itself. In other words, they were asked to emulate a class of natives who were widely condemned by British observers for their apparent mimicry of the British, but without themselves becoming mimics.

As the great mimic man of colonial society, the baboo is the ever-present shadow at the back of the Chiefs' College — deracinated but without a compensating cultural, moral or political authority. While selecting teachers for Mayo College, Lewis Pelly, political agent for Rajputana in 1873, wrote to Aitchison:

> The object in view is to train the young aristocracy of Rajpootana, to fulfil worthily their high positions in social life, and to fit them for command and even for independent rule. It is to be borne in mind that the object of this College is not to educate youths for social and practical life *in Europe* where their whole existence would be an exotic one; and where the severance of their habits of thought from all association with the ideas and prejudices of their homes might prove an advantage. The object of this College is to engraft on the Native aristocracy something of the bearing, habits and modes of thought of our nobility, and then to *return these youths to their own capitals* and States, where they will have to rule tribes and States composed mainly of unenlightened Hindoos. [Emphases in original]

> Solidity of character and strength of mind are more necessary than is sharpness of intellect — we should bring up these youths to be wise rather than clever, to grow indeed with our growth, but to do this without forgetting the soil to which their social roots reach down. For our purposes one or two conscientious experienced Hindoo gentlemen of what is called the old school, and who might not even have thrown off their own religion, would be preferable to many of the clever young

Indians that may be found in polished boots and a thin veneering of civilization, but who, while they have emancipated themselves from the restraints imposed by their own customs and superstitions, have yet failed to become a law unto themselves.[54]

Those who had 'failed to become a law unto themselves' were essentially still children; they could not be expected to assume or teach authority. They could, however, teach insubordination, much like older children in the reformatory. The anti-intellectualism of the Chiefs' College was a stance against the 'cleverness' of the 'new school' that the baboo may have attended in his own youth. The remark about shoes, reminiscent of upper-caste attitudes towards Dalit footwear, reflects a resentment of Indians who usurped European sartorial privileges.[55] This, too, was a habit that the princely child could not be encouraged to acquire; if he wore boots, it had to be the dusty shoes of subordinated military service in the ICC, and not an accessory that reminded Pelly and Aitchison of the opening of well-shod white bastions to clever natives.

Pelly was quite clear about the experimental nature of emulation at the Chiefs' Colleges. The new schools, he wrote, constituted 'an experiment on the practicability or otherwise' of teaching English habits to Indians.[56] This was quite different from Macaulay's infamous vision of brown Englishmen in the *Minute on Indian Education*. To emulate was not to mimic; it was to admire, and to submit to a superior political, aesthetic and moral authority. The emulated and the successful emulator, in Pelly's perspective, should both be 'wise'. To be wise was to be safely antique, traditional, apolitical and irrelevant in the modern world of political competition. It was also to be loyal and subordinate, 'engrafted' with some English habits but excluded from European identities, geographies, rights and privileges, and restricted (or 'returned') to a limited geographical, cultural/racial and political place. The idea of return, imagined as an arrangement of subordination, is critically important to the Chiefs' Colleges. Pelly, Aitchison, Daly and others recognized that going to such schools and emulating adults other than princely parents constituted a departure for Rajput children. It was not intended to be a continuing departure, or one that became permanent; the emulating child was expected to 'return' to native society, retaining some traces of the enclave. The experience of the enclave, moreover, was itself a 'return' to a Tod-inspired model of Rajput manhood that had apparently decayed.

Although the middle-class Indian could inhabit this experiment only as an absence, worthy native objects of emulation did exist. Howard believed he had found some 'learned' Indians who might teach Sanskrit and Marwari in the schools of his fantasy, and serve British scholars as research assistants in the libraries of Jodhpur and Jaisalmer.[57] This was consistent with his vision of princely education as part of a larger project of reviving Sanskritic knowledge and transforming Rajputana into a modern archive of this knowledge — an authentic India that might exist at a historical and cultural distance from the colonial state. He thus had a certain respect for native scholars of Sanskrit and the vernaculars, provided that they were adequately subordinated to white administrators.

The Chiefs' Colleges that actually emerged did not reveal much interest in a Sanskritic revival, installing polo and Tod as their civilizational signposts. Nevertheless, Howard's successors continued to try, fitfully, to locate Indian teachers of the right sort. Pelly claimed to have found in Jaipur 'a Hindoo gentleman — named Baboo Kanti Chunder Mookerjee — who appeared to me to unite in his own person all the characteristics and qualifications one could desire to discover'. One of the many Bengalis who worked in the durbars of Rajputana as advisors and educators, Mookerjee apparently possessed 'a genius for organization and for rule by moral power'.[58] Such a man, Pelly concluded, could be consulted on the recruitment of junior teachers for Mayo; if the recommendations were misguided, Englishmen would soon discover and correct the mistake. Mookerjee was what Pelly would have considered a native of the 'old school'. As the Rudolphs have noted, however, he was hardly a precolonial character,[59] and Pelly's admiration of his organizational skills and 'moral power' indicates something familiar and valuable in an Arnoldian sense.[60] What made Mookerjee acceptable is the lack of cleverness — a certain deference, his subordination to the judgment of Englishmen, and the lack of a visible interest in usurping Englishness and its shoes.

For all his enthusiasm about Mookerjee, Pelly believed that such men were a dying breed, and he was unconvinced that 'native gentlemen' could in fact teach anything but mimicry of the most contemptible kind. He advised Aitchison that the teacher of English at Mayo — the individual who would wear the mask of conquest — must always be an Englishman, not an Indian. Pelly conceded that an Indian teacher would be less expensive and might possess impressive academic credentials. Such credentials, however, were an impediment in his anti-intellectual vision of the colonial school. Even the principal could be merely 'an average scholar', he wrote, without detracting from the effectiveness of the institution.[61] While the imitative nature of the child was to be encouraged, it had to be shielded from the imitativeness of the native adult, which did not include the necessary element of return to an appropriately subordinate place in the colony. Pelly wrote:

> We know how readily and almost insensibly youths imbibe the ideas and imitate the tone and even gestures of those to whom they are taught to

look up. The essential point with the English Master as with the Principal is that he should be an educated English gentleman. We might then rest assured that whether in at [sic] lessons or in the school field he would diffuse the manners and habits of a gentleman and would teach the boys English and not 'Cheechee'.[62]

Pelly's formulation shows how imitation, which is the nature of both the child and the native and also the sign of an underdeveloped will and intellect, could be utilized in the school to produce a colonial order of race and authority. Language could be equated with moral and political character: Indian English, or English spoken with an Indian accent, could represent the imitative, seditious, effete and overeducated wog. The wog was a pseudo-man as well as a pseudo-adult when compared with the English gentleman, for whom even an average education ensured manhood and adulthood in the colony. By articulating the formula, colonial administrators posited multiple models of childhood and adulthood — the ignorant Rajput adult with a residue of manliness (thanks to Tod), the manly and ideal English adult, the culturally authentic and apolitical native adult (like Mookerjee), the effete Rajput child whose juvenile plasticity mitigates his native flaws (but also threatens to erase native identity altogether) and the contemptible adulthood of the baboo. The object of the experiment was to press the child to grow towards the first three adult types, while avoiding the pitfalls of the last.

It was in Curzon's time, however, that the experiment in emulation was articulated with the greatest authority and coherence. Curzon approached the Chiefs' Colleges with a clear purpose: he intended to build political support for the ICC, over the objections of his own military officers and the indifference of the princes.[63] He was committed to regenerating the aristocrat, across racial lines but not on equal terms, in an imperial polity that was slipping into the hands of commoners. The Chiefs' Colleges could conceivably provide the ICC with a ready source of cadets who had already been subjected to a reparative education, and whose aristocratic pedigrees had been generated by their membership in an institutional community. This was overtly an exclusionary exercise. In 1900, Curzon wrote that restricting the ICC to students from the Chiefs' Colleges would effectively block 'the newer aristocracy, who, if the criterion were one of wealth, or education, or precocity in European manners, would flood us with a stream of applications supported by every sort of examination test, but resulting in the very last type of young officer that we should desire to procure'.[64]

Aristocracy could thus be imagined as a contested category in colonial society, with the middle and business classes reconstituted as a perverse 'new aristocracy' that had to be kept out of the training grounds where the 'old' were refashioned into a wholesome newness. There would be no direct contact between the two aristocracies, or direct emulation, in the Chiefs' College as there was at Eton or Oxford. The competitive instincts of the middle-class meritocrat, which Curzon desired for his regenerated aristocrats, would be imparted entirely by European adults who could mediate between the classes in the native society. The reference to the Englishness of middle-class Indians as 'precocious', is also revealing. Curzon was hardly opposed to Indian children learning English; in fact, he insisted that ICC cadets be English speaking. It was the identity and the allegiance of the teachers, and control over the learning process, that demarcated the well-raised child from the precocious child. Like the delinquent child, the middle-class child was seen as having asserted a premature and thus insubordinate adulthood, in sites (schools, homes, literature) where British authority was at best shaky. The Chiefs' College, in this vision, was a location in which a colonized child could be a true child, and grow up to be a true adult as well as a true native, provided he was effectively insulated from the frauds.

Child, Adult and Authority in the Chiefs' College

Post-Mutiny schooling for native aristocrats was intended by Howard, Daly and Curzon to imprint the normative categories of the colonial state over the perceived disorder of native childhood — a state of affairs where the lines between Rajput and Maratha, aristocrat and arriviste, child and adult were not always clear; in which mothers, servants and native teachers competed with white/male/experts; and in which the home encroached upon the dormitory much as the CT encroached upon the reformatory. The education of princely children was therefore both an instrument and a site — it was a tool of conquest, but it was itself a contested political theater. It was through contest, as much as conquest, that the school produced its body of knowledge.

By the mid-1870s, it was already clear that as a space occupied by purpose-designed buildings, and by students, teachers and assorted others in highly specific relationships to each other, the school was a political and moral lesson. This pedagogical function was not limited to the Chiefs' Colleges, of course. Contemporaneously with the opening of the Mayo and Rajkot Colleges, S C Bayley, the Commissioner of Patna, wrote about a relatively humble institution in his city:

> Space will...be required for a botanical garden without which lectures in Botany cannot be illustrated. There is besides the general consideration that such a building as the College should have as much free space as possible around it for the purposes alike of health and recreation and of

seclusion, which is requisite to prevent mental distraction during the time of study, and lastly, the field in its present state renders the approach to the College very disagreeable, for being near the public road and unenclosed, it is freely resorted to by the public for necessary purposes, and the smell...is most offensive.[65]

Bayley was, at the time, engaged in a discussion with his Deputy Commissioner for Public Instruction, who told him that enrolment at the college was growing, and that 'these facts distinctly prove that the schools are getting more popular and better understood'.[66] As much as the curriculum, the school itself has to be 'understood' by the colonized parent and child. This lesson includes the importance of gardens, segregation, health, recreation and not defecating in the yard. Enrolment statistics measured the degree of this moral communication between ruler and ruled. It is significant, also, that the school is marked off in the imagination as an enclave. It is a 'free space' that is free because it is enclosed, a space that is in India and distinctly colonial but subject to persistent echoes of metropolitan nostalgia (greenery, playing fields), a space where bodies are disciplined and the senses are not assaulted, a space that is permanently besieged by smelly undisciplined natives who make it impossible to sustain the fantasy of enclosing walls.

The political and moral significance of academic space manifested in the Indo-Saracenic architecture of Mayo College has been pointed out by Metcalf.[67] Metcalf has not paid as much attention to the layout of the campus, but here also, much can be learned. For the college named after him, Lord Mayo had envisioned a schoolhouse set in the middle of a garden, adding, 'Round it might be placed the bungalows for the boys with stables, accommodations for servants, etc'.[68] Since the garden was set with playing fields, it evoked the English public school rather than the Indian pleasure palace. As the campus reached the advanced stages of planning after the Viceroy's assassination, the Agent to the Governor General for Rajputana reminded his political agents, 'What Lord Mayo had at heart was a college like one of our own great Universities, with the residences of different States wrestling [sic; some chagrined official has scribbled "nestling" in the margin of the document] round it'.[69] This was the architectural representation of a political vision — Oxbridge at the centre, surrounded by neatly separated state dormitories, linked by their shared allegiance to the center and nestling in docile subordination (or wrestling with manly energy). The public school and Oxbridge effect, however, was immediately undercut by design features such as servants' quarters. The student was supposed to learn and respect the authority of Eton and Oxbridge, but not seize it for himself.

The much noted but not fully understood clock that topped the campus,[70] likewise, imparted a lesson in the hierarchy of power in a colonial school. At Mayo in the early twentieth century, the stipulated daily routine was as follows:

Morning bells, 6:15, 6:45 and 7 AM

Roll-call, 7 AM taken by College Monitors

Morning exercise, 7–7:30 AM

8–9 AM, preparation hour in the Boarding Houses. Boys who obtain the special permission of their housemaster prepare their lessons in their own rooms. Others sit in the House Common rooms.

9–10 AM. House for bath and breakfast.

School Hours —

Mondays, Tuesdays, Thursdays: Morning School 10 AM–1 PM, Afternoon School 2–4 PM

Fridays: Lessons of 1 hour each.

1–2 PM: Recess hour

Wednesdays, Saturdays: School 10 AM–1:30 PM. Lessons (1) 10–10:45, (2) 10:45–11:30, (3) 11:30–12:15, (4) 12:15–1, (5) 1–1:30.

Evening games, 4:30–6:30 PM except on Wednesdays and Saturdays, when they are from 3–6 PM.

Dismissal bell at 6, when all boys return straight to their houses.

6–7:30 PM: Dinner hour

7:30–8:30 PM: Evening preparation under the same conditions as in the morning.[71]

Obviously, the regularization of time compensated for, and molded the undisciplined natures of the natives and children and located in space a population that, like indifferent factory workers, was prone to vanishing from the sight of the educator-overseers. As in other areas of colonial society, however, the clocks in the new colleges also produced the limits within which the colonizer adult might exercise his authority.[72] At the turn of the century, one principal complained to Walter Lawrence, Curzon's personal secretary, that the Daly College campus was too sprawling for him to go rapidly from building to building, and that this had allowed the boys to escape supervision in the evenings. Lawrence told the Viceroy, 'It might be thought that one Englishman could manage twenty four boys, and no doubt he can manage them in school time.'[73] Power and order were thus synchronic with 'school time'; adult/white authority over the native child was produced by the discipline of the institutional enclave, represented by time and communicated by clocks. The colonial enclave was temporal as well as spatial.

The clocks did not just produce the authority of the categories of white, native, adult and child; they produced the categories themselves. It was within 'school time' and the larger cycle of a calendar year measured by terms, that the student was unambiguously a child. Much as the duration of sentences and the ages of admission and release produced childhoods in the reformatory, school administrators measured the childhood of students by their location within a time when they might be receptive to the authority of the colonizer. A F Pinhey, the Resident in Udaipur, wrote:

> I would not fix the minimum age of entry [into a Chiefs' College] at ten, nor would I advocate superannuation [i.e. forcing boys to leave when they turned eighteen] as long as the boy's character was good. There are boys of nine or even eight who are quite sufficiently developed to be sent to school, and whose early separation from their home influences would certainly be for their benefit, while the more stupid a boy may be, the more reason there is for keeping him under the wholesome influences of school life.[74]

At the Ajmere conference on the Chiefs' Colleges, the minimum age of admission was set at eight and maximum at fifteen. All boys would leave at eighteen or twenty years of age, depending on their 'capacity and attainments'.[75] Pinhey and his colleagues were engaged in determining the limits of impressionable childhood; he in particular was also distinguishing that impressionability from a state of infancy when the claims of the natal family could not be denied without major ideological and political innovations, and when the nature of the child was too liquid for institutional impressions to endure. Such gradations, however, could be produced only in a time of pedagogical confidence. When that authority waned, as it did whenever students left the circle of 'school time' and returned to the dormitory or the home, their ages seemed to disappear; they then became sullen, undifferentiated and unknown. Investigating the dormitories of Daly College, Lawrence wrote about students at what was by common consensus the most troubled of the Chiefs' Colleges:

> They were a very unequal lot, small clever boys sitting side by side with grown up loutish youths mostly in one room. No proper register of ages

is kept up, and no one seemed to know what a boy's real age was. There was a languid air about the place, and no one seemed in earnest.[76]

'School time' was thus a rather small circle of time-as-authority, which Pinhey, Gunion and Lawrence sought to expand even as they recognized its enclavist confines. When the hours of instruction ended and the student left the classroom, he left his status as a child and became an uncertainly colonized native.

Within school time, the physical space of the Chiefs' College was to enfold, and mold, a new political community of the princes. In the words of St. John, the campus would 'bring together the young men of different States, and afford opportunity of friendships which, continued into mature life, could not fail to be of the highest benefit to themselves and their subjects.'[77] The hope that a student body might become a political community is hardly unusual in the establishment of schools; it is evident in the creation of Aligarh, Jamia Millia and any number of nationalist pedagogical projects, real and fantastic.[78] The new schools for princely children, however, came with a nearly explicit ordering function in which the designers and enforcers did not include themselves in the communities that they ordered. Howard, for instance, imagined a network of colleges as a key step in identifying a set of landowning elites who might be designated as 'chiefs', and sought to reify Rajput ethnicity at a moment when the category was acquiring new significance in colonial politics.[79] The Chiefs' Colleges were intended to facilitate an ordering of the princes — distinguishing between Kathiawari Rajputs and Mewari Rajputs, or 'major' and 'minor' Rajputs. Each category was assigned its own space, and it caused Gunion considerable anguish when he had to compensate for poor enrolment by accepting Rajput children into a school intended for Marathas.[80] Rajputs in the neighbourhood of Indore could certainly be counted as 'chiefs', but their presence muddied the waters that Daly College was supposed to clarify.

The perception that something had been muddied, however, provided educators with opportunities to hold forth on the peculiarities of native communities, and to establish in discourse what could not always be established in practice. Chiefs' Colleges were remarkably similar to reformatories that produced criminal communities through anthropological analyses of their own failures. The educational schemes for princely children indicate that the colonial regime did not try so much to isolate the chiefs from each other as McLeod has argued,[81] as to bring them together in orderly groups that were produced by the schools themselves. In the process of planning a Chiefs' College for the modest chiefs of Baghelkhand,[82] the Foreign Department decided that it would make more sense to combine them with the chiefs of Bundelkhand, and observed:

> It seems a thousand pities that the Baghelcund Chiefs are not disposed to unite with those of Bundelcund in this memorial. The union of the Chiefs of both provinces would give a wider and less provincial scope to the undertaking, and by the intimate association of the young Baghel and Boondela Chiefs at such a College good results may be hoped for in the way of abolishing the traditional animosities and jealousies which prevail between these two Rajpoot tribes.[83]

Princely education could provide a way of bridging the geographical ('provincial') and political gaps between the chiefs, and of creating regional, or even pan-Indian, princely identities and political structures. Children were particularly useful in such an exercise, because they were hypothetically capable of taking on the ethnological shapes that experts and institutions wanted them to exhibit.

Such communications and manipulations would, of course, be mediated through masters, political agents and curricula. The expert educator was a model for emulation to a much greater extent than the reformatory administrator; princely children were, after all, encouraged to be socially at ease with Europeans, albeit without contesting the racial-political hierarchy. In certain contexts, therefore, the educator was expected to function as a peer of his wards; in others, he was to be a stern father who, by virtue of his race and expert credentials, was also a better, more influential parent than the old Rajput chief. Whereas the natural father could only freeze the child in his 'old' shape, the expert father would change the princeling to fit the needs of colony, empire and civilization, and thus reveal his true childhood. The Chiefs' Colleges thus facilitated experiments in surrogate parenting that might destabilize the princely child with precision, political purpose and discursive profit.

This model of the educator, as it emerged in the 1870s, was internally stratified by race, age and function. When Meade was engaged in taking over the upbringing of Syajee Rao, he wrote to Aitchison about his plans for a 'Rajah's School' in Baroda. The senior masters must all be well-paid Europeans. The ideal principal in the eyes of Meade and his colleagues was Chester Macnaghten of the Rajkot College — youthful, innovative, Cambridge educated, athletically inclined, heroic in his presence on the Kathiawari frontier, commanding yet affectionate in his relationship with his students and extremely well-paid.[84] (When the Home Department suggested a salary of Rs. 300–400 a month for the principal of the Chiefs' College in Bundelkhand, the Foreign

Department protested, 'You cannot possibly get a *gentleman* for that sum. [Emphasis in original] And if you do not, and only select a schoolmaster, will the thing work at all? Mr. Macnaghten gets Rs. 1500 a month.'[85]) Regarding the choice of a principal for Mayo College, Meade wrote to Aitchison:

> The gentleman selected for the office should be himself competent to supervise and direct the education of the boys. The physical instruction of the boys will be the subject of special attention on the part of the Principal and his subordinates, and every proper effort will be made to establish a healthy interest among the pupils in the exercises and sports practiced with this object. The requirements of the case would be best met by the appointment...of a Covenanted Civilian of six or eight years standing, whose erudition would qualify him for the scholastic duties of Principal.[86]

The great attention paid to sport in these educational schemes was, at one level, a public school affectation that Lelyveld has noted in the case of Aligarh.[87] It was, however, more than that. It reflected the anti-intellectualism of princely pedagogy, literally demonstrated to effete boys that their masters were not effete (while providing the boys with the remedy for the failing), and generated a shared imperial field that was, in theory, orderly and hierarchical.[88] Sport at the Chiefs' Colleges, as at some other colonial schools, formed the basis of a pedagogic triumphalism. The colonizer's triumph, in this context, was not so much over the weakness of the native body as over the unreason and effeminacy — the wilfulness as opposed to the will — of the native soul. A development of the body and its habits functioned as signposts in this triumph. Such triumph was possible only with the child, whose growth into adulthood, or the passage of time observed as 'age', could also be interpreted as a progressive alteration of nature. Wrestling with boys, so to speak, could generate visual, measurable, reportable displays of change: progress, muscles, health, growth, enthusiasm. Adults who had exhausted their physical potential for change could not provide such satisfaction. Meade's insistence that the European teachers play with the students also indicates his desire for younger men — a civilian with six to eight years of experience would, ordinarily, be barely thirty years old. Meade, therefore, imagined an active role-model and older friend, rather than an aloof father figure, as the bearer of authority.

This was not a universal preference. Pelly had wanted an older army officer to be selected as the principal of Mayo College.[89] Only men accustomed to commanding natives and the childlike, Pelly believed, could effectively impress their authority upon native children. His view reflected the close proximity between the adult-masculine ideals of colonial child-correction and militarism, or what might be considered the right wing of imperialism.[90]

Nevertheless, Meade's inclination to involve younger men remained a powerful impulse within an experiment predicated on exposing native children, especially adolescents, to desirable models of youthful behaviour. Meade wrote about personal tutors for young princes:

> The Tutor should, from the first, endeavour to associate with and be a companion to [the prince], as much as may be possible out of school hours. It is…most important that a feeling of personal attachment should spring up between them.[91]

The European tutor was thus asked to find a precise balance between familial attachment and expert-authoritative detachment. He was expected to inspire attachment on the part of the colonized child, while himself developing an 'adult' attachment to his ward — one that rose above love and was invested with the authority of superior knowledge. Since it is unlikely that Meade was thinking either in terms of manipulating the tutor (although the tutor is in fact manipulated by the arrangement) or in terms of a coldly instrumental manipulation of the prince, the imbalance in the 'attachment', i.e. the relative statuses of adult and child, is rooted at least partly in the racial nature of the protagonists.

Europeans did not, of course, work alone in the schemes for the education of princely children. They were outnumbered by an assortment of ill-paid Indian teachers, whose presence inspired in British administrators a broad contempt that was tempered by an acknowledgment of need and by the utility of natives in lessons in hierarchy. Gunion, at Daly College, attributed his various problems at the turn of the century (poor enrolment, high rates of withdrawal, indiscipline and academic standards that were low even by the standards of the Chiefs' Colleges) to the influence of 'timorous self-seeking native Masters' who undermined his own good work.[92] Gunion's ire was heightened by his awareness that some of the Indian teachers at Daly were not affiliated with the college at all — Lawrence found that the princelings from Rutlam and Jaora had brought their own tutors with them. He noted, 'These tutors were not in any way under the control of the Principal of the College, and there had been friction.'[93] At the Rajkot College, Lawrence found twenty-nine private tutors, and commented, 'These Tutors are useless and often injurious. They should be abolished.'[94] Teachers on the college staff did not impress Lawrence more favourably:

> I noticed at Rajkot, as elsewhere, an obsequious deference paid by the Native masters to the pupils. I was told that here as at Ajmere, the Native masters, instead of teaching in English, would lapse into vernacular

when the Principal was out of hearing. The remedy is plain. More English masters are wanted — young Englishmen, and old Native masters. The Natives can teach most things save English and science.[95]

The contempt for spineless native masters reflects an impatience with (or misunderstanding of) the patron-client relationship of Indian teachers and the princes. Native masters and tutors could only represent a counter-authority — they were both ineffective as moral influences (because they were effeminate) and threatening (because they introduced the inauthentic and insubordinate upstart into an exercise that was supposed to be an antidote to that specific phenomenon). The white administrator's position *vis-à-vis* native teachers can be described in terms of 'dominance without hegemony'[96] — the natives retained a substantial autonomous space within the colonial relationship that the British could not ignore or forgive.

This led observers like Lawrence, Meade and Pelly to arrive at a formula of age, race and authority. They preferred older natives to younger men as teachers of princely children because the former — like Kanti Mookerjee — were presumed to be deferential to whites, and to be respected by native children even without the authority of white skin. Young white teachers, on the other hand, derived their authority from the vitality of youthful masculinity and whiteness itself, qualities that young natives did not possess. The reluctance to let natives teach English and science reflects the intellectual content of whiteness as well as of masculinity. Thus, while young white masters and guardians could be 'role models' or even 'friends' to native children, young native masters could only be quasi-juvenile (and hence servile) themselves.

Native Son: Panna Singh and Rawdon McNabb

The kind of white educator that Meade had admired in the 1870s might be glimpsed in Rawdon McNabb in the early years of the new century. Having followed his father James as a political agent and guardian in the princely states, McNabb went from the Residency at Indore to a job at Mayo College as guardian to the Kumar of Indore, Panna Singh. He then accompanied Panna to the ICC just before the outbreak of the World War. When he went to France to fight in the war, his own son Archie inherited his career as tutor to the children of the princes. In his letters to his father, Rawdon would typically describe Panna as 'my boy' and it is impossible to miss the competitive pride that he took in the child when Queen Mary visited Mayo College, or when Panna attended the Delhi durbar.[97] His attachment to Panna was proprietorial and controlling, but it should not be divested of affection and seen solely in terms of power and manipulation.

It would, nevertheless, be a mistake to downplay the elements of manipulation and investigation in the relationship between McNabb and Panna Singh. During encounters with the imperial monarchy, children like Panna would be made to play games such as musical chairs (to the great amusement of Queen Mary), behave correctly at tea parties and dinners with colonial officials, and do homage to the King Emperor.[98] The rituals reflected the function of princely education as the inculcation of loyalty to an imperial order, but the children also featured as performing seals watched anxiously by their trainers. They performed Englishness, but they also performed a native identity defined by mimicry — what made the events touching and funny to the queen, and satisfying to McNabb, was that these were not, in fact, English boys.

McNabb reserved for himself the authority to assess Panna's impressionability and capacity for reform, to measure the levels of inherited nativeness and acquired political fitness, and to prolong or terminate his childhood. In 1913, he wrote to James that Panna might soon be ready to take charge of his state, adding, 'My boy has improved a lot in the last few months; I had begun to be afraid that he would be perpetually childish and unresponsible [sic], and to foresee that we would have to put off the date of his getting his powers.'[99] As a general trend, the age at which young princes inherited their powers receded as minority administrations became increasingly rigorous in their enforcement of childhood.[100] Here, the juvenilizing functions of the expert parent and the political agent converged.

These were functions that Indians could not be entrusted with. As he prepared to leave for Europe in 1914, McNabb fretted about who would inherit a boy that would soon become a ruling chief but remain a minor. The Agent to the Governor General (AGG) had ordered that Archie be the guardian until Panna acquired his 'powers' in January of 1915, and 'Friend and Advisor' for a year afterwards. Rawdon was nevertheless furious, because the AGG had also decreed that the Indian dewan would replace Archie as the primary father figure after 1915. Rawdon fumed that the dewan would fail 'unless there is a Sahib there to back him up'. If that happened, 'my deputation [as guardian] will end in a failure'.[101] Some of McNabb's anger, no doubt, stemmed from his hopes that his son would inherit a powerful role in a minority administration. ('If he is allowed to run the State as well as be Guardian it would suit him very well,' he had told James about Archie.[102]) More pertinent, however, is McNabb's perception that Indian guardians could not maintain parental authority or enforce the childhoods that princely education sought to create. The danger was two-fold: the child might backslide in civilization (as if he had gone back to his natal parents) and also escape from colonial supervision, acquiring unpredictable political habits.

Like Meade before him, McNabb located the dangers in maternal influence. Panna's mothers seemed intent upon immersing their son in the irrational world of the married native child, with its illiterate females, unmanly rituals, bejewelled excess and silly religion. During the boy's wedding, McNabb wrote James:

> The boy's mothers have been giving a lot of trouble. Yesterday they crowned everything by insisting on the boy doing all his last ceremonies from the house they are living in two miles from the city and not leaving it till he does his final procession round the town plastered with jewellery with a gold head-dress with a jewelled gold peacock's feather arrangement on top of it. When he has finished some quite trivial and unnecessary religious ceremonies, I shall have to collect and check the boy's and his brother's jewellery and take it off two miles to the Treasure room and lock it up. I'm sorry but these women are very trying.[103]

The civilizational content of this struggle over the young kumar's education, loyalty, movements, dress, religious habits and capacity for reason is as significant as the issue of which parent controls the prince. The plurality of mothers should be noted, although McNabb, accustomed to Rajput households, does not bat an eye. It indicates precisely the kind of moral and cultural environment that he competed with, and it is clear that he could not take his success for granted.

Success could not be assured because the British did not want to erase the 'authentic' cultural markers of the native child. This generated a peculiar ambivalence in educators like McNabb: even as he fulminated against the irrationality of the mothers who arranged Panna's marriage, he actively collaborated with Panna to frustrate the boy's reformist father-in-law (the chief of Bhavnagar), who wanted his daughter to come out of purdah.[104] There were many more 'liberal' or cosmopolitan parents in McNabb's time than there had been in Meade's, given the greater mobility of the princes in the twentieth century and the fact that the graduates of the Chiefs' Colleges had become parents themselves, with their own ideas about their place in the empire and the family. Such parents gave colonial guardians no comfort; rather, they made it more urgent that the guardian assert himself as the mediator of habits. It is unclear whether McNabb acted out of a sense of loyalty to the reactionary child when he undermined Bhavnagar, out of loyalty to the principle of reactionary authenticity, or out of a reluctance to give the father-in-law a say in the boy's life. All three reasons would seem to apply, but it is likely that the second and third were the most influential.

McNabb and his colleagues were, after all, groping towards a redefined notion of 'home' for the princely child. Given the peculiarities of their educational project, home was necessarily a schizophrenic place. This is evident in McNabb's tendency to wonder about the benefits and dangers of taking Panna there. He rambled to James:

> You are I think not very sure about the wisdom of bringing my Maharaja home. He has always wanted to go home ever since I have known him, and as soon as he gets his powers he will not rest till Government let him go home, it is a matter for Government to decide how long they can reasonably go on refusing to let him go, but personally I should put it at three years at the outside, if he is behaving properly and running his State well and so on, all I say is that if he is to go home at all in the next five years he had better go before he gets his powers, i.e. while he is still in my charge. The visit would do him nothing but good if I could only guarantee that he should meet none but the right sort of people. I'll allow that if Society began to lionize him, and he would make a fairly good lion, it would do him a deal of harm.[105]

'Home' could be England for the native who had been educated to loyalty, and whose identity had been modified so as to dislocate him from his natal family. At the same time, only the near-adult, who had completed his education, become politically mature and less plastic, could go 'home'. Princely education thus marked a transition between two kinds of home — the old, feminine, childish, Indian home, and the new, manly English home that might be visited, learned and loved, but not inhabited. For the embryonic adult, whose maturity was fragile not only because it was new but also because he was a native, the new home had its own dangers, being partially outside colonial power relations. The white 'father' therefore had to accompany him there, to ensure that the essentially colonial vestiges of his childhood were preserved, or protected from those who might inadvertently encourage the native to assume the privileges of metropolitan adulthood.[106]

Native Place: At Home in the Dormitory

The expert's attempt to assert his authority over the childhood of his ward generated a third template of 'home' in the dormitory of the Chiefs' College. The dormitory was neither England nor the *zenana*, and both of these negatives became constant terms of reference as European educators and administrators sought to define it as a secure colonial enclave. Yet the dormitory had been a compromised home from the outset. In 1870, Daly had written

Aitchison that the colleges they were building would have to make concessions to the homes that the children might leave, by downplaying or disguising the element of departure:

> No education worth the name can be imparted to a young Chief at his own home: the *zenana* and its intrigues entangle him in the early days of boyhood; fawning parasitism, inseparable in the East from rank and coming power, stifles independence there, and jealously resists his removal elsewhere. Education, therefore, must be brought as near home as is compatible with its purpose.[107]

Daly's reference to 'intrigue' is significant — it indicates a discomfort with the strategic familiality that Sumit Guha, adapting Wink's theory of *fitna*, has identified in the princely milieu of the eighteenth century.[108] The British were themselves willing to participate in these manoeuvres, well before the Doctrine of Lapse.[109] The disdain for 'intrigue' after the Mutiny shows a heightened determination to control the autonomous realignments within the princely home, and an awareness of the difficulty of managing its distance from the colonial enclave. The architecture of the colleges was itself discovered by Curzon and Lawrence to have capitulated before the homes that the boys were supposed to outgrow. Students lived in lavish and widely separated dormitories built by their own states, socialized only infrequently with boys from other states, and retained their personal cooks. This replication of home defeated the principle of institutional identity, or 'school spirit' and a shared monasticism. In the process, it challenged the idea of the school as a moral lesson that embodied the authority of a new set of adults.

The menial who had accompanied the student to the dormitory was identified as the face of the challenge. Lawrence reported to Curzon that students arrived at the schools with absurdly large contingents of servants (the princeling from Kota had taken one hundred and eighty retainers to Mayo) and musahibs, the latter being agents of their home states. He went on about dormitory life at the Rajkot College:

> The Musahib is selected by the State to which the student belongs; he is usually a selection of the boy's mother, and he is always with the boy except in the schoolroom and on the playground. I saw a large number of these Musahibs, and they impressed me unfavourably. The boys have each a sitting room, an inner bedroom, and a bathroom. On going round the rooms, in the first I saw a dirty servant lying on a bed in his Master's apartment talking to a repulsive looking Musahib. The Principal did not know the men. One night to find out the exact state of things, [C Mayne,

the principal] went very late into one of the wings where eighteen Kumars were sleeping. He counted in the rooms fifty nine persons.[110]

None of this was a new development; it was fallout from the original attempt to bring the school closer to 'home' while still producing a distance between the two. As Ramusack has pointed out, the acquisition of a semi-independent residential establishment with its own servants was for the princes a rite of passage into adulthood.[111] In the mid-1870s, thirty-odd students at Mayo had brought some five hundred servants into the college, to the despair of St. John, who complained that the boys socialized with their servants but not their own peers.[112] He read the tendency as a perversion of proper class consciousness, a violation of modern expectations of hygiene (which included a sexual anxiety), and an indifference towards the age-bound peer group that renders childhood socially and conceptually self-evident even when the children are in their middle teens. Servants thus contaminated the state of childhood that the new education sought to isolate, breeding a threatening independence from the authority of masters.

At the same time, servants marked a contemptible dependency on the part of the students. Mary Procida has noted the anxiety of Anglo-Indians about their own dependence upon 'dirty' servants in their colonial homes, which signalled an abdication by Englishwomen of their domestic responsibilities, and Marriott has highlighted the unease that accompanied the reliance upon natives of dubious moral and political inclinations who straddled the line between private and public space.[113] Lawrence and others reflected this anxiety, and the 'dirt', into the dormitories of Rajkot and Mayo. Here, large retinues represented the wild excesses of native effeminacy, and established why the Chiefs' College was inferior to the English public school.[114] 'Boys drive to school and back in luxurious carriages,' Lawrence noted disapprovingly in 1901.[115]

This decadence was, moreover, inseparable from a permanent crisis of British authority — Lawrence observed about Daly College that the 'effect of contact with the English Principal in school is frustrated by the long houses of association with servants described by [the principal] as "unusually great blackguards"'.[116] Educators felt that they could not expel these representatives of a barbaric child control regime, because it was only by admitting the *zenana* into the dormitory that they could persuade native parents to send their sons out of the home. Lawrence was certain that the compromise had undermined the project of relocating the child from his natal family. About residential life at the Rajkot College, he observed:

> The boys do not mess together, but eat sitting on the floor of their bedrooms. In Kathiawar, up to quite recent times, there has always been a

fear of poison. An old boy told me that this fear did not now exist at the College, but in their houses, the Chiefs still decline to eat with their wives or mothers.[117]

This is an enclave in which the inmates are stubbornly resistant to learning and live lives of secrecy, in spite of detective surveillance reminiscent of Sleeman among the Thugs. The reference to poisoning signifies a pre-colonial disorder: the primeval 'chaos' of India in which the British have not defeated the poisoners even within the enclave. The disapproval of the boys' refusal to eat with women relatives appears counterintuitive, because British guardians typically wanted to get male children away from the *zenana*. Within a critique of the perverse society of the dormitory, however, eating apart reflected a failure of civilized familiality, and a relapse of the child into the habits of the native home.

In Lawrence's broad vision, life in the dorms is thus seen, although it is more often imagined, as multiple transgressions of Victorian domesticity and colonial policing — racial, spatial, class-based, aesthetic and sexual. Visiting the Aitchison and Mayo Colleges, he discovered much hand-wringing on the part of teachers who felt that a soft haze of sex and alcohol had infected the clean, hard, masculine environment of the dormitory in spite of the best efforts of the school authorities. He informed the Viceroy:

> Col. Loch [principal of Aitchison College] is an admirable manager. The buildings and the park are excellently kept, and the boys are neatly dressed. But...the boys drank, and had intercourse with prostitutes [and] ran a risk of becoming profligates. It is common gossip in Rajputana that the Chief of Alwar contracted his vicious habits at Ajmere. I suggested [to the Maharaja of Jaipur] that he may have acquired his propensities during the holidays. But a fellow Chief...assured me that the vice was acquired at College.[118]

Pinhey backed up Lawrence's account, providing additional stories about boys concealing alcohol in the dormitories with the collusion of servants, bullying and sexual abuse of the younger boys by older students, and the impossibility of maintaining any supervision over the boys at night and during holidays.[119] Not even school time was safe — Lawrence learned that at Raipur College, which was a secondary Chiefs' College for the smaller landed elites of Chhattisgarh, boys had been found to be suffering from venereal disease 'contracted...while under instruction'.[120] The colonial enclave, here as elsewhere, shared a fluid set of geographical, temporal, cultural and sexual borders with native society, and the expert who might police and enforce the borders had to remain permanently vigilant and at war. The idea that some boys developed a taste for sex and alcohol in the dorms, not unlike catching a disease in a hospital, is also similar to the idea of the reformatory as a site of moral contagion. Lawrence was keen to relocate the contagion to the native home and outside school time (whereas the parent chiefs were eager to blame the school) but he was clearly unsuccessful, not least because the school, as a moral habit, was supposed to accompany the boy even when he went 'home' or into town.

Lawrence could, however, try to convert failure into authority by investigating the moral character of specific chiefs and children, and delineating the imaginary, if not actual, boundaries of two opposed worlds that the colonial child might inhabit. He made specific suggestions for the segregation of older boys from the younger students in the residential quarters of Aitchison College — an exercise in the production of age groups and sexual natures that would have been familiar to any reformatory administrator of his time. The Chhattisgarh students' lack of 'self-control' could be explained by noting that their families had been 'left undisturbed' on their estates by the British for many years.[121] Chhattisgarh represented a lesser and spurious aristocracy, whose inferiority was marked by the physical signs of sexual deviance and disease on the bodies of children. The establishment of British authority might cure disease and indiscipline, but even if it did not, it would establish a discursive connection between indiscipline at home, disease in the body, and authority in a political geography. Regarding Hukam Singh of Bikaner, an Aitchison College alumnus and potential recruit for the ICC, Lawrence – who generally admired the Indian princes[122] – complained:

> A heavy, sodden young man who said at once, that he did not want service. Two years' residence at his home…had turned him from a bright hopeful youth into a sensual drunken boor."[123]

The natural promise of Hukam Singh's childhood (praised by Loch as well as Lawrence) could be presented as raw material that the college had molded, but that had warped into a deceptive adulthood marked by immorality, effeminacy and disloyalty as soon as the boy stepped back across the border of the juvenile institution. The authority of the expert lay not so much in policing that border as in locating it.

Following Lawrence's report on the Chiefs' Colleges, Curzon called a conference in Calcutta to discuss the problems uncovered and potential remedies.

Opening the conference, the Viceroy speculated that birth parents must resent the immersion of their children in the residential life of the colleges:

> Their hostility or indifference springs...from the *zenana* influence which is frightened at the idea of an emancipated individuality, and the Court surroundings, every unit of which is conscious of a possible loss of prerogative....should a young recruit from the West appear upon the scene, and begin to stir up the sluggish Eastern pools.[124]

Sluggish pools, however, had formed within the college itself, rendering the residential quarters altogether un-English:

> In England a boy is continuously exposed to [desirable] influences from morning till night. He is not only taught in the classroom...for brief periods at stated hours. His housemaster, who is really responsible for his bringing up, is always teaching him too, by watching and training his combined moral and intellectual growth. But in your Indian Chiefs' Colleges the reverse plan is adopted. You therefore shut him up in a boarding house, where he is surrounded by musahibs...who are separated off from the staff, the curriculum, and the educative influence of the College. You divide his College career into two watertight compartments. The boy is transferred from the one to the other at stated intervals of the day or night, and you sacrifice the many advantages that accrue from a single existence with an undivided aim.[125]

Thus characterizing the Chiefs' College as a grossly incomplete total-institution, Curzon articulated two zones of authority within the colonial boarding school: the classrooms and playing fields, which were under the control of European educators and where boys might be molded into good colonized men, and the dormitories, where European authority was non-existent and children might lapse into effete, childlike creatures of the *zenana*. 'Control of the boarding houses is in the hands of the Natives,' Lawrence had told him disgustedly about Daly College, adding, 'They deliberately attempt to undo all the good that is done in school hours.'[126] In the conflict with the classrooms and playing fields, the dormitory seemed to be winning. As the work of Arnold and others indicates, this was a common dilemma — like the colonial world outside the enclave, the enclave itself contained pockets of indiscipline that required unending counterinsurgency campaigns.[127] The establishment of the Chiefs' Colleges, therefore, was not the culmination of an agenda of conquest, but the enclosure of the process of conquest within a juvenile 'laboratory' where it might continue indefinitely, and the creation of a lager that blurred the lines between conquest and defence.

Curzon's reference to musahibs is especially pertinent in this context. Musahibs and Indian tutors were not simply a compromise with parents. They were an ideological necessity, preserving a distance between Rajkot and Eton, the native child and the English child. There were roles in the new education for which white men were manifestly unsuited, and natives necessary. Lawrence, for all his suspicion of Indian tutors,[128] could not get rid of them because he was even more uncomfortable with the idea of Englishmen as private tutors:

> I regard the system now in vogue of placing a young chief under a special English Tutor, picked up from the Bengal Cavalry or the Police Department, as disastrous. The Tutor has enormous influence as Tutor — he has also the crushing influence which an Englishman always has over the single-handed Oriental. The English Tutor is an unconscious vampire. He sucks out the very soul of the boy. He anglicizes his mind, and unfits him for his position in India. Individual teaching by an Englishman is fatal. Class teaching by Englishmen is healthy and profitable.[129]

Lawrence's view indicates the limited scope of the modification of nature that a colonial institution might attempt to achieve in the child. The classroom, which meant not only a peer group of native boys, but also an apparatus limited by time, curriculum and institutional regime, was a necessary restraint upon the English teacher's authority over the individual student, but some learning had necessarily to occur outside of class. To eliminate native intermediaries would raise the spectre of deracination. Curzon wrote, 'For Hindu lads...the [musahib] is generally necessary; he occupies, to a certain extent, the place of the parents, who rely on him to see that the bath, puja, etc. of the boys are duly performed in accordance with local usage'.[130] Unable to dispense with musahibs, Curzon tried to impose conditions, limits and authority upon their competing presence. He noted that a majority of educators had recommended that musahibs should 'be relatives of the Chief of the State concerned, and should be elderly men of high character'. He ordered political agents to enforce these rules, and to ensure that each state sent only one musahib for all its boys at a particular college. He added hopefully, 'In any case the [musahibs] will be under the control of the Principal and liable to be dismissed by him.'[131]

The educators themselves tried out similar measures. Expressing a desire to 'sweep away all these Tutors and Musahibs, and...cut down the number of servants', Mayne urged that such staff be supplied by the College and work under the orders of the Principal.[132] Not surprisingly, little came of his fantasy, and the musahib remained a problem, highlighting a British ambivalence about how much of the parenting role could be taken oven by the colonial educator, and calling into question the expert's ability to reorder native childhood without destabilizing a wider order in colonial society. His political and ideological importance in the college gave him an undeniable measure of power — the classroom might belong to the master, but the dormitory was the musahib's territory. In the dorms, the musahibs and servants, not the principals and masters, became the intermediaries between native nature and colonial nurture. Curzon's fiat giving principals the right to fire the musahib was a fig leaf. It merely preserved the appearance of adult authority in a space where the guardians of children were themselves childlike anti-adults, and where, consequently, the inmates had taken over the asylum.

Failure and the Production of Nature

By the turn of the century, it had become nearly impossible for experts to talk about princely education without also talking about the collapse of a grand project. Yet the project was not discontinued — guardianships proliferated, and the colleges were not closed in spite of Lawrence's conclusion that Daly College and possibly Aitchison College ought to be abandoned. (Mayo and Rajkot could be saved, Lawrence had decided, if significant numbers of young, well-paid, Oxbridge-educated Englishmen were inducted as masters to offset the native adults.) Clearly, the encounter with aristocratic children continued to be useful within other, larger, colonial projects — the search for a viable political relationship with the princes, the search for a utilitarian colonialism that was nevertheless informed by the romantic, the search for children who might test the expertise and institutions of colonial child-correction, and investigations of the content of race.

It is necessary, therefore, to look closely at the experience and interpretation of failure. I shall return briefly to the phenomenon of 'Eton in India', or the durable trope of the English public school in the construction of the Chiefs' College.[133] The public school was to the Chiefs' College what metropolitan child-correction, with its admirably modern network of detention centers, remand homes, juvenile courts and parole officers, was to the colonial reformatory. In each case, the metropolitan institution was occasionally held up by peripheral experts as a signifier of the universal. Exposure to such an institution, it was anticipated, would normally produce a predictable set of responses from the child. At the same time, it was patently clear to the expert that the responses were not the same, and that the institution itself had not been 'accurately' translated in the colony. The induced slips between expectation and experience constituted the experiment, and produced the experimental child of the juvenile periphery. Ultimately, Eton could not be replicated in India because the English public school was necessarily defeated by the shoddy nature of the native child and the wider shoddiness of the native.

Universalistic models of childhood and education were reasonably prominent in the discourse of the Chiefs' Colleges, in the sense that those who planned the schools often believed that roughly similar educational regimes could be imposed upon elite children in India and in England, and that the children were similar enough to respond similarly. Pelly, in 1873, wrote Aitchison about his curricular intentions for Mayo College:

[The teachers] should be acquainted with the Indian classics; but what is far more essential is that they should understand men and the true bearings of history — and that they should be able to read the signs of the present time aright. Doubtless some boys may addict themselves to Sanskrit, but the majority, like our own youths, would regard the classics as a task. Teach him as much Sanskrit as we will, when the young Raja from Jodhpoor returns home, he will talk Marwaree just as certainly as the Shah of Persia postpones the languages of Saadi and the Koran in favour of Toorkee when conversing with his tribal relatives. I would leave [the principal] as much as possible unfettered in his choice of material. His mental tendencies may resemble those of a Dr. Arnold or a Carlyle, or they may rest on the theories of a Steuart Mill or a Compte, and it would avail little to tell a Principal imbued with German ideas that the only road to truth was through Whately or Senior. Firstly, I would render these youths sufficiently acquainted with the principles of physical science; secondly, and according to their several bents, I would endeavour to induce them to practice themselves in some mechanical or fine art, or in the study of some branch of natural history, so that they might come to delight in thus employing their leisure, and thus be weaned from the sensualities and other evils of idleness; thirdly, I would teach them to read history and realize its bearings on their own careers, especially I would explain to and impress upon them the characters and the modes of action of those men who have most peacefully, widely, and permanently developed societies or influenced the human race; fourthly I would teach them politics as applied to societies and wherein the elements of time and circumstances must be taken into consideration; fifthly, I would train their bodies by manly athletic exercises.[134]

In Pelly's view of children at study, English, Iranian and Rajput boys would respond similarly to the 'classics' and classical languages. Even middle-class native children are implicitly accounted for; he does not feel the need to teach princely children a different history from what the baboos have studied, insisting only that its significance be properly mediated by the English educator-administrator-adult. This does not necessarily mean that Pelly assumed that the children were identical. Rather, it reflects his perception that institutionalized pedagogy, judiciously adapted to differences of environment, temperament and political circumstance, could generate similarities of nature, and a universally modern aristocratic childhood. While he was flexible in his prescription of pedagogical method, his terms of reference are all modern, European, informed by the Enlightenment, and informed also by a decisive separation of childhood and adulthood. A colonial Eton, in this formulation, is not necessarily fraudulent.

Nevertheless, it is also true that Pelly sought to modify the public school curriculum, the major modification being the effort to compensate for unscientific and ahistorical temperaments, and bodies habituated to idleness. Daly too had suggested that something in the nature of the native would make it difficult to place the children of the princes in public schools. In Daly's correspondence with Aitchison, the Eton parallels were qualified and nearly dismissed, not so much on account of an inherited racial difference as because of the overwhelming weight of custom and environment.[135] Daly implied that since the gelled moral failure of the native was a premature acquisition of adulthood, it was substantially impervious to British intervention. That resistance made colonial pedagogy a heroic enterprise, but it ensured that Eton — an institution for true children — would remain an ironic reference at best. The public school ideal was also overwhelmed in Daly's thinking by the colonial agenda of gender, which denied the native male the ability to combine manliness and academic achievement.[136] Some natives must be effete and imitative intellectuals, others manly dimwits.

By the turn of the century, the fragility of the Eton comparison was apparent to a wide range of critics of the Chiefs' Colleges, and noted regularly in their critiques. In a long editorial in 1902, the *Pioneer* attacked Curzon's hopes that the colleges might provide a platform for recruitment into the ICC. The editor began by dismissing the public school parallel. He explained that English public schools were founded on 'democracy', in which 'mere class' was irrelevant, and peers and commoners met on a level field. The Chiefs' Colleges, on the other hand, were founded on the 'pretensions' of birth and privilege. The 'healthy rivalry' of interhouse competition in the public school was different from a residential system in which 'boys are divided into blocks according to their religion or States'. Moreover, 'The manliness and self-reliance of the Public School boy cannot be developed under a system which...encourages guardians and muhsahibs and the presence of a large retinue of servants.' Therefore, 'It is better to look the facts in the face and not to let flights of fancy lift our feet from the solid ground. If the Public School system is thought to be feasible in India, by all means let it be adopted; but we must create new institutions, and not rely on mere Chiefs' Colleges.'[137] The editorial went on to make a distinction between 'real' public schools that might be established for a genuinely useful class of Indians, and useless and ornamental schools for a useless and ornamental class.

Curzon himself might be expected to reject any automatic correlation between the useless and the ornamental. While the ICC was closest to his heart when it came to creating useful imperial ornaments, the Chiefs' Colleges were not far behind. He did not hold back from using the Eton metaphor, and he appeared, at times, to share Pelly's faith in the suitability of the metropolitan juvenile institution to colonial children. At the conference in Calcutta in 1902, Curzon declared:

> Chiefs' Colleges in this country...are the outcome of a growing desire...to keep abreast of the times and to give to the rising generation in India an education that shall enable them to hold their own in a world of constant change and ever increasing competition. The founders of these institutions, deliberately selecting the English Public School as that which had best succeeded in doing a similar work among the higher ranks of English society, sought to reproduce its most salient features here. Indian boys of the upper classes were taken away from the narrow and often demoralizing existence of their homes, and were thrown together in the boarding house, the classroom, and the playground. In all these respects the Chiefs' Colleges...have followed, at a distance it may be but with anxious fidelity, their English prototypes.[138]

So far, so good. Curzon then abruptly rejected the adaptability of races and their institutional molds, which had been a basic assumption of unthropologist-educators like Campbell.[139] He continued,

> But there I am afraid the resemblance stops. In the world of nature a plant cannot suddenly be shifted from some foreign clime, and expected straightaway to flourish in a novel temperature and a strange soil. So it is with the Public School system in India. In its essence the system is contrary to the traditional sentiments of Indian parents of the aristocratic classes, and to the hereditary instincts of Indian sons. One of the chief sources of a healthier result in the English system is a feature that

is difficult of reproduction, and ought not…to be forcibly reproduced here. Eton is an aristocratic school organized upon a democratic basis. The scions of the nobility are commonly sent there by their parents, but there is nothing to prevent the son of a parvenu from being sent too. All mix together on a footing of social equality. That is impossible in India, and will be impossible — even if it were desirable, which I think it is not — for many a long day to come. Here the class distinctions are…ingrained in the traditions of the people, and they are indurated by the prescriptions of religion and race. You have to deal with a more primitive state of society and with feelings whose roots are intertwined in the depths of human nature.[140]

Curzon was able to reconcile the two rather different perspectives by paying lip service to a kind of gradualism, noting that Eton had evolved slowly into its present state of 'democracy' and that a similar evolution might be possible in the Chiefs' Colleges over the course of a century. What might transpire in a century, however, was insignificant compared to the there and then. Curzon's ambivalence about the Eton metaphor is unmistakable. On the one hand, he recognized its value — 'Eton in India' was a potent fantasy that could be publicly shared by some administrators, some princes, some educators and as Cox points out, by missionaries,[141] as a fictitious cultural bond and a political tie, not to mention a prestigious and remunerative set of professional credentials. On the other hand, Eton provided Curzon with a base for a vicious cultural critique and a strong assertion of different natures, which might be revealed by the children's institution but not significantly altered. It is clear that the 'temperature' and 'soil' that might reject the English public school are actually the natives themselves, with their 'hereditary instincts'. The age of Risley is evident in this vision, but in spite of his talk of heredity, Curzon did not assume a fundamental difference between the natures of the native and the European. He grounded the incompatibility between Indian children and public schools in a conception of race and inheritance that was informed by social habit, and in a human nature that — unlike the nature of English children — had not been shaped and refined by history.

In Curzon's construction of the problem, the nature of the native child, while not inherently different, had been rendered different by its 'primitiveness', i.e. by a prolonged and congealed existence outside history and progress. The child in the Chiefs' College was therefore a more or less fully formed representative of a civilization and a race that had been stunted in childhood. Like the child who was a delinquent by habit, the aristocratic native child was discovered to be minimally plastic, and thus resistant to growth and true adulthood. The institutionalization of such children might provide the beginnings of history, plasticity and growth, but like other proponents of trusteeship in colonialism,[142] Curzon was sure that 'adulthood' would not come in the foreseeable future, and unsure that it should come at all.

This brings us to a second area of ambivalence in Curzon's perception that the public school could not accommodate Indian children. With his interest in constructing an undiluted class bias for native society that was both (explicitly) better than and (implicitly) inferior to the democratized class prejudice of England, he sought in the very decrepitude of the colonial Eton a confirmation of a primitive and natural elitism that had been eroded by history in England, and by colonial hybridization in British India. He announced,

> [Exclusivity of class] is...founded upon sentiments inherent in human nature; it is congenial to the East; it is compatible with the finest fruits of enlightenment and civilization. I [do not] want to see these Colleges reduced to dull drab uniformity of the Board School, with an English Principal and a cricket ground thrown in to give a dash of colour. Let us keep them as what they were intended to be, and not turn them into a composite construction that is neither one thing nor the other.[143]

In the 'congenially' primitive east, Curzon implied, the educator-administrator ought to highlight, rather than demolish, the very traits that rendered the native child a misfit in the public school. The child and the school were thus caught in the trap of a colonialism that produced the primitive as a measure of its success and a source of its pleasure, even after its agents — from Macaulay to Howard and Curzon himself — explicitly set out to mold natives with some of the characteristics of Englishmen.

At times the pleasure is close to the surface. Just as Giffard was gleeful at having found Jack Sheppard in the Chingleput Reformatory, and Forrester paraded his 'jackals' and 'tigers' with more satisfaction than dismay, Curzon was pleased to have discovered that native princes were like Klingons — aristocratic savages who might be given a veneer of civilization and competence in the modern world, but never actually brought in from the periphery of either true childhood (marked by plasticity) or true adulthood (that followed upon a plastic childhood, and was marked by the rational exercise of authority). At most times, however, such pleasure could not be openly acknowledged by experts who had set out to correct the native child. The gap between Eton and Daly College — or between Mettray and the juvenile ward of the Alipore Jail — was, in those circumstances, interpreted as the regrettable failure of the modern juvenile institution in the face of the shortcomings of the native child and its parents.

The perception of specimens that defeat the laboratory is present at the very outset of the project of re-educating the princes. Howard had written about various pedagogical experiments in the princely states, initiated by British political agents as well as by progressive native commoners, that had quickly ground to a halt — good intentions had been foiled and good institutions marred, by basic inadequacies in the native worldview and knowledge systems.[144] For Howard, the dangers of failure and embarrassment were ever present just around the corner, but he had expected that a system of schools backed by the British-Indian government would flourish where local initiatives had withered. When the Chiefs' Colleges became operational, however, their principals continued to echo Howard. At Mayo, St. John worried that children would forget during the holidays what they had been taught in school time, and 'forget' even that they must return to school, especially when a long journey was involved.[145] In fact, the 'graduation' of the first student to enrol at Mayo — the subsequently 'vicious' ruler of Alwar — had been irregular. The boy had gone home at Christmas and not bothered to come back. St. John also noted that two boys 'have withdrawn on account of hopeless incapacity, mental and physical'.[146] At Aitchison College in 1902, the principal observed that most boys enrolled late and left early in their childhood, and the expectation that boys would be at school between the ages of ten and eighteen had no basis in practice.[147] He had, earlier, declined to nominate any of his students for the ICC, telling Lawrence that 'the status of his pupils was such that they might lower the prestige of the Corps and seriously detract from the success of the scheme'.[148] Alumni of the Aitchison College, Lawrence had learned, 'are mostly vegetating on their jagirs'.[149]

At various points, St. John at Mayo, Godley at Aitchison and Gunion at Daly all envisioned their students as lazy, sullen prisoners who escaped back to their criminal tribes at the first opportunity, foiling the experts' ability to produce them as children, let alone as adults.[150] The stupidity of princely students achieved legendary proportions among educators who worked in and around the Chiefs' Colleges, and by 1903 political agents were debating the pros and cons of expelling boys who failed to perform academically. Humiliating princely parents, however, posed obvious political problems in a project that struggled continuously to attract students from a limited aristocratic pool. Moreover, the established anti-intellectual culture of the colleges, and their deliberate rejection of meritocratic benchmarks like final examinations and degrees,[151] had left it very unclear whether academic failure was in fact a failure at all. At the same time, since these were undeniably academic institutions with an explicit mission to impart a 'liberal education' (and, in some prescriptions, the skills of modern landowning gentlemen or military cadets[152]), intellectual shortcomings could not be altogether ignored. The Rev.

Macalister of Jaipur, who was consulted on the subject by the British Resident, advised that stupidity would have to be not so much tolerated as accommodated within the institution:

> It may be necessary in the case of persistent evil conduct, for the safety of others, to dismiss a boy, but he should never be dismissed for mere stupidity: make the best of a stupid boy: he is infinitely safer under the discipline of the College than running riot at home. He is more likely to be a better boy for what he learns and sees at College than if he had never been there.[153]

Macalister's defence of the stupid boy reflects a belief that the Chiefs' College was a holding space where deviance might be contained rather than corrected. It is not coincidental that similar formulae were articulated by 'failed' reformatory and prison administrators; in all cases, the colonial institution served to produce and exhibit the evidence of its own exoticism.

It was, however, a reassuring and rewarding exoticism. As instruments that measured the mismatch between colonial enclave and native inmate, British educational schemes in India in the later nineteenth century actually reminded the scientists of race and childhood that their own natures, manifested in their identities as public school boys, expert administrators and headmasters, had been shaped by a different set of nurturing environments. The contours of this nature generated a Self that was in fact authoritative even when it did not leave its mark upon the native, because it continuously discovered the limits of the experiment in the shape of children and adults who were, literally, beyond the pale.

Conclusion

The idea of the child necessarily comes attached to the idea of emulation. In other words, the plastic individual exists so that he might take on, gradually, a shape that he does not yet possess. The Chiefs' Colleges and guardianships that emerged after the Mutiny were based on the idea that the Indian princes had to be molded into cultural and political shapes that were more congenial to a colonial regime that was, on the one hand, facing an insubordinate class of mimic men, and on the other hand, pushing relentlessly into the remaining uncolonized spaces on the periphery of an empire. Children, as soft receptacles of adult influence, appeared to be a point at which the initiative could be pressed. From the outset, however, educators and administrators were plagued by their own ambivalence about who princely children might emulate. Whereas the Macaulayan middle class of Indians was unsuitable, British surrogate fathers and their juvenile selves emerged from this experiment as largely inimitable by natives. Consequently, the child was reified as an unchanging and substantially unchangeable entity that inhabited a cultural, intellectual, political and gendered limbo. This frozen state was imagined by pedagogical authorities as the native state, or as the perverse native home that could, in fact, be discovered within the colonial enclave. In 1902, the *Lahore Observer* wrote about the Chiefs' Colleges:

> They have hitherto failed…because they have had to adopt means and methods of education which were meant for another class of boys. The ordinary textbooks of common public schools, the system of examinations depending on an unintelligent parrot-like knowledge of certain books, sufficient to obtain pass marks, and the placing of a certain pass as a goal before the mind's eye, have contributed to destroying…that speciality of these Colleges which the founders contemplated to cultivate. No Chiefs' College can justify its existence and cost unless it sends out its alumni into the world, well-equipped with information necessary for success in high life and with their faculties fully developed for the creditable performance of the duties to which they are called by their birth. To keep a chief in an institution for eight or ten years and then send him out with a certificate of having barely passed the Middle School or Entrance exam is an ideal far from attractive.[154]

The editorial is as contradictory as the object of its ire. On the one hand, it demands a rigorous academic education and the cultivation of utility for princely children, and sees the Chiefs' Colleges as having failed in these regards. But it also rejects the academic training of Macaulayan education as having produced 'parrots', who lacked real intellectual content and adulthood. The imagined ideal remains the child in the English public school — an institution that was intellectual without being effete, rigorous without encouraging imitation, and different from colonial schools of both the middle-class and aristocratic varieties. It is held up as a model, but one that could not — and, in Curzon's thinking, should not — be replicated in the colony. Colonial schools thus functioned as necessary failures, successfully generating difference, pessimism and wonder regarding the nature of the native child.

6

THE POLITICS OF DERACINATION

In 1912, the government of Bombay decided to send Mohabat Khan, the twelve-year-old Nawab of Junagadh, to school in England for a year and a half. The decision set off a small firestorm of criticism in India as well as in England. The boy's mother, Asha Bibi, had not been consulted in the decision. In a series of petitions to British authorities at every level — the political agent, the Governor of Bombay, the Viceroy, the Secretary of State for India and the King — Asha Bibi demanded that her son be returned to her. Sections of the English press took up her cause; the *Nation* called the episode 'kidnapping by order'.[1] Nevertheless, the decision stood. The *Nation's* editors were dismissed by old India hands as naïve about the realities of imperial government and colonial society, and Asha Bibi was labelled a hysterical woman who did not understand her son's best interests.[2]

The Mohabat Khan affair was emblematic of the larger conflict over the upbringing of the children of the princes. The new child-rearing schemes were welcomed by many Indians, including the princes themselves. The latter, in particular, recognized that this education increased their ability to move vertically and horizontally within the empire at a time when they were in some danger of becoming irrelevant. They embraced the ideological goals of colonial education, and the opportunities it provided for the reinvention of the Indian prince. At the same time, this education was highly controversial. Just as British observers feared that colonial education would produce rootless wanderers who would disrupt the racial order of the empire, Indian critics feared that the project would create a class of 'denationalized' leaders and disenfranchised parents in native society. Whereas the British worried about an undermining of the racial-political hierarchy of empire, the infiltration of England by insubordinate natives, sexual escapades across the lines of race and a diminution of the colonial fantasy, including the fantasy of the despotic Oriental ruler, Indians feared moral misadventures involving liquor and white women. They worried that foreign trips inculcated in princes the habits of wasteful spending. They worried, especially, that colonial education alienated the loyalty of the princes at a time when anticolonial resentments demanded conformity between race, culture and political allegiance.

The princely milieu was not, of course, the only stage on which these anxieties were articulated. Syed Ahmed Khan made strenuous efforts to convince the *ashraf* community that their children would not become aliens as a result of the Aligarh experience. Levyveld has argued that Syed Ahmed — not unlike H D Daly — approached the problem through a series of apparent compromises that sought to reassure the Muslim elite that the college was an extension of 'home', even as the institution and the experience inexorably altered students' conceptions of home and abroad.[3] A similar set of anxieties can be identified in the battles over the education of Indian women at the turn of the century, when, as Minault and Forbes have both noted, the objectives of companionate marriage and professional motherhood had to be balanced against the fear of cultural collapse.[4] As early as the 1820s and 1830s, sections of the Calcutta elite were up in arms about what their sons were learning at Hindu College.[5]

What is different about the controversy that surrounded the princes is, firstly, the peculiar geography in which their education took place. Unlike students at early colonial schools like Hindu College, the princes of the post-Mutiny era were among the first Indians to enter institutions where the residential geography was removed from parental supervision. While the alarm of Calcutta parents could be contained by firing a dangerous teacher like Derozio, it was considerably more difficult to make similar adjustments in the learning environment of princes at Mayo College or Cambridge. Aligarh was also a boarding school, of course, as was Deoband. There was, however, no overt British control over education at Deoband, which, Barbara Metcalf has noted, utilized modern pedagogical techniques to teach students how to turn away from the colonial state.[6] At Aligarh, British educators were subordinated, however imperfectly, to *ashraf* trustees and Syed Ahmed himself. *Zenana* teachers were not fully independent of the Indian males within the household. A Chiefs' College, in comparison, was a British enclave, where Indian political influence was either counter-institutional (as in the servant-infested dorms) or relatively weak. When the princes travelled to England, it only exacerbated a concern that their identities were being molded in territory that was beyond the control of other Indians, including parents and families.

The second variable that differentiates the education of the princes is that the schools that were created for them had different professional and political trajectories from Aligarh and Hindu College, not to mention the Deoband madrasa and *zenana* teaching. The princes who attended these schools were expected and encouraged by the British to be highly visible public figures with considerable power within their states, and occasionally, not inconsiderable influence in a wider field of imperial politics. Such expectations placed enormous weight upon the novelty of their education. When the students became ruling princes, their schooling was immediately seized upon by British as well as Indian observers as a hallmark of their modernity and a harbinger of political reform. When these reforms were less than satisfactory, however, the critics would see the ruler's education as evidence of his moral, cultural and political incompetence, and declare that he was too deracinated to be acceptable as an Indian prince. Under the circumstances, it is apparent that colonial education for the princes was contentious only superficially because it raised the specter of a moral and cultural meltdown. The discourse of moral and cultural loss functioned as a shorthand in which the fluctuating Indian responses to colonialism — the pleasure as well as the anger — could be articulated. The deracination of native children was not the loss of morality and culture; it was the blurring of boundaries in a political conflict.

Education and Racial Anxiety

The British conviction that princely children needed a comprehensively new education found considerable support among Indians. The professional and merchant elite in the provinces and the princely states tended to share a Howardian view of the princes as atavistic and repressive.[7] Kamakshi Narayan, the editor of *The Indian Social Reformer*, came out in favour of educating Mohabat Khan in England, and added that without such relocation, the Indian princes would remain a spoiled, immoral and parasitical class.[8] Sumit Sarkar has observed that Indian critics of 'traditional' familiality spoke as least as much from the uncomfortable material, intellectual and conjugal circumstances of middle-class families, as from their desire for a 'western' model of the domestic.[9] Sarkar's argument was made in the context of Vidyasagar's Bengal, but it is not altogether unhelpful in understanding the animus of middle-class reformists like Narayan towards the 'orthodox' aristocratic family in which a vast assortment of clutching relatives and sharply varying levels and types of education might plague the modern individual.

On occasion, the princes themselves voiced similar sentiments, because by doing so they demonstrated their own reformed status, their allegiance to the Crown and their sympathy with the middle-class desire for modernity.[10] The princes were also willing to accept the reparative agenda of colonial education. The heroic past was a part of the princes' own image of themselves as a class, and while this image often had autonomous roots in family histories and bardic narratives,[11] by the late nineteenth century, those roots had become intertwined with British narratives — not only Tod, but also narratives by relatively obscure officials like Howard, who followed Tod's lead and constructed their narratives interactively with the princes.[12] It was possible, therefore, for colonial administrators and the princes to agree very generally about the character of the Indian civilization that was to be resuscitated through education.

The agreement, however, was not especially deep, and some cracks were evident from the outset. By the time of the Great War, certainly, it was evident to the colonial government that princely families had remained half-hearted in their enthusiasm for the military careers that were valorised in the Chiefs' Colleges.[13] At the same time, the ambivalence that British educators frequently expressed about the racial-political location of English-educated native children was echoed by Indian critics of sending princes abroad for their education. When the plan to send Mohabat Khan to England was first announced, Asha Bibi and L Robertson exchanged a series of increasingly testy letters about whether England was in fact a morally safer environment than India, and whether 'the dangers and temptations which come with adolescence' might not actually be greater there.[14] Sex was not, however, the only moral issue at stake. In her petition to the Viceroy, Asha Bibi wrote, 'I do not think it at all desirable that a Mahomedan Prince should constantly associate at the same table with people to whom drinking wine is perfectly legitimate.'[15]

Concern with the racial boundaries of morality framed the issue of 'denationalization', to which Asha Bibi referred explicitly in her letter to the Viceroy. The anxiety was greatest in the native press, i.e. the newspapers with Indian editors and readerships based in presidency cities like Bombay, Pune and Calcutta. Here, the hostile reaction to the Junagarh episode reflected a barely concealed resentment of the heavy-handedness that the colonial authorities had demonstrated in overruling the objections of Mohabat Khan's mother. This was perceived as an extension of British arbitrariness in other areas of colonial politics.[16] There was a keen awareness among Indian critics that the politics of education in colonial India was, among other things, a clash between Indian parents and British administrators, and a part of the colonization of the 'Indian home'. At the same time, the content and structure of the experience that awaited Mohabat Khan was also a part of the debate. Here, the native press reflected the schizophrenia surrounding the political values attached to race in colonial India, and the impact of the new education upon racial identity. Deracination was both welcomed and feared. When there was a strong possibility that English-educated princes would be sympathetic towards the newly assertive middle and upper-class commoners in their states, deracination was seen as intellectual and moral progress, and welcomed by the native press. When the princes turned their backs on these classes, however, deracination was seen as disloyalty, and condemned.

The coverage of the Mohabat Khan affair in the native press demonstrates both sides of this process. The *Praja Bandhu*, which was frequently critical of the western-Indian princes in its editorial policy, was cautiously optimistic about Mohabat Khan's English sojourn, but added that it should be brief, 'for we hold that for a Native Ruler to lose touch with his State or his subjects spells nothing but disaster'.[17] Even as the editor of the *Kathiawar Vartaman* conceded that modern princes required a 'liberal' education, he urged the Government of Bombay to delay sending boys to Europe until they had 'acquired some knowledge of the language and customs of their own country'.[18] Other papers couched their discomfort with sending Mohabat Khan to England in terms of support for the Rajkot College, and argued that the boy could have been educated there with less damage to his cultural identity.[19]

Yet, even those Indian observers who expressed support for the Chiefs' Colleges remained apprehensive about the political implications of a residential college in a colonial society, especially its imbedded critiques of the native family, culture and history. In 1903, Pandit Sukhdeo Pershad, a mid-level official in the Western Rajputana States bureaucracy, sent his superiors a long memo detailing his views on Mayo College, as part of another review by the colonial government of the performance of the Chiefs' Colleges.[20] A richly layered document penned by a native official with one foot planted strategically in authentic racial identity and the other in political loyalty to a colonial regime, Sukhdeo's memo contains and combines the elements of agreement, advice and dissent, each qualifying as well as reinforcing the others. Sukhdeo agrees that the project of reforming princely children in residential colleges is broadly valid. He agrees, also, that the children are resistant to reform, averse to discipline, prone to homosexuality and corrupted by servants and musahibs. He calls for a more austere culture of intramural discipline, and for more English masters whose watchful eyes might deter sexual activity in the dorms.[21] He alleges that princely fathers showed an interest in their children's education only when they were sure that the Viceroy was watching. In all this, he is broadly aligned with British perceptions of what had gone wrong with the Chiefs' Colleges.

From this secure position of ideological and political loyalty, Sukhdeo launches bold attacks against the assumptions of his superiors and readers. This is a familiar strategy for the native bureaucrat engaged in debates about state intervention in native society; for Sukhdeo, as for Indians talking to the regime about female infanticide in the 1870s,[22] delinquent girls in the 1890s, and hook swinging in the same period,[23] agreement and loyalty generate the political space for dissent and advice, the latter being a subversive encroachment upon the territory of the white expert. Sukhdeo's first attack is actually a defence of that most maligned area of Rajput child rearing — motherhood. He writes:

> The mother's influence on the boy's habits and character is always of a salutary kind in Rajput families. She is usually very conservative, seeks to bring up the boys in a love for the old national traditions and ways, about which there is nothing objectionable. And in this, she is a strict disciplinarian too.

The mother is thus rehabilitated as a disciplinarian in her own right. Sukhdeo not only manages to recuperate a range of 'old national traditions and ways', he also locates and insulates Rajput women within a discourse of womanhood which is bound up with national traditions.[24] The blame for spoiling children at home and at school is shifted from gender to class, caste and religion — like his contemporaries who were engaged in debating the boundaries of the Rajput family, he identifies Gola and Muslim servants as the culprits, and demands that they be replaced as the children's associates by 'some relation (from the mother's side, if possible), or…by any *pure* Rajput'.[25] [Parentheses and emphases in original].

The other target of Sukhdeo's derision is the curriculum at the Chiefs' Colleges. He declares himself 'cordially unable to concur' with the determination of H W Orange (the Director of Public Instruction, who chaired the investigation) that lessons at the colleges be geared to introduce the boys to 'England and English life, English Public Schools and the doings of the Indian Chiefs who visit England'.[26] Instead, Sukhdeo writes:

> I feel confident that a great deal will be found in the Indian ideals of life, thought and action worthy of imitation by the future Chiefs and Nobles of Rajputana among whom, as the destined leaders of their people, it would be advantageous to preserve and foster that respect for and touch with their national traits and traditions, which will endear them to their people. The better side of English life had best become familiar to the boys only through the example of their masters.[27]

If this was not subversive enough, Sukhdeo insisted that the history and geography that the boys learned at school, and the clothes they wore, must all 'relate to Rajputana and India'. He also wanted less time devoted to sport and more to academics, and teetotaller masters who might set the right example for the children in their charge.[28] At the same time, it is clear that he is not opposed to history and geography as intellectual disciplines, or even to the teaching of European history in the higher grades. He chides colonial educators who had resisted reformist proposals (by J B Hutchinson, for instance) that the Chiefs' Colleges provide students with a practical education and examination-based degrees that would support professional careers,[29] and he is explicit that the boys' native clothes ought to constitute 'a compromise between the simplicity and grace of the native fashion, and the smartness and effectiveness of the Western mode'.[30]

Thus, while apparently dressing Rajput children in the masks of conquest, Sukhdeo is appropriating the masks as well as the children. His agenda is identical to that of middle class journalists: it is upper-caste, Hindu, nationalist and modern and it manages to critique British educators like Gunion and Orange, critique the princes, prescribe correctives and absorb the princes, all at once. The call for temperance was by this time well-established within Indian middle-class morality, and a part of the middle-class critiques of European social habits as well as aristocratic degeneracy.[31] Sukhdeo's polemic seeks to redirect the affiliation of aristocratic children from England to India; it is only tangentially concerned with the content of their 'character'. The importance given to the examination and the degree is indicative simultaneously of the middle-class resentment of aristocratic privilege, British protection of such privilege and the middle-class investment in a competitive system of modern qualifications.

It appears, therefore, that while the Chiefs' College could be represented as a lesser evil than the transportation of princely children to England, its flaws were obvious to some Indian observers. The editors of the *Indu Prakash* expressed a straightforward apprehension of racial and moral alienation at the college, and connected that to a larger pattern of cultural decline under colonial rule:

> It is necessary that the princes attending [such] institutions should not be allowed to drift from their ancient traditions and religion. We are prompted to this remark by the sight we sometimes see of princes who have practically no religion. Do the Colleges turn out princes who are aware of their responsibilities and who have always in view the high traditions of their ancestors? We are afraid some of them turn out merely frivolous, pleasure seeking young men.[32]

A more common criticism, however, was one that saw the Chiefs' Colleges not so much as a misdirected institution as the failure of a worthwhile mission and implied that this failure had exacerbated the political subjugation of India to the British. *The Parsi*, for instance, was hardly a consistent critic of British cultural influence, but complained nevertheless that students at the college learned nothing about politics and administration, and were reduced to the status of 'puppets' in the hands of their political officers.[33] The *Kathiawadno Himayati* issued a more forceful condemnation of education at the Rajkot College, calling it impractical as well as harmful, and adding that the college turned out 'worthless and incapable administrators'.[34] The *Gujarati* literally exclaimed that English education had failed the princes intellectually, morally and even physically:

> Many of these princes are constitutionally very weak. A railway porter is stronger than an Indian prince! As for their morals…the less said the better! Their intellectual development is such that they avoid university

examinations, and their mental and intellectual training is supposed to be complete if they can converse in English for five minutes!'[35]

The reference to weak bodies was particularly cutting, given the centrality of sport to the educational model that was held up by the British to the Indian princes at the end of the nineteenth century. While large sections of the Indian elite shared the British perception that they lacked and needed athletic bodies, they wanted to control the process by which those bodies were created, to dominate the spaces where strong, disciplined and modern men were assembled, and above all, to claim the finished product. When they were uncertain of this control, they rejected the English-educated bodies as deracinated.

The desire to own the educated body politically is evident in the discourse of princely government in the native press, which is marked by a sharp disappointment. To understand this disappointment, we must take into account the high expectations that were attached to English-educated princes by Indians as well as the British. When Bahadursinhji returned to India and became the ruler of Palitana in 1919, E Maconochie, the political agent for Kathiawar, said at his coronation, 'You have seen the best of English school life as a member of the most distinguished of public schools and have learnt to 'play the game' in all departments of life. After this long absence from your home and your people you now have to reorganize your life as a Rajput Ruling Prince.'[36] Virtually identical sentiments were expressed by the native press in 1907 when Ranjitsinhji became the Jam of Nawanagar.[37]

In each case, the expectation was that English education had made the prince something more, or other, than simply Indian or Rajput. That otherness could be described as enlightenment, which in this context was a combination of four traits: responsibility in fiscal policy; willingness to undertake public works; commitment to a legal regime based on the British colonial model; and responsiveness. Obviously, these were nebulous traits with considerable room for disagreement on whether the individual ruler had in fact been enlightened by his education. The fourth trait — responsiveness — was particularly contentious, because whereas the native press typically interpreted it as a desire to make government more democratic, the British would read it in terms of a willingness to listen to the political agent. Moreover, in colonial India, the British had effectively reversed their tendency to equate despotism with decadence and effeminacy; here, in a discursive rearrangement that suited the Raj as well as the princes, it was autocracy that was held up as masculine, provided that autocracy was enlightened.[38] Under these circumstances, it was not difficult for English-educated ex-children to fail what might be described as the 'enlightenment test'. When this happened, the standard complaint from Indian onlookers was that English education had denationalized and degraded, rather than enlightened and elevated, the prince formerly known as a child.

An echo of the connection between alienation and princely education is audible in the diary of Amar Singh, a junior member of the Jodhpur ruling family. While in the ICC, he wrote contemptuously about a fellow cadet, the ex-Etonian Vali Uddeen Khan, 'He does not know Indian things and is practically an Englishman. We none of us liked him… He was quite unable to put on his own turban.'[39] Another classmate was described thus:

> This boy had been brought up in England and looked down upon Indians as mere animals. I am always against bringing up boys in England. This makes them used to English life and they always afterwards hanker to go there. They get English ideas and like English food, dress and women.[40]

Yet Amar Singh was a product of the new education, steeped in Plutarch, polo and military professionalism. He was literally the prototype of the new native soldier — a veteran of the Boxer 'rebellion' and the first non-white to be commissioned as an officer in the Indian Army. He was himself criticized by relatives who found 'these English educated children' vicious, disrespectful and smug.[41] Amar Singh's hostility reflects a schism within the ranks of the English-educated, separating those who had been trained in India from those who had been to England. In this divide, English women and Indian turbans indicate the individual's political loyalties, rather than any significant moral exoticism. They reflect, also, the privileges and disadvantages that came with the 'clothes' in a prince's political closet. Amar Singh grumbled, '[Rajendra Narain] has been brought up in England, and consequently has everything in his favour.'[42]

Amar Singh's resentment of Rajendra Narain and Vali Uddeen Khan — the latter was emasculated with the nickname 'Rosy' — is foreshadowed in a story that appeared in the *Sahachar* in 1896. An unnamed prince in Bengal had told the reporter that his education at a Chiefs' College had rendered him alien and friendless in his state, his government and even his family. So great was the prince's trauma, the *Sahachar* declared, 'that in sheer disgust he took to the English vice of drinking'.[43] The newspaper did not, however, issue a blanket condemnation of colonial education for the princes. Its response was more nuanced than that, trying valiantly to separate education into categories which might be described as 'skills' and 'lifestyle'. The article said:

> It cannot be said that this falling off was due to the Prince's English education. The Prince fell off because he was taught to imitate English habits and manners. There are many native Princes in Bengal who have received English education, but not at the Rajkumar College, and they

are not Anglicized. The Maharaja of Darbhanga was taught the English language, literature and science, but was never taught to imitate English habits and manners. The pupils at the Rajkumar College are taught on the same method as the scions of noble families in England are trained up at Eton. But the Eton system does not suit Indian Princes, who have to live among relatives and rule over people who are perfect strangers to the language, the religion and the manners of the English people.[44]

What the *Sahachar* objected to was not the skills, but the life that seemed to come with the skills. For instance, the paper was substantially in agreement with the *Poona Observer*, which — like Sukhdeo and Hutchinson — insisted that the agricultural sciences were essential to the education of a modern prince.[45] The princes often agreed. Ranjitsinhji sent his nephews to study agriculture at the University of California[46] and Bahadursinhji trained in agriculture when he was in England.[47] Nevertheless, like Curzon and Amar Singh, the *Sahachar* did not see it as desirable that Indian princes should be encouraged to become English, attend English public schools, or 'join' English society, because these obscured the princes' true identities and loyalties in colonial politics. The reference to the Maharaja of Darbhanga is revealing, because tutoring him had been Chester Macnaghten's first job in India. It would seem, therefore, that the corrupting influence was not so much the content of colonial education, but the environmental, structural and the political context of that education. It might be argued that the geography of colonialism, including India as well as England, was itself a part of this flawed educational context, because within this geography, there was no escape from the tensions of the 'true' identity of the educated.

The Other Side of the Contested School

Middle-class journalists were obviously not the only Indian critics of colonial pedagogical agendas. As is evident from Asha Bibi's reaction to the British removal of Mohabat Khan, Rajput parents were themselves ambivalent about colonial projects for the education of their children. To unpack this ambivalence, it is first necessary to problematize and gender the idea of the parent, or the assumption that adults with legitimate authority over children are family members — particularly fathers — who have opinions, who make decisions about their children's schooling and who interact with educators. The word 'parent' is an upper-class Victorian signifier in search of a practice that colonial observers struggled to discover in India except in occasional and inconsistent fantasies, and that obstructed their attempts to assert the authority of the white colonizer, teacher and pedagogical expert.

To some extent, this underlies the difficulty experienced by experts who sought to recreate in the colony metropolitan institutions like the public school and probation. The tendency of colonial educator-officials to complain about ineffective native fathers is inseparable from their simultaneous inclination to see mothers as the primary spoilsports, or from their despair about the profusion of servants and musahibs. In each case, the 'cleanness' of a recognizably modern late-nineteenth-century relationship between father and teacher had been muddied by the mediation of those who not only were unqualified by virtue of gender, class, biological relationship to the child and political position within the colonial state, but who also eroded the authority of the white surrogate parent whose racial-political location in colonial society might compensate for his lack of a biological tie. The result was the production of pathological adults who could only preside over the production of pathological children: the interfering mother, the unmanned and apathetic father, and on occasion, even the defeated and emasculated white educator. In 1901, while explaining to Curzon why the Daly College was 'moribund', Walter Lawrence declared that 'Mr. Gunion has been Principal since 1889. He is a man of learning, but he is despondent, and has certainly lost all enthusiasm'.[48]

To understand this sense of defeat, which might also be read as effective resistance on the part of the obstinate native parent, it is useful to begin by noting that even when ruling princes contributed money towards the Chiefs' Colleges, they were far more reluctant to contribute their sons. These latter were sent only after much hesitation, negotiation and argument with white educators. The reluctance was a part of a broader confrontation between princes and the British over education, carried on through what Manu Bhagwan has called the 'chicken wire fence' of the native states.[49] In his study of debates on higher education in Baroda and Mysore, Bhagwan has pointed out that the princes rejected the authority of universities based in British India, and attempted to establish universities in their own states. These attempts, Bhagwan has argued, constituted implicit critiques of colonialism and support for Indian nationalism, a 'reclamation' of modernity from the ornamentalist regime by the disgruntled princes and organized elites in the native states, and a bureaucratic and ideological secession from the colony.[50] Up to a point, the reluctance of princely parents to send their children to the Chiefs' Colleges reflects a similar unwillingness to participate in the pedagogical instruments of their subordination.

Bhagwan, however, creates a false dichotomy between a British resistance to changing a political *status quo* and the princes' own eagerness for change. His analysis deals with imagined universities that are accepted or rejected, demanded or refused, and not institutional spaces and living inmates subject to chronic, fluctuating skirmishes over authority. There can be little doubt that the princely responses to the Chiefs' Colleges contained, in both senses of the word, the realization that children marked a site of contestation between parent-princes and educator-officials. The contest was manifest in British attempts to place princely children in domestic spaces that were less perversely feminine than unmodified native habitats; it was apparent also in disagreements and compromises about corporal punishment, religious education, sexual morality, architecture, curricular content and the racial identity of teachers. What these confrontations and their partial resolutions indicate is that Rajput parents were neither eager partners nor irrational obstructionists in the new schooling for their children, which is how British enthusiasts for the education often depicted them. They were, instead, engaged in the articulation of a nuanced and flexible set of positions which preserved their authority as parents, their status as members of a political elite, their manoeuvrability as colonial allies and adversaries, and their interest in a modernity that went beyond the ornamental.

By the turn of the twentieth century, the ruling chiefs in large and mid-sized states in western and central India were heavily invested in the Chiefs' Colleges. In Punjab, the princes and the colonial government had shared an initial cost of nearly half a million rupees towards infrastructure, scholarships and salaries at Aitchison College.[51] The rulers of Gwalior and Indore had contributed tens of thousands towards dormitories at Daly College, and the Rajputana states — especially Marwar and Mewar — had given well over a million rupees to endow Mayo College with appropriately impressive buildings.[52] The Maharaja of Jodhpur had declared his full support for 'this laudable undertaking' and pledged money towards a dormitory for students from Marwar.[53] The college in Rajkot ran entirely on princely money, without any consistent financial support from the colonial treasury.[54] Moreover, the princes participated actively in the various conferences that the colonial government, particularly Curzon, organized to discuss the progress (or failure) of the schools.[55] It is against this appearance of enthusiasm that we must interpret the reluctance of the princes to send their children to the schools.

In 1901, political officers engaged in evaluating potential candidates for the ICC noted that none of the bigger chiefs of central India had sent their sons to Daly College, leaving the school to the children of Bhils.[56] As early as 1873, the political agent for Marwar and Jaisalmer mused that 'it is no use disguising the truth that many of the Chiefs do not really care about education for their children, and it is only by very careful measures and by humouring them as much as possible that we shall ever persuade them to send their sons to [Mayo] College'.[57] Matters had not improved two, or even three, decades later: in 1892, one Aitchison College master noted with disappointment that 'we have not…been able to attract the sons and near relatives of the larger

Punjab Chiefs.'[58] In his 1901 memo to Curzon, Lawrence observed, 'Mr. Godley, who has been Principal [of Aitchison College] since 1895, considers that the attempt to interest and associate ruling Chiefs in the management of the new institution has proved an unqualified failure'.[59] There was no demand for the scholarships to Aitchison, and even at the relatively well-received Mayo, only fifty-six of the one hundred and thirty-nine places were filled.[60] Asked to explain why there were no Mewar boys at Mayo in 1903, A F Pinhey weakly informed his superior, 'The Maharaja [is] personally in favour of sending them, but the boys themselves and their guardians are most unwilling'.[61] In the same letter, however, Pinhey also reported that he had convinced the ruler of Mewar to start a feeder school in Udaipur to prepare local boys for Mayo College.[62]

Pinhey believed he knew how to explain these paradoxes. There was a broad consensus among colonial bureaucrats that to the princes, the new colleges represented not so much educational institutions as opportunities for political display, or the demonstration not only of competitive enlightenment but also of the 'traditional' generosity that might be expected of a native king. As Ramusack notes, such behaviour would be broadly consistent with contemporary Indian kingship.[63] In 1873, the Foreign Department observed that whereas fifteen Rajputana chiefs had promised large sums of money towards Mayo College and squabbled energetically with each other over the relative opulence of the dormitories they might build, they had shown little urgency in actually making the funds available.[64] 'They regard the [Aitchison] College as a deserving charity,' Lawrence wrote acidly a generation later, 'but they don't send their relatives to it.'[65] Encouraging the Punjab government to ensure that the Raja of Jind — an enticing orphan of eleven — be sent to Aitchison, the *Civil and Military Gazette* warned in 1890:

> If he is not sent here, the conclusion will inevitably be drawn that the College is not fulfilling its function. Apart from the natural disappointment of those who contributed to support the undertaking under misapprehension, this conclusion will be a very undesirable one for the College itself. 'If', another Raja may well be excused for thinking, 'the Aitchison College is not good enough for Jind, it is not good enough for my son and heir.' And once distinctions of this kind begin to be drawn, they show a marvellous aptitude for sliding downwards.[66]

Not all observers read this backsliding as the irrational competitiveness of a backward native elite. Reporting to the Foreign Department on his conversations with the fathers of boys who had not been sent to Daly College, Meade discovered 'a mistrust of the way the boys are brought up'.[67] Lawrence was aware that many princes regarded the residential arrangement of the colleges as cesspools of homosexuality and drinking.[68] (There was an English parallel to this behaviour, but Lawrence would have seen it as a feature of a past that had been superseded by progress.[69]) He also noted that some princes were dissatisfied with the standard of English that was taught at the colleges.[70] While he read this as evidence of the inferiority of native teachers, it is not unreasonable to read it as an indication that far from being indifferent to the academic content of the Chiefs' Colleges, princely parents were in fact too demanding in their expectations of the new institutions. Through a conversation with Yar Mohammad Khan, the administrator of Jaora (and the uncle of the minor nawab), Lawrence also discovered that the princes believed 'too much attention was paid to sport, too little to education; [and] the Native community was bitterly incensed at our insidious policy of half educating the young Chiefs, weaning them from their own people, but giving them none of the advantages of Western education'.[71] In the course of the same conversation, Lawrence learned that the uncle was unhappy that the nephew 'is proficient in English, but cannot speak or write in his own vernacular'.[72]

Yar Mohammed Khan's critique of the Chiefs' Colleges — too much sport, not enough academic training — indicates a rejection not so much of the public school model, but of the inferiority of the transplanted public school. Like middle-class observers, he perceives that colonial education is geared to produce subordination, or men who are deliberately under-equipped for political power. The point about his nephew not knowing his vernacular might be read as a metaphor of a larger cultural anxiety. The trick, Yar Mohammad Khan tells Lawrence, is to be modern without losing authenticity, and this is a trick that the educator-administrators who devised the Chiefs' Colleges to produce a different configuration of modernity and authenticity had not learned to perform convincingly.

That Curzon himself was aware of the failure is apparent in his correspondence with the Secretary of State for India, George Hamilton. The Viceroy wrote to Hamilton in 1903 that common messing, which had long been central to the educators' agenda of restructuring the social and spatial habits of princely children, should be made voluntary, excusing those boys whose feathers of 'customs and caste' might be ruffled by such association. He added that the rulers of Baroda, Nabha, Gwalior and Rewa had all voiced their 'want of confidence' in the Chiefs' Colleges, and made it clear that this lack of faith was due to the schools' neglect of 'moral and religious training'.[73] Eager to reassure the unhappy parents, Curzon had ordered C W Waddington, the Principal at Mayo, to recruit a *shastri* for the school so that the neglect might be rectified.[74]

While Curzon's reactions are aligned with his broad inclination to support aristocratic privileges, the princes' unhappiness about the lack of religious education and caste violations should not be taken at face value. Caste, messing and moral education did not emerge with any comparable regularity in colonial conversations about the ICC, which was also a residential educational institution, involving the same classes of Indians, and to which the same princes who remained aloof from the Chiefs' Colleges were often eager to send their sons.[75] The reluctance reflects the reality that the ICC was for older boys, who were no longer considered children. They were less vulnerable to the dangers that surrounded the more plastic inmates of the Chiefs' Colleges, and did not require the same kinds of parental responses. The princely complaints about the moral climate of the Chiefs' Colleges, like the fears of vernacular atrophy, were shorthand for wider anxieties about the British manipulation of their children, most often packaged in terms of 'religion' because religion occupied a widely accepted colonial niche as a legitimate and comprehensible native concern,[76] as well as a place within the older, Victorian, British discourse of the reforming institution for children.

Religious education featured prominently at the 1904 conference on the Chiefs' Colleges, held at Ajmer. The Rajput princes were present in force even in Curzon's absence, belying Sukhdeo Pershad's allegation that they never visited Ajmer unless the Viceroy was in town.[77] At the conference, it was resolved (with the broad support of princely fathers and uncles) that religious services and teaching would become mandatory at the Chiefs' Colleges.[78] For Hindu boys, a fixed period every morning would be 'devoted to Sandhya' and general religious instruction, while Muslim boys would devote the time to namaz and reading the Koran and Wazifa. The Bhagavad Gita was given the status of a 'textbook' for Hindu students, pending approval by a committee of four pandits. At Aitchison, Daly and Rajkot, the college shastris and maulvis would be paid by the princes; at Mayo, which was located in British territory, the colonial government would pay the salaries. At all institutions, religious instructors would be subordinate to the musahibs and subject to their supervision.[79]

The Ajmer conference of 1904 thus marked the partial decolonization of a colonial children's institution. Like contemporary Arya Samaj meetings and Aligarh, the Chiefs' Colleges and its students were confirmed as the sites and manifestations of reconstructed native identities that might claim textbooks and college chaplains.[80] What is noteworthy here is that when religion emerged in the state-sponsored colonial juvenile institution, the initiative came not from the old advocates of Christian reform, but from native parents who borrowed the old frames but insisted on supplying their own images, effectively occupying the frames. The parallels with the reformatory in the era of Indian expertise are obvious, although not perfect. In each place, the method of decolonization was to concede a principle while insisting upon practices that subverted — or wrested control of — the principle.

The chief of Sailana appeared to accept the principle of common messing, but this did not prevent him from adding that rules for compulsory messing would represent an intolerable intrusion.[81] His fellow chief from Jaipur took an identical position, except that he cited Curzon in his own defence, pointing out that even the Viceroy believed class prejudice to be a perfectly natural sentiment.[82] Sailana supported the teaching of 'dead languages' but (resuscitating Howard) insisted that the dead language taught at the Chiefs' Colleges be Sanskrit, 'which is as highly essential for their religions [sic] as Latin and Greek are for Europeans'.[83] The acquisition of the dead language in the modern classroom was too valuable an ideological signifier to eschew, but the sign had to be Indian, even as the European parallels established the modernity, universality and value of the exercise.

The Maharaja of Jaipur clarified that the religious instruction he envisioned did not constitute surrender to the Christians. 'The object…is not to give any sectarian training to the boys,' he declared, 'but to picture before the young lads the principles of truth, justice, charity, etc. so that potent examples of moral precept, instituted into the young minds from the illustrious lives of their forefathers, may always keep them on the right path.'[84] The note of ancestor worship was a familiar pre-war Victorian-Edwardian posture,[85] but the displacement of laudable moral principles into vague religious compartments was also a familiar colonial maneuver, not altogether different from the deism of the Brahmos and other reformist natives who had flirted with Christianity through much of the nineteenth century but stubbornly and subversively insisted upon a congregational distance.[86] It was also a quiet victory of the native home over the colonial school, widening a space on campus that was domestic, being native and under the control of natives, as well as modern and recognizably reformed.

There was, of course, the danger that the encroachment was in fact in the opposite direction — that by making religion a function of the school, the Chiefs' Colleges had usurped and transformed an important marker of native/parental sovereignty. Certainly, this what Bhugwat Singhjee, the Thakur of Gondal, feared. Disagreeing strongly with the resolution on religious education at school, he declared:

> Religious instruction should be left entirely in the hands of parents, and we should be most careful not to say or do anything that can, by the wildest stretch of the imagination, be construed to suggest anything like compulsion or interference in the matter. Home is undoubtedly the proper place for religious instruction, which should be carried out under the direct supervision of the parent or guardian by the family priest.[87]

To support his point, Bhugwat Singhjee referred not to the content of religious education at home or at school, but to its potential effect on the body, and indirectly, upon habits as they congealed into nature:

> If a boy is dosed with two hours of religious instruction every day in addition to the class work, which, with the new Curriculum will…be anything but light, the boy will get so sick of it that there will be danger of creating in him a positive dislike for the subject for the rest of his life. An hour or so devoted to the subject during the vacation will not seriously cut into the holiday, and the brain is not overtaxed with class work, the boy will be better able to concentrate his attention, and acquire the knowledge with profit.[88]

Thus, just as there was a recognition on the part of the princes that religious education at school could be a necessary form of resistance against the colonization of their children, there was also a recognition that it could be a part of the colonizing process: not only the inculcation of learning that the child might not receive at home and that might manipulate his identity, but also the displacement of a parental/domestic role. In each case, the native speaker found it advisable to reinforce his position with languages that were only tangentially about religion — textbooks and clock-bound instruction on the one hand, the vulnerable physiology of the child on the other. It ought not to be surprising, in this context, that the rulers of Jaipur and Bikaner, who supported the resolution calling for religious instruction, both insisted that the shastris be English speaking and endowed with a cosmopolitan erudition, and not 'too old fashioned and orthodox'.[89] Each position was a stance that enabled the reclamation of the contested school, the contested child and the contested nature of the re-educated native prince.

It is worth noting that a nearly, but not quite, identical articulation of the princes' demand for religious education at the Chiefs' Colleges had been made a year earlier by the Rev. Macalister. Writing to the Resident in Jaipur, Macalister had begun with a sentiment that is perhaps predictable in a missionary, but then gone on to make more startling suggestions:

> The fact that no provision is made for the religious instruction of the youths of India is the bane of the English system of education. The tendency of Western education is to shake a boy's faith in the religion of his fathers, until gradually he comes to believe in nothing. A good Hindu or a good Mussulman is a much better man than one destitute of religion. A Hindu Pandit should be appointed to teach the boys the fear of God. The Pandit should be a thoroughly well-educated man, with an English education, if he is to command the respect of the boys. He should be

broad and liberal minded and well-acquainted with other religions than his own. An old fossil will never do; he would be likely to enjoin what the boys would despise.[90]

Macalister was one of the 'experts' in 'Rajputs and their ways' that Curzon's administration had consulted during its attempt to understand the princes' reluctance to send their sons to the Chiefs' Colleges. Like Jaipur, Sailana and to some extent Gondal, he voices his desire for a metaphorical Brahmo or even a Vidyasagar as religious instructor for the princely child, i.e. for an English-educated native who is nevertheless 'grounded' in his native identity.[91] Cox has argued that for missionaries in the colony, the utilitarian institution, or 'machine', was itself a reforming 'presence' that allowed for compromises and concessions on the racial, religious and gendered identities of the operators and products of the machine.[92] Macalister's, however, is a defensive position: as a missionary who has clearly given up on proselytization and Christian education within the colonial school, Macalister sees any religion as a restraint upon the combined natures of native and child. In the hands of the princes, Macalister's defensiveness is transformed into an aggressive polemic against deracination, or against the colonization of the native child. Macalister himself is chasing a ghost — he assumes that it is within the prerogative of his own expertise to determine the content of native identity at a time when it is precisely that prerogative that is being wrested by the inmates of the asylum.

The contests over religious instruction overflowed easily into issues that had no obvious connection to religion. Like Yar Mohammad Khan, Jaipur attacked colonial educators' faith in the value of games, declaring:

> Play and games should not be given a more important place than useful study and moral training. This is one of the causes for which people are not disposed to send their boys to the Chiefs' Colleges.[93]

Sailana was more abrasive, calling for a curriculum that

> will bring [the Indian princes] in contact with the Western civilization, and will prepare them to meet the exigencies of the time, so that they may be able to maintain the traditions of their houses and rule their territories wisely, appreciating at the same time the paternal protection of the Sovereign,...and will repay the trouble of the noble Lord Curzon, who is actuated with the best of motives and noble intentions to make us administrators, statesmen and the like, instead of polo players, cricketers, and appearing at the race course and at English Hotels under the mask of foreign dress but with perfectly empty minds.[94]

He went on to complain at length about an athletic regime that seemed to consume more time than academics, that crippled children in gymnastics accidents, and that forced orthodox boys into alien clothes. The moral and the sub-national discourses slipped easily into the sporting arena: athletic events attracted European guests, Sailana observed, and these guests had to be served alcohol, 'which creates a very bad impression upon young minds, and tempts them to acquire the habit sooner or later'. In fact, 'The practice [drinking] is one of the chief causes of the downfall of the Rajput nation.'[95] At the same time, Sailana insisted that he recognized the importance of 'ordinary exercise' as a source of health, and even the value of sports. The specific sports that he named, however, were lancing, fencing and riding: quasi-military exercises that had been reshaped and integrated into colonial-princely culture, to be sure, but much less so than polo (which he decried), and that had acquired distinctly pre-colonial roots in the Rajput as well as the middle-class nationalist self-image.[96]

Sailana's remarks showcase the utility of social conservatism as anticolonialism, borrowing subversively from precisely those Britons who saw the Chiefs' Colleges as experiments in social engineering. Through a subversive and probably sarcastic use of language, Sailana re-articulates colonial pedagogical goals (the sporting prince) as well as colonial disdain (the princely moron and dislocated mimic), and implies that they are incompatible with the third language — that of the modern partner in imperialism. The reference to alcohol reminded British officials and educators present at the conference that the princes knew about, and disapproved of, the ease with which their sons obtained liquor at the Chiefs' Colleges.[97] But it was simultaneously a critique of European moral habits, and an indirect defence of a Rajput/native cultural identity that was periodically criticized by European observers for its recreational use of opium.[98] When Sailana invokes the rural martial skills of middle-class nostalgia, it is surely not coincidental. In each case, it is the fantasy of a recovered masculinity that is substantially extra-colonial and potentially anticolonial, and that is counterpoised against the colonized, and thus self-contradicting, manliness of the student cricketer at a Chiefs' College. For Sailana, as for middle-class observers, disapproval of athletic education could function as a code in which an anticolonial position of moral superiority might be articulated.

Middle-class critiques of colonial pedagogy are also echoed in the remarks of Bhugwat Singhjee, who tied athletic education to the failure of an agenda of modernization that was autonomous of Curzon's objectives:

[There is] an impression in the Province that the College is established to teach the Rajkumars English games and not to give them a sound intellectual education. We see that after a course of two or eight years the acquaintance of most of the Kumars, with the various subjects they have read, is quite superficial and disappointing. I do not in the least object to manly sports. They should be encouraged by all means but not to the detriment of intellectual education. In these days of all-round progress, intellectual culture is of the highest importance to the Rajkumars.[99]

The nearly ubiquitous critiques of athletic education for children, coming from the princes, belie the British assertions that the princes were more interested in games than in academics, and contest the implication that princely children were so naturally unintellectual that their education could only be athletic. The parents were not altogether without support from British 'experts' on appropriate education: A P L Tucker wanted polo banned in the Chiefs' Colleges as it was 'not a game for schoolboys' and, in a curious echo of Sailana's concern about the moral content of sport in the colony, because it might lead to an interest in racehorses and gambling.[100] Tucker, however, was in the minority — a rare skeptic about the cult of the athletic schoolboy in the decades between Tom Brown and the Great War. Most educators reacted defensively to criticism of their faith in teaching children on the playing fields, even as they conceded that the academic performance of the schools was unsatisfactory. C Mayne, then officiating as principal in Rajkot, protested that 'the complaint that too much attention is given to games is…unfounded. The weakness in work has hitherto been due to the inadequacy of the native staff'.[101]

The Ajmere conference indicates that the chiefs were far from uninterested in the refashioning of their children's education, which encompassed not only the broadest confrontations over cultural meaning, such as the meanings of alcohol and religious instruction, and the relative virtues of cricket and swordplay, but also the specifics of control over the body of the native child. The last was still a ground to be claimed, conquered, reclaimed and recaptured.[102] When the issue of corporal punishment at the Chiefs' Colleges came up at Ajmer, the subject proved to be so contentious that no resolution was possible, other than a vague statement that 'no Chief's son ought to receive corporal punishment'. Waddington noted that although he reserved the right to beat his students, he did not actually exercise this right, preferring to sentence offenders to solitary detention in his room.[103]

Corporal punishment at the Chiefs' Colleges, as at Aligarh (where only Syed Ahmed, in his role as surrogate father in the relocated home, could beat the students[104]) or at missionary schools,[105] represents the starkest instance of the struggle between native parents and colonial educators, with the body of the child representing not only parental privilege but also the political prestige of native elites. Waddington's retention of a theoretical but unutilized right to beat students is a political compromise, but it is also a face-saving measure in a compromised pedagogical exercise. The recourse to detention indicates a re-enactment of the tensions of the reformatory. Unlike in the reformatory, however, the movement in the Chiefs' College is towards imprisonment, indicating that dealing with a different class of children could produce inadvertent movements towards modernity in their punishment.

The ideological misalignment between parents and educators is summarized in the well-known disagreement over the architecture of the Chiefs' Colleges. In 1872–73, when designs for the Mayo campus were still being evaluated, Lord Mayo and the executive architect (J Gordon) wanted the structures to resemble 'modern buildings constructed by Hindoos', by which they meant Indo-Saracenic design.[106] The princes, however, were less interested in authenticity than they were in a 'classical European design', which the Governor General's Council rejected as a 'preposterous' desire for 'a Grecian temple'.[107] 'Grecian temples' obviously do not make for modern school buildings, but the Europeanness of this 'classical' tradition could function as a metaphor of modernity. The princes read this implied modernity as more cosmopolitan, less narrowly 'native', less ornamental and more useful than the colonial fantasy of a 'modern Hindu architecture' within which Curzon and Gordon sought to contain native children.

By seeking to control the politically charged buildings and playgrounds of the Chiefs' Colleges, the chiefs attempted to break out of this field of containment in two directions. One was English-speaking, useful and universal. The other was marked by Sanskrit and Urdu, Hinduism and Islam, and parochial pre-colonial 'traditions'. The two directions of resistance were not necessarily distinct. In fact, they were necessarily compatible; the parents who wanted religious education in the Chiefs' Colleges also wanted useful academic training for their children. The combination of the two creatures — the native child and the modern child — could be acceptable only if the 'native' could be transcended in the process of combination, and this could happen only if the agents of combination were politically legitimate. In the eyes of princely fathers at the turn of the century or even at the outset of the Chiefs' Colleges project, the modern native child could only be fraudulent.

The dialogues examined above are, of course, conversations between fathers and male educators about boys. Given the centrality of gender in the pedagogical agenda of the Chiefs' Colleges, it is important to listen for female voices like that of Asha Bibi, and to determine if mothers articulated positions that were significantly different from those of fathers. Maternal voices, not surprisingly, appear less frequently in the official record, and it is by no means clear that the women represented a uniform hindrance to colonial educators. Unlike Asha Bibi, some mothers went along with British intervention in their relations with their sons. Jumnabaee, the Queen Mother of Baroda, appears to have given her cautious support in the 1870s to Meade's efforts to provide a new education for Syajee Rao. Meade had qualified his determination to remove the boy from the palace by adding that he would intervene 'excepting when [Syajee is] with the Maharanee herself'.[108] To some extent, this reflects a concession made to the political improvidence of crossing the queen. It also reflects, however, Jumnabaee's own inclination to accept Meade's plans to educate Syajee outside the feminized palace. He decided, eventually, to relocate the boy and his mother to a new residence, a garden house which 'is a favourite place of residence of the Maharanee's'.[109] The queen mother seems to have negotiated a working compromise, by which she retained a substantial measure of control over her son, but agreed to give the political agent a place within a redefined residential and domestic arrangement.

Other women negotiated differently. The mothers of Panna Singh may have vexed McNabb with the frequency and the cultural content of their interference, but it is not at all apparent that they were narrowly or even broadly opposed to his pedagogical methods.[110] Rather, it seems that they insisted only upon retaining a place for themselves as participants in Panna's upbringing, by choosing his clothes at the coronation ceremony and enforcing the religious components of the ritual.[111] The roles that they chose may have conflicted with McNabb's paternal assertion of authority over 'my boy', but they were entirely aligned with maternal functions that middle-class Edwardians like McNabb himself would have accepted as normative. The norm, however, was metropolitan. Its applicability in a colonial context was complicated by the agendas of altering the nature of the native prince, which required that mothers be displaced by white, male guardians like McNabb.

It is this displacement, with its emotional and political ramifications, that led Asha Bibi to protest the colonial government's seizure of Mohabat Khan. It is not surprising that she chose to highlight the moral dangers that awaited her son, since she was protesting in the acceptably maternal roles of moral guardian and social conservative. The invocation of moral jeopardy provided native parents of both sexes, but particularly mothers, with a language in which they might attack British intervention in the Indian family, and this language was more familiar and even acceptable to the British audiences, than it was alien or bizarre.

Conclusion

Indian anxieties about the education of princely children, like British anxieties, revolved around the familiar specter of the educated native who had gone out of control in the colonial theater. The specific fears, however, were different from those of British educators. Whereas the British were concerned that English-educated princes had come too close to England for comfort, Indian critics condemned as deracinated those princes who had apparently remained too distant from India. There is no doubt that 'India' was a political position to be asserted and defended against England in a contest in which morality served as the ammunition, rather than as the target itself. This is evident in an editorial which appeared in the *Bombay Chronicle* as late as 1920:

> The kind of education — or miseducation, which the Indian Princes receive nowadays — is responsible for their disorientation, or distortion. In the colleges where they are sent, what do they learn? Are they taught there the history of their country or family from the proper point of view? Do they even learn the Indian languages — including their own mother tongues — properly there? Alas, no! They only aspire to become intellectual and moral *Eurasians* of the lowest order, and thereby lose their true individualities.[112] [Emphasis in original]

This too was a pitfall of emulation. Colonial education could be viewed by Indian critics as the mechanism of moral downfall even as it was understood that the content of this education was necessary for national revitalization. The apparent inconsistency did not depend upon any fundamental ideological division between proponents and opponents of this training. Both accepted the assumptions about race, gender and 'enlightened' political behavior that underlay this education. All sides in the debate — Indian and British enthusiasts, Indian and British skeptics, the princes themselves — saw re-educated princes as a resource in Indian and imperial society. The anxiety over deracination hinged, rather, on the question of who might control the terms and the location of education, and even more so, the question of who might control the behaviour and affiliation of the educated. English education appeared illegitimate when it was seen as an arbitrary British intervention in Indian society, geared to capture young Indian men from their families, race and nation. The deracinated prince was not somebody who had received the wrong education. Rather, he was a man who had received the right education in the wrong setting. He was a powerful symbol of Indian self-assertion as well as of Britain's colonial mission, who had failed to identify himself with — and limit himself to — the right group in the politics of empire.

CONCLUSION

Liberal-utilitarian projects in colonial India were not based solely on the optimistic assumption that modern metropolitan strategies of intervention in the societies, bodies, minds and habits of undisciplined populations would produce modifications that were desirable to the colonizer. In the case of the child-correction project, we find that the optimism was accompanied from the outset by serious doubts about whether modifications could be induced in even the 'softest' of all native populations. As experiments with reformatories for juvenile delinquents and boarding schools for savage princelings continued into the twentieth century, these doubts accumulated into a pervasive sense of failure. This, in itself, is not surprising. It is overwhelmingly established in the post-Foucauldian historiography that disciplinary strategies rarely worked as expected, either in the peripheral space of the colony, or in the enclaves of juridical power within the metropole. Much of the time in India, reformatories and boarding schools, like prisons and hospitals, did not produce a discernible modification; they were, therefore, 'failures'. Colonial disciplinary institutions, from this familiar perspective, were defeated by the resistance of inmates, the autonomy of their native staff, the apathy or hostility of the wider society of natives, and the British need to negotiate constantly with inmates, staff and outsiders.

The appearance of a defeated discipline is, however, misleading; there are other ways of reading the dysfunctional colonial institution. One is to use the 'rock / water' analogy that Sudipta Kaviraj has used to describe the interplay between strategy and tactics in the politics of marginal urban populations.[1] In this analogy, the rock of strategy (such as the police force or the prison) is surrounded, eroded and ultimately reshaped by the swirling, fluctuating waters of subaltern tactics. The colonial school for princely children and the reformatory can both be seen in this light, as strategies for the molding of colonized children, that were themselves molded by the tactics of the colonized — by the habits of habitual offenders, the dirtiness of musahibs, the effeteness of Rajputs, the sexual experiments in the dormitories and wards, the interference of mothers and the indifference of fathers. They are molded, eventually, by the ambitions and agendas of Indian modernizers, who usurp some of their strategic functions even as they tactically criticize other strategies, converting institutionalized children into representatives of a larger colonized population that included the Indian expert, and colonial institutions into signifiers of an unacceptable gap between the modernity of the metropole and the primitive state of the colony.

The juvenile institution is partially decolonized, therefore, when the strategists become tacticians, locating themselves — however contingently and metaphorically — within as well as without the experiment. We see this process most clearly with the reformatory, where an increasingly assertive group of Indian observers seeks to insert itself simultaneously into the community of incarcerated 'children' as well the community of incarcerating 'adults'. In the years after the First World War, the reformatory is transformed by their tactics — not completely or consistently, but significantly enough. The Indian expert in the colonial reformatory shifts the focus of the experiment from the undisciplined inmate to the practice of discipline in a colonial institution, identifying the latter (and implicitly, its patron regime) as the proper object of reform. We see it also in the case of princely education, in which the pedagogical project is both supported and criticized by Indians, who see themselves reflected in the eyes of the deracinated and colonized students but also in those of the teachers of a discipline that might sustain the strategies of nationhood.

A second way of interpreting the colonial juvenile institution is to acknowledge that the apparent 'failure' of attempts to modify the nature of the native in fact constituted a successful project. The gap between the metropolitan model and colonial practice that Indian observers perceived and regretted was not accidental; nor was it merely the consequence of tactics of resistance or negotiation. It was a feature of the design of the peripheral institution that was required to produce evidence of its own experimental status. Divergence from institutional ideals, be it Mettray or Eton, was crucially important not only to the expertise of the administrators and exponents of colonial child-correction, but also to the authority of the larger project of colonialism. The reformatory and the Chiefs' College existed, not so much to reform the native child, as to produce a child that was beyond reform.

Since the metropolitan model of childhood emphasized the element of plasticity, to be beyond reform was also to be beyond childhood. The colonial institution for native children was thus deeply self-contradictory: it produced native children by identifying, ordering and describing a juvenile population, but it also implied that this population was not childlike. It produced this failure as a 'deviance' in the context of the reformatory, but it constantly implied that this deviance was in fact normative within the broader context of native natures. By doing so, it highlighted a set of metropolitan constructions of childhood, adulthood and nature, positioned these at the centre of a political, moral, familial and institutional modernity, and consigned natives of all ages to the margins. If the native child was not truly a child, then the native adult could not be a true adult — not only because he had misconceived the flawed child, but also because he was the culmination of a flawed childhood. The peripheral location of the colonial juvenile institution — which might be described as the distance between Eton and Mayo, or Mettray and Chingleput — was thus produced continuously by institutional practice. It gave the colonial expert his authority and simultaneously denied the possibility of authority and adulthood to natives of all ages.

NOTES

Introduction

1 Cohn, 1997, 5.
2 Cunningham, 1995, 134–62.
3 Marriott, 2003, 41–56.
4 Sen, 2004a, 5:2.
5 Eisenstadt, 2002, 1–29.
6 Cunningham, 1995, 189–90.
7 It is useful to recall Mill, 'It is in the case of children, that misapplied notions of liberty are a real obstacle to the fulfillment by the State of its duties.' Mill, 1947, 107. Thapar has indicated that romantic and liberal visions of the 'child' overlapped significantly, with the former perceiving a naturally childlike quality in the native, and the latter something unnaturally childish. Thapar, 1999, 200–19.
8 For a typical study, see Gillis, 1974, *passim*. Cunningham, Aries and DeMause do not touch upon colonial developments at all. Walvin makes some connections between English childhood and the history of white settler colonies, but the non-white empire does not feature in his analysis. Walvin, 1982, 149–58. Garland also refuses to venture east of Suez, and is unconcerned by the convergences and divergences between metropolitan and colonial child-correction regimes even as the content of his study cries out for such comparisons. Garland, 1985.
9 Dawson, 1994, 84–114, 223–40; Springhall, 1977, 111–20.
10 Springhall, 1977, 111. See also Hall, 1904, *ix–xi*.
11 On the fragility of imperial oppositions, see Cooper and Stoler, in Cooper and Stoler (eds), 1997, 3, 8.
12 Nandy, 1983 and 1992; Kakar, 1981.
13 Kakar, 1981, 2–8.
14 Chatterjee, 1995; Kumar, 2000; Maskiell, 1984; Lelyveld, 1996; Metcalf, 1982; Whitehead, 2003; Viswanathan, 1987.
15 Viswanathan, 1987, 11–22.
16 Lelyveld, 1996, 128–56, 265.
17 Maskiell, however, highlights the cautious and piecemeal nature of these early experiments. Maskiell, 1984, 1, 4, 11–14.
18 Dirks, in Cohn (ed.), 1997, *xv*.
19 Sarkar, 2001; Chakrabarty, in Cooper and Stoler (eds), 1997, 373–405; Grewal, 1996.
20 Sarkar, 2001, 191–225; Sinha, 1995, 138–80.
21 Nandy, 1983,15–6; 1992, 56–7.
22 Chatterjee, in Sangari and Vaid, (eds), 1990, 233–53.

23 Bhabha, in Cooper and Stoler (eds), 1997, 152–62.
24 Chatterjee, 1993, 5–6, 116–34.
25 Behlmer, 1998, 1; Anderson, 1983, 6.
26 Beisel, 1997, 202–14.
27 Dirks, 1987; Price, 1996; Ramusack, in Breckenridge (ed.), 1996; Ramusack, 1978; McLeod, 1999; Copland, 1997; Bhagwan, 2003; Sen, 2004b.
28 Rudolph, Rudolph and Kanota, 2001; Bhagwan, 2003, 1–31.
29 Sreenivasan, in Chatterjee (ed.), 2003, 47; Guha, in Chatterjee (ed.), 2003, 73–94.
30 Nasaw, 1979, 99–100.
31 Banerjee, 2004, Paper presented, 15 October; Sen, 2004a.
32 Prakash, 1999, 5–7.
33 Joshi, 2001, 1–10.
34 Chatterjee, 1986, 43–50.
35 Elias, 1978, 141; Aries, 1962, 33–49; Nandy, 1992, 59–62.
36 Elias, 1978, 73–4.
37 DeMause, 1974, 3–4.
38 *Ibid*, 6–10.
39 Cunningham, 1995, 189–90.
40 *Ibid*.
41 Sandner, 1996, 67–81, 143–4.
42 Stokes, 1959; Metcalf, 1995.
43 Foucault, 1979.
44 Levine, 1996, 55:3, 587–89; Singha, 1998, 168–228.
45 Sen, 2000; Mills, 2000; Anderson, 2000.
46 See Donzelot, 1979, 108–10. For critiques of Donzelot and Foucault, see Behlmer, 1983, 26–7, and Ignatieff, in Cohen and Scull (eds), 1983, 98.
47 Arnold, in Arnold and Hardiman (eds), 1994, 148–87; Anderson, 2004, 15–16.

1. State of the Experiment: Experts, Parents and the Reformatory

1 HJ, June 1875, 107–12.
2 Barton, 2004.
3 On the negotiated character of Macaulayan law in India, see Singha, 1998, 119–20.
4 Fitzpatrick, in Coleborne and Kirkby (eds), 2001, 11–22.
5 Marriott, 2003, 4, 15–21; Cohn, 1997, 4.
6 The metropolitan precedents of these claims might be identified in the 'Children's Charter' passed by Parliament in 1889, and contemporary French legislation. In Britain, however, the state eschewed financial responsibility for the actual protection of the rights of the child, leaving the responsibility to civil society. See Behlmer, G, 1982, 109–10.
7 Chatterjee, Sangari and Vaid (eds), 1990, 233–53.
8 Garland, 1985, 76.
9 Ignatieff, 1978, 5–26; Sen, 2000b, 131–4; Mills, 2000, 29–30.
10 Pr. NWP&O, 21 March 1889, 612-VI-40B.
11 On Napier's role in articulating an imperial architecture for India, see Metcalf, 1989, 34–6, 57–8.
12 President's Minute, 3 November 1867, HJ 4.4.1868, 4D-4F.
13 *Ibid*.

14 Dirks, 2001, 43–60.
15 President's Minute, 3 November 1867.
16 *Ibid.*
17 *Ibid.*
18 Ballhatchet, 1980, 96–122.
19 HJ 4 April 1868, 4D–4F.
20 RJLPBP, 1867, HJPr, 1868.
21 Edgerton, F W, to Thorburn, S S, 15 May.1896, LDPr, 3.1897, 87–136.
22 RJLPBP, 1867, HJPr, 1868.
23 *Ibid.*
24 ARRS Alipore, 1882.
25 President's Minute, 3 November 1867
26 Lyall, A C, to Viceroy, 2 September 1874, HJ, 1.1875, 130–2.
27 RCTJDB, 1928.
28 *Ibid.*
29 Walkowitz, 1992, 41–80; Baker, in DuBois, and Ruiz (eds), 1990, 66–91.
30 Sargant, 1987, 11–27; Burton, 1998, 34–8.
31 Ghose, 1998, 107–26; Strobel, 1991, 49–71.
32 Carpenter, 1967, 1–22.
33 *Edinburgh Courant*, 15 October 1867.
34 Sen, 2002a, 39:4, 417–38.
35 HJ 18 January 1868, 21–2; 9 January 1869, 55–72.
36 *Ibid.* Well into the twentieth century, reformatory administrators clung to this theory to explain why few released children actually took up the occupations they had learned in the institution.
37 HJ, 18 January 1858, 19.
38 Brandt, F, to Madras, 15 August 1867, HJ 4 April 1868, 4D–4F.
39 HJ 4 April 1896, 4D–4F; RJLPBP, HJPr, 1868.
40 JJDI, HJ 9 January 1869, 49.
41 HJPr, 1868.
42 It was only in 1922 that the Indian Jails Committee recommended that while probation officers should ideally be officers of the state, 'private individuals may also be recognized'. HJ, 1922.
43 Act XIX (1850) of the Criminal Procedure Code allowed magistrates to 'apprentice' children under the age of fifteen, instead of sending them to jail. The practice was not uniquely Indian. On similar schemes with 'neglected' children in America, see Nasaw, 1979, 10. In England, apprenticeship was common as an arrangement for destitute children and, until mid-nineteenth-century changes in the labor market, a (contentious) mechanism of transmitting economic skills. It was also a factor in the assessment of 'life cycles', marking a set of boundaries for childhood Kirby, 2003, 10, 60–8.
44 HE, 2 February 1858, 1–2.
45 HE, 31 November 1863, 20–2.
46 Carpenter, 1868, 180–1.
47 *Ibid.*
48 The idea that some native parents viewed the reformatory as a shelter from monetary and corporal punishment or as a free boarding house for children was frequently expressed by colonial administrators. In 1864, the Committee on Jails and Jail Discipline used its fear of such 'subterfuge' to justify its preference for the whipping post over the

reformatory; HJ, 23 June 1864, 47–51. However, some officials, such as Richard Temple in Bengal, believed that Indian parents were too devoted to their children to resort to such opportunism, and this conviction was instrumental in the passage of the RS Act of 1876. Bengal to GOI, 11 November 1875, HJ, 6.1877, 303–17.

49 Mills, 2000, 132–44. For examples of such appropriation and negotiatior in a colonial African context, see weitzberg, 2005.
50 Foucault, 1979, 234. Garland disagrees, arguing that while mid-Victorian reformism was merely corrective and infrastructural, late-Victorian Europe witnessed disillusionment with the prison itself. Garland, 1985, 59–60. Such a shift is not evident in India, where doubts about the efficacy of incarceration can be found at the very origins of the reformatory. Indian professionals in the twentieth century demanded better prisons, not an end to imprisonment.
51 Mitter, O N, to Larymore, A D, 13 June 1896, LDPr.
52 Comins, D W D, to Bengal, 13 June 1896, LDPr.
53 HP, 23 April 1858, 43.
54 *Ibid.*
55 Larymore, A D, to Bengal, 8 June 1897, LDPr.
56 Metcalf, 1995, 203–13.
57 ARRS Hazaribagh, 1885.
58 ARRS Chingleput, 1892.
59 *Ibid.*
60 *Ibid.*
61 *Ibid.*
62 The officiating superintendent at the Jubbulpore Reformatory in 1899 was U Sen. Jaideo Dixit officiated in 1903 when P M Greany was on leave. ARRS Jubbulpore, 1899–1909.
63 Bishumber Nath, 6 January 1897, LDPr.
64 Nihal-ud-Din Ahmed to NWP&O, 14 June 1896.
65 Napier had observed: 'Religious teaching in connection with the superstitions of India, is, of course, out of the question, and…moral teaching loses much of its force when not associated with the influences of Christianity.' President's Minute, 3 Novmeber 1867. See also the remarks of Bayley, E C, and Phillips, H D, HJ 4 April 1868, 4D–4F. In Nihah-ud-Din's time, Indian 'superstitions' were no longer out of the question, whereas Christianity had become even less viable than previously. As late as the 1920s, however, reformatory administrators in Assam felt that missionaries were under-utilized as surrogate parents for delinquent children, who, if reformed, might make good tea-plantation workers. HJ 1922, 280.
66 Dayaram Gidumal to Judicial Dept, Bombay, 27 May 1896, LDPr.
67 Johnston, R L, to Judicial Dept, Bombay, 4 June 1896.
68 McLane, 1977, 332–57; Rosselli, 1980, 121–48.
69 Kirby, 2003, 74; Gillis, 1974, 141–55; Haley, 1978, 141–60.
70 ARRS Hazaribagh, 1893.
71 *Ibid.*
72 Westmacott, E V, to Political Dept, Bengal, 23 May 1885.
73 ARRS Hazaribagh, 1897.
74 Viswanathan, 1987, 11–22.
75 Wiener, 1991, 5–6.
76 For critiques of caste, *'homo hierarchicus'* and the idea of a culturally sabotaged modernity, see Dirks, 2001, 19–42; Beteille, 1992, 15–58; van der Veer, in Breckenridge and van der Veer, (eds), 2002, 23–44; Eisenstadt, 2002, 1–29.

77 Panikkar, 2001, 2–9.
78 Mitter, O N, to Larymore, A D, 13 June 1896.
79 Obbard, R, to Commissioner of Hyderabad Assigned Districts, 5 June 1896, LDPr.
80 Chief Commissioner of Burma to Legislative Dept, 21 July 1896, LDPr.
81 RIJC, HJails 1922. On the English Children Act, see Behlmer, G, 1982, 220–2.
82 HJails, Madras Children (Amendment) Act, 1928.
83 HPolitical, 20 May 1932.
84 Section 3, Bengal Borstal Schools Act, 1928, HJ 1928.
85 *Ibid*.
86 *Ibid*, Sections 11 and 13.
87 Fox, 1952, 352–91
88 Minutes of Raja Kshaunish Chandra Ray, Bengal Legislative Council Pr, 23–4 August 1927, HJails, 1928.
89 Minutes of Kshaunish Chandra Ray.
90 *Ibid*.
91 Minutes of Campbell Forrester, J, Bengal Legislative Council Pr, 23–4 August 1927, HJails 1928.
92 Minutes of Raja Bhupendra Narayan Sinha, Bengal Legislative Council Pr, 23–4 August 1927, HJails 1928.
93 Sarkar, 1973, 39.
94 Joshi, 2001, 1–6, Hasan, 2004, 142, 152. Hasan has noted, a more upper-class context, Muhammad Ali's fascination with the work of Havelock Ellis.
95 Minutes of Babu Bijoy Krishna Bose, Bengal Legislative Council Pr, 23–4 August 1927, HJails 1928.
96 Minutes of Babu Jogindra Chandra Chakravarti, Bengal Legislative Council Pr, 23–4 August 1927, HJails, 1928.
97 Minutes of Kshaunish Chandra Ray,
98 Bengal Legislative Council Pr, 23–4 August 1927, HJails 1928.
99 Minutes of Tambe, S B, 15 December 1926, Central Provinces Legislature Pr, HJails 1928.
100 ARRS Chingleput, 1898.
101 Elias, 1978, 53, 140.
102 On the Jabbalpur school, see HPolice, 21 October 1863, 13–19A. On thuggee, see van Woerkens, 2002. For a critique of van Woerken, see Sen, 2004c, 72:2, 566.
103 HE, 25 November 1859, 1–3.
104 *Ibid*.
105 HEcc, 19 June 1861, 1–3; HEcc, 27 March 1862, 11–3; HP, 4 December 1861, 4–9; HP, 25 February 1863, 45–6; HEcc, 29 April 1859, 1–3. The proximity between mission-operated 'orphanages' and 'industrial schools' has been noted by Cox, who points out that orphans were accessible to missionaries when other unfortunates, such as widows, generated an uncomfortable scrutiny of moral and political motives. Cox does not, however, suggest that the idea of the orphan might be a tactical maneuver to produce that access. Cox, 2002, 163–5.
106 The Midnapore school was in the charge of Bhoobunmohan Banerjea; the supporting staff were also Indians. HE, 25 November 1859, 1–3.
107 HP, 5 March 1863, 1–2.
108 The missionaries liked what they discovered. African children were judged to be 'born to hard labour', athletic, 'sympathetic and docile' without being 'cleverly precocious' like Hindu children, 'sincere' and 'affectionate' without 'the servility of the natives of

this country', 'wild and shy but apparently tameable'. Much attention was paid to facial features ('their eyes were moist and quick-glancing, like the eyes of wild animals'), musculature, hair, singing ability, etc. The younger children were generally considered more bestial than the older ones; the young/bestial were seen as the most interesting, whereas the older children were regarded as satisfying signs of successful reform. HEcc, 29 April 1859, 1–3.
109 Sen, in Mills and Sen (eds), 2004, 58–79.
110 The colonial government remained skeptical of non-Christian attempts to establish reforming orphanages. In the 1920s, it refused official recognition to the Masjid Madrasa Rounaq Islam school and 'orphanage' in Rangoon (managed by Syed Yousuf Ali), even as it recognized and aided 'orphanages' run by the Salvation Army. Syed Yousuf Ali's application, the prison reform committee's recommendation and the Burma government's decision all show that the creation and reform of native orphans was, among other things, a gesture towards the racial identity of children and putative parents. RCTJDB. The Salvation Army also ran camps for Criminal Tribes in this period. See Tolen, 1991, 18:1, 106.
111 The Lawrence Asylum was founded in 1856 on Henry Lawrence's initiative, with an initial grant of Rs. 10,000 and subsequent support from the colonial government once the Home Department was convinced of the 'efficiency' of the institution. After receiving the inmates of an earlier orphanage in Kidderpore, the Lawrence Asylum came to house nearly seven hundred children, making it one of the largest quasi-reformatory institutions in the history of colonial India. HE, 19 February 1858, 1.
112 Ballhatchet, 1980, 123–4.
113 Nandy, 1983, 64–79.
114 HE, 9 March 1874; BPrC, 1874.
115 *Ibid.*
116 *Ibid.*
117 Bayley, E C, to Ellis, 3 April 1868, HJ, 4 April 1868, 4D–4F.
118 Lord Napier, 3 November 1867, HJ, 4 April 1868, 4D–4F.
119 Howell, Jails and Jail Discipline in India, HJ, 9 January, 1869, 49.
120 Bengal to GOI, 11 November 1875, HJ, June 1877, 303–17.
121 *Ibid.*
122 Aikman, R S, to NWP&O, 31 January 1890, LDPr.
123 Handley, F F, to Larymore, A D, 5 June 1876, LDPr.
124 LDPr, March 1897, 87–136.
125 Behlmer, 1982, 235–8.
126 RJP, 1871.
127 Central Provinces Children Act (Act X, 1928), HJails, 1928.
128 *Ibid.*
129 *Ibid.*
130 *Ibid.*
131 See Chapter Two.
132 Anderson, 2004, 4, 7.
133 ARBPAA, 1938; ARRS Dharwar Borstal School, 1935–8.
134 In Bombay in 1938, the CT Act was used against a Bhil boy who repeatedly violated the territorial restrictions of his Borstal license, and who had 'enticed away a woman'. D A Dhruva, who filed the report, did not see the offense as reflecting a communal norm, instead blaming 'difficulties in the [boy's] home'. *Ibid.*

135 Howell, A, to Bengal, 16 December 1874, HJ, January 1875, 130–2.
136 Mackintosh, J S, to NWP&O, 27 June 1896, LDPr.
137 Gray, P, to NWP&O, 3 June 1896; Bird, H M, to NWP&O, 4 July 1896; Hooper, J, to NWP&O, 22 July 1896, LDPr.
138 Trethewy, A W, to NWP&O, 10 July 1896, LDPr.
139 'Gopal' and 'rakhal' are imaginings of the cow-herding child-God, Krishna, the former benign and domesticated, the latter wild. Bandyopadhyay, 1991, *x*.
140 Sen, 2004a.
141 Spivak, in Breckenridge and van der Veer (eds), 1993, 134–57; Mee, 2003, in Tabish Khair (ed.), 90–108.
142 Mackintosh, J S, to NWP&O, 27 June 1896.
143 In the Bareilly reformatory in 1890, administrators experimented with schemes in which children wrote letters to their (typically illiterate) parents, and occasionally met with them. Letters and meetings were both monitored by the superintendent, and it is worth noting that the meetings were held not at the family home, but in the nearest district jail. Muhammad Tajummul Husain ('native visitor' to Bareilly Reformatory) to Redfern, T R (Sessions Judge, Bareilly), 6 February 1890, LDPr.
144 ARRS Bareilly, 1890.
145 There was not universal — Bayley, predictably, was hostile to the idea that large numbers of native children existed in a vacuum of moral guidance and emotional sustenance within their families. Criminalized natives, Bayley believed, could be recognizably good parents. He meant that they were instructive parents within their own moral universe, and there is in Bayley's position an implication that this universe was not so exotic as to be incomprehensible to the British. Bayley, E C, to Ellis, R S, 3 April 1868, HJ, 4 April 1868, 4D–4F.
146 Gordon, J D, to Chief Commissioner of Mysore, 5 September 1876, HJ, June 1877, 303–17.
147 Bengal to GOI, 25 August 1896, LDPr.
148 Prison administrators in Burma in 1928 concentrated on 'children, principally in the large towns, who have parents unable or unwilling to control them or no parents at all, and who are leading a precarious life on the brink of the abyss of crime'. RCTJDB
149 Lyall, A C, to Viceroy, 27 July 1874, HJ, January 1875, 130–2.
150 ARRS Chingleput, 1892.
151 *Ibid.*
152 RCTJDB. The committee was headed by Justice W Carr, and included F B Leach, the Commissioner of Pegu, and J S Morris, the Superintendent of Therrawaddy Jail, M S Merrikin, the Police Commissioner of Rangoon, and F G French, the headmaster of the Government High School in Rangoon. It also included P K Tarapore (IMS and the IG-Prisons, Burma), and U Ba Kin, the Deputy Commissioner of Hanthawaddy.
153 ARBPAA, Dharwar, 1937–45.
154 Behlmer, 1982, 230–71.
155 Probation officers often arranged the marriages of their wards, to the fury of parents. ARBPAA, Dharwar, 1937–1945.
156 RCTJDB.
157 ARBPAA, Dharwar, 1939.
158 Metcalf, 1995, 28–65.

2. The Nature of the Beast: The Content of Institutionalized Childhood

1 Nasaw, 1979, 7.
2 Bates, in Robb (ed.), 1995, 219–59.
3 Foucault, 1979, 257–92.
4 ARBPAA, 1938.
5 Heeley, W L, Mackenzie, S C and Lambert, J, Report on reformatories, HJ, June 1875, 107–12.
6 LDPr, March 1897, 87–136.
7 HJ, June 1875, 107–12.
8 Harvey James, S, 14 August 1894, LDPr, March 1897, 87–136.
9 Miller, A E, August 1894, LDPr, March 1897, 87–136.
10 Chief Commissioner of Burma to Legislative Department, 21 July 1896, LDPr, March 1897, 87–136, deliberations on Act VIII of 1897, to amend the Reformatory Schools Act (Act V of 1876).
11 Duncan, J, to Madras, 1 June 1896, LDPr.
12 HJails, 1922.
13 HE, 25 November 1859, 1–3.
14 NWP&O to GOI, 18 November 1876, HJ, June 1877, 303–17.
15 In 1908, C E Hill, the Director of Public Instruction in the Central Provinces, expressed his surprise that reformatory populations had remained stable in a period of economic hardship. This was an extremely unusual observation. Even in the days of the 'famine orphan', material deprivation was seen as a factor in the criminalization of adults, but not of children. Hill, C E, to Education and Medical Department, Central Provinces, 19 March 1908, ARRS Jubbulpore, 1908.
16 Sen, 2000, 48–54.
17 *Ibid*, 42–8; Freitag, in Yang, Anand (ed.), 1985, 141–5; Radhakrishna, 2001, 1–12.
18 This could be rather literal; the Salvation Army, which ran several concentration camps for the CTs, was eager to 'bring up little boys bubbling with crime…in an atmosphere of agriculture', Radhakrishna, 2001, 99. See also Tolen, 1991, 18:1, 106.
19 Lyall, A C, 27 July 1874, HJ, January 1875, 130–2.
20 Bayley, E C, 28 July 1874, HJ, January 1875, 130–2.
21 Cowlishaw, 1988, 80–1.
22 Chatterjee, 1997, 11.
23 Edgerton, F W, to Thorburn, S S, 15 May 1896, LDPr.
24 Metcalf, 1995, 6–15, 24–7.
25 ARRS Hazaribagh, 1885.
26 Greeven, R, to NWP&O, 18 June 1896, LDPr.
27 ARRS Chingleput, 1891–92.
28 In Punjab, the maximum term for CT children in the reformatory was seven years. Other children could be held for five years. Pr. LGP, HJails, 27 May 1907; see also ARRS Delhi, 1905–07.
29 Garland, 1985, 61.
30 Gordon, J D, to Commissioner of Mysore, 5 September 1876, HJ, June 1877, 303–17.
31 Apart from the CT, the English 'street Arab' provided a second precedent for the habitual juvenile offender that emerged in the Indian reformatory and Gordon had no qualms about making the connection explicit. This did not, however, establish a

common 'bad nature' that transcends race, because the English Arab is an internal exotic. The street Arab provided an English handle by which the English observer might grasp the Indian child, just as 'Arab' provided the Oriental handle for the English delinquent. On street Arabs, see Carpenter, 1868, 193.
32 ARRS Chingleput, 1892.
33 ARRS, Delhi, 1906.
34 On prison dress, see Anderson, 2004, 101–40; on clothes and colonialism generally, see Cohn, 1997; Yegenoglu, 1998, 95–120.
35 Sanders-Slater, J, to Judicial Dept, Bombay, 8 June 1896, LDPr; ARRS Chingleput, 1891–92, 1905.
36 RCTJDB.
37 Minutes of Richard Temple, 11 March 1875, HJ, June 1875, 107–12.
38 Wullschlager, 1995, 12–13.
39 Lyall, A C to Baring, E, 2 September 1874, HJ, January 1875, 130–2.
40 RJLPBP, 1867, HJ Pr, 1868.
41 Greeven, R, to NWP&O, 18 June 1896, LDPr.
42 *Ibid.*
43 Kennedy, T J, to Chief Court of Punjab, 20 April 1896, LDPr.
44 Nasaw, 1979, 99–100.
45 HJails, 1922.
46 *Ibid.*
47 Lord Napier, President's Minute, 3 November 1867, HJ, 4 April 1868, 4D–4F.
48 Lyall, A C, to Baring, 2 September 1874.
49 RJLPBP, 1867.
50 The Home Department noted that NWP&O objected to the existing definition of 'youthful offender' because it excluded boys between seven and twelve years of age who had been acquitted under Section 83 of the Indian Penal Code, which blocked convictions on grounds of 'immature understanding'. NWP&O wanted to lock them up anyway, using the RS Act. LDPr, 1897.
51 RJLPBP, 1867.
52 Burma to GOI, HJails, 1922.
53 Brander, W B, to GOI, 10 February 1922, HJails, 1922.
54 Heeley, W L, Mackenzie, S C and Lambert, J, Report on reformatories, HJ, June 1875.
55 *Ibid.*
56 Kirschner, J G, ARRS Alipore, 1880.
57 Court of the Judicial Commissioner to the Commissioner of Central Provinces, 7 April 1890, LDPr 1897.
58 ARRS Alipore, 1880.
59 Fox, C E, to Burma, 3 October 1892, LDPr 1897.
60 Lynch wrote in 1867, 'The diet of the children, whose ages ranged from eight years to sixteen years, had, prior to their separation, been that of adults — an alteration was made by reducing the quantity of rice from ten chittacks to six chittacks, and of dal from two chittacks to one chittack.' RJLPBP, 1867, HJ Pr, 1868.
61 LDPr, March 1897.
62 *Ibid.*
63 Pitcher, D G, to NWP&O, 27 January 1890, LDPr, March 1897.
64 Fulton, E M H, to Legislative Dept, 18 May 1892, LDPr, March 1897.
65 LDPr, March 1897.

66 Gillis, 1974, 55–61; Cunningham, 1995, 163–85.
67 HJails, 1922.
68 The British committee of 1842 defined those below thirteen as 'children', and those between thirteen and eighteen as 'young persons'. Kirby, 2003, 20 (n. 5).
69 Under the central government's plan for famine orphans, each child would receive an allowance of Rs. 50 per annum until they were eighteen, and then a golden handshake of Rs. 30. All eight hundred and seventy children covered by the plan were under twelve years old at the time; the average age was seven. HP, 25 February 1863, 45–6.
70 Minutes of Kshaunish Chandra Ray, Bengal Legislative Council, 23–24 August 1927, HJails 1928.
71 Central Provinces Children Act, 1928, HJails, 1928.
72 Sarkar, 2001, 191–225; Sinha, 1995, 138–80.
73 The specific issue was the amendment of Section 373 of the Indian Penal Code, which prohibited trafficking in minors. This required redefining a minor to mean a person under sixteen, as opposed to one under eighteen.
74 HJ, January 1875, 48–67.
75 Elliot, C A, to Bayley, E C, 29 April 1872, HJ, January 1875, 48–67.
76 Mangles, R L, internal memo of the Mysore Commissioner's office, 22 April 1872, HJ, January 1875.
77 Foucault, 1990, 17–35.
78 Fytche, A, Chief Commissioner of British Burma, Memo on Prison Administration for 1869–70, HJ, 4 March 1871, 10.
79 RJLPBP, 1867; HJ Pr, 1868.
80 Kirschner, J G, ARRS Alipore, 1879.
81 Horn, 1997, 181.
82 Nandy, 1983, 64–79.
83 Heeley, W L, Mackenzie, S C and Lambert, J, Report on reformatories, HJ June 1875.
84 The NWP&O rules were drawn up by Dr Mair, the superintendent of Bareilly Central Prison and District Jail. LDPr, March 1897.
85 Duncan, D, to Madras, 1 June 1896, LDPr.
86 Central Provinces Children Act, HJails, 1928. Act X also made it a crime to 'encourage' a female under sixteen to have sex with anybody other than her husband or associate with a prostitute or 'person of known immoral character'. Sex with husbands was always 'legitimate', automatically rendering girls both consenting and adult, but sex with other men always illegitimate, turning girls into victims, children or whores.
87 Hall, 1904, *ix–xi*.
88 Kakar, 1981, 69–71.
89 ARRS Alipore, 1878.
90 ARRS Alipore, 1881.
91 IG Jails, Lower Provinces, to Bengal, 30 September 1876, HJ, June 1877, 303–17.
92 Bengal to GOI, 11 November 1875, HJ, June 1877.
93 LDPr, March 1897.
94 United Provinces to GOI, 15 February 1922, HJails, 1922.
95 RIJC, HJails, 1922.
96 One Calcutta newspaper had editorialized, 'Both mind and body are fully developed in this country on the attainment of the eighteenth year. It is not proper to keep them in a state of tutelage, especially the married ones, after that period.' *Amrita Bazar Patrika*, 1 July 1875, NNR Bengal.

97 The Madras Children (Amendment) Act, HJails, 1928.
98 Burma to GOI, HJails, 1922.
99 ARRS Madras Presidency, 1939.
100 Nasaw, 1979, 88.
101 Bose, 2003, 5.
102 Garland, 1985, 82–4.
103 Chatterjee, 1986, 38.
104 Central Provinces Act IX of 1928 allowed Borstal administrators to send 'incorrigible' adolescents to the adult jail. HJails, 1928.
105 Radhakrishna, 2001, 5.
106 HPolice, 21 October 1863, 13–9.
107 RJLPBP, 1867.
108 Calcutta High Court to GOI, 14 July 1896, LDPr.
109 Duncan to Madras, 1 June 1896, LDPr.
110 ARRS Chingleput, 1891–92.
111 ARRS Chingleput, 1895.
112 Anderson, 2004, 163–6, 183–9; Springhall, 1977, 110–20.
113 Burma to GOI, HJails, 1922.
114 Minutes of Campbell Forrester, J, HJails, 1928.
115 *Ibid.*
116 Dirks, 2001, 213–5; Bates, in Robb, (ed.), 1995, 219–59; Anderson, 2004, 181–202
117 ARRS Chingleput, 1898–99. Murderers were uncommon within the colonial reformatory (most were sent to jail), but the 'progress' of the few that were present was followed with great interest by reformatory administrators.
118 HE, 25 November 1859, 1–3.
119 See RCTJDB.
120 Bengal to GOI, 25 August 1896, LDPr.
121 ARRS Chingleput, 1902–1905. H Thomson, the acting superintendent in 1902, observed that 'a high rate of crime is the result of a densely aggregated population, which produces a weak and ineffective people, and a juvenile in this position is always tempted to enter upon a criminal career'. His successor in 1905 complained, 'These boys come to us full of the vice and cunningness of city life, and their large numbers in the school help to keep alive the memory and associations of the past.'
122 Bhupendra Narayan Sinha, HJails, 1928.
123 Contractor, S C, to Madras, 26 April 1940, ARRS Madras Presidency, 1940.
124 *Ibid.*
125 Middleton, 1998, 30–1.
126 Kakar, 1981, 2–8.
127 Hartnack, 2001, 1–5.
128 *Ibid*, 128.
129 ARBPAA, 1945–46.
130 President's Minute, 3 November 1867.
131 Howell, A, JJDI, HJ, 9 January 1869, 49.
132 Comins, D W D, to Bengal, 13 June 1896, LDPr.
133 Larymore, A D, to Bengal, 8 June 1897, LDPr.
134 ARRS Chingleput, 1898.
135 RCTJDB.

3. Experimental Childhoods: Pain and the Reformatory

1. RIPP, 1853.
2. Arnold, in Arnold and Hardiman (eds), 1994, 148–87; Ernst, 1991, 164–73; Ernst, in Harrison, and Pati (eds), 2001, 137–64.
3. Bentham, 1995, 85–6.
4. Ignatieff, 1978, 5–26.
5. Walvin, 1982, 44–7, 56–60.
6. Behlmer, 1982, 197. Behlmer points out that these conversations took place in the context of a diminished tolerance for the violent treatment of children.
7. HJ 23 April 1864, 47–51.
8. Zinoman, 2001, 50n, 208.
9. RIPP, 1873.
10. Acceptance and resistance are both evident in the Punjab government's hesitant move to fund the institutionalization of famine 'orphans' in 1861–62. The link between orphans and juvenile delinquents was best manifested in the orphanage at Sikandra. Many of its over 600 inmates were sent there by magistrates who had convicted them, or their parents, of famine-related crimes, HP, 12 April 1861, 4–9; 15 April 1862, 17–36.
11. RIPP, 1853.
12. RIPP, 1853.
13. SRJP, 1872.
14. JJDI, 1867–68, HJ, 1 September 1869, 49.
15. RIPP, 1867.
16. SRJP, 1870.
17. RIPP, 1867.
18. RIPP, 1863.
19. SRJP, 1870.
20. SRJP, 1872.
21. HJ, 4 April 1868, 4D–4F.
22. RJP, 1863, 1869.
23. RJP, 1866.
24. RIPP, 1853.
25. RIPP, 1864.
26. Sen, 2000, 100–9.
27. Collini, 1985, 5:35, 45–6.
28. RIPP, 1863.
29. Foucault, 1979, 135–69.
30. See Chapter One.
31. RIPP, 1862, 1863.
32. RIPP, 1867.
33. RIPP, 1863.
34. RIPP, 1867.
35. RIPP, 1863.
36. JJDI, 1867–68.
37. RJP, 1870.
38. *Ibid.*
39. SRJP, 1870.
40. RIPP, 1869; SRJP, 1869.
41. Carpenter, 1868, 172.

42 HE, 25 November 1859, 1–3; HJ, 4 April 1868, 4D–4F.
43 JJDI, 1867–68.
44 SRJP, 1869.
45 RJP, 1870.
46 Behlmer, 1998, 263–4.
47 Foucault, 1979, 3–31.
48 Modern penal techniques based on medical supervision and dietary deprivation are also forms of corporal punishment. See Sen, 2000, 131.
49 Semple, 1993, 62–94.
50 RJLPBP, 1867.
51 RIPP, 1853.
52 Mouat, F J, to Bengal, 12 Ocotber 1867, HJ, 18 January 1868, 21.
53 Greeven, R, to NWP&O, 18 Junr 1896, LDPr.
54 Lethbridge, A S, to Bengal, 9 April 1886, ARRS Hazaribagh.
55 Report by Heeley, W L (IG Jails Bengal), Mackenzie, S C (Superintendent of Presidency Jail) and Lambert, J (Deputy Commissioner of Police, Calcutta) to Richard Temple (Governor of Bengal), 1874, HJ, June 1875, 107–12.
56 See Chapter Five.
57 Heeley, W L, Mackenzie, S C and Lambert, J, to Temple, R, 1874.
58 NWP&O to GOI, HJ, June 1877, 303–19.
59 RJLPBP, 1867.
60 *Ibid*.
61 *Ibid*.
62 *Ibid*.
63 *Ibid*.
64 On Walker in the Andamans, see Sen, 1999, 30:1, 29–59.
65 RCJJD, HJ, 23 June 1864, 47–51; JDDI, 1867–68.
66 RJLPBP, 1867.
67 Stone, 1977, 287–91.
68 Mouat, F J, to Bengal, 12 October 1867, HJ, 18 January 1868, 21.
69 RJLPBP, 1867. Mouat's vision of premature sexuality was fully aligned with contemporary British readings of child marriage and native physical development, especially in Bengal. See Sinha, 1995, 138–80.
70 SRJP, 1869.
71 RIPP, 1864.
72 RIPP, 1864.
73 RIPP, 1864.
74 PrLGP, HJails, 10.18.1872, 3102
75 RIPP 1853
76 PrLGP, HJails, 27 May 1907.
77 HJ, 18 January 1868, 21.
78 RIPP, 1864.
79 Rosselli, 1980, 86, 121–48.
80 Handley, F F, to Larymore, A D, 5 June 1876, LDPr, March 1897.
81 RIPP, 1863.
82 Harrison, 1999, 1–24; Redfield, 2000, 49–108.
83 RIPP, 1863.
84 Arnold, 1994, 148–87.

85 RIPP, 1862.
86 HJ, 13 February 1869, 11–32.
87 RIPP, 1864.
88 Ignatieff, 1978, 5–26.
89 Orwell, 1962, 38.
90 HP, 8 January 1858, 281–2.
91 Mukherjee, 1998, 41–6.
92 HPB, December 1880, 59–61.
93 HJ, June 1877, 303–17.
94 RCJJD, HJ, 23 June 1864, 47–51.
95 Dumerge, J W F, memo to Madras, 4 July 1896, LDPr.
96 HPolitical, 20 May 1932.
97 Boy-Picketers to be Whipped, 1932, *The Hindustan Times*, 30 January.
98 Sen, 2000, 61–75.
99 Emerson, H W, to Thompson, John, 24 February 1932, HPolitical, 20 May 1932.
100 SRJP, 1872.
101 RIPP, 1864.
102 RIPP, 1862.
103 Pr. NWP&O, 612-VI-40B, 21 March 1889.
104 RIJC, HJails, 1922, F.280.
105 See Chapter Four.
106 HJ, 4 April 1868, 4D–4F.
107 *Ibid.*
108 When the Government of Burma expressed its contempt for 'weakly sentimental considerations' in the treatment of juvenile offenders, it called for 'a more masculine attitude towards crime whether committed by adolescents or adults'. HJails, 1922, 280.
109 HJ, 4 April 1868, 4D–4F.
110 Arbuthnot, A J, 31 Decmeber 1867, HJ, 4 April 1868, 4D–4F.
111 RIPP, 1867.
112 Pr.LGP, HJ, 14 December 1871, 1748.
113 RJP, 1871.
114 *Ibid.*
115 Napier, 1867, HJ, 4 April 1868, 4D–4F.
116 JJDI, 1868.
117 Bayley, E C, to Ellis, R S, 3 April 1868, HJ, 4 April 1868, 4D–4F; Duncan, D, to Madras, 1 June 1896. The fact that Duncan — an official in the Department of Public Instruction — had become an authority on juvenile delinquency indicates a partial colonization of the children's prison by the school.
118 HJ, 4 April 1868, 4D–4F.
119 Some colonial jailors viewed flogging as an especially humiliating and effective punishment for adult middle-class prisoners, because such men threatened their authority. See Sen, 2000, 264–71. When the offenders were children, however, the 'wild' habitual offender was a bigger challenge to colonial authority than the relatively docile offspring of the 'respectable'.
120 HJ, 4 November 1868, 14–22.
121 RIPP, 1864.
122 ARRS Alipore, 1879.

123 *Ibid.*
124 ARRS Alipore, 1880.
125 ARRS Alipore and Hazaribagh, 1891. Violent assaults by juvenile inmates against senior staff remained a chronic feature of the colonial reformatory, which seems to have increased in frequency with large-scale anticolonial agitations outside the colonial institution. There were several such assaults by older juvenile inmates in Bombay in 1935 and 1936. ARRS Dharwar, 1935–36.
126 ARRS Chingleput, 1895.
127 ARRS Chingleput, 1899, 1902.
128 Monro, A, to Central Provinces, 2 April 1902, ARRS Jubbulpore, 1902. It is worth noting that the Sleeman-era Thug prison had been condemned as unsafe by the Public Works Department, but was being used as a juvenile reformatory anyway, reflecting the link between infrastructural problems and the reliance on flogging.
129 ARRS Alipore, 1879, 1880; ARRS Chingleput, 1899.
130 HJ, January 1875, 130–2; June 1875, 107–12.
131 PrLGP, HJ, 14 December 1871, 1748.
132 Lethbridge, A S, to Bengal, 22 April 1887, ARRS Hazaribagh, 1887.
133 On prison medicine in colonial India, see Sen, 2000, 131–34.
134 RJLPBP, 1867.
135 Political and Judicial Records, 1880, L/PJ/6/12/599 (OIOC).
136 ARRS Alipore, 1880.
137 ARRS Hazaribagh, 1885.
138 ARRS Chingleput, 1892.
139 ARRS Alipore, 1882.
140 ARRS Hazaribagh, 1883.
141 ARRS Delhi, 1905.
142 ARRS Chingleput, 1901.
143 ARRS Chingleput, 1899.
144 *Ibid.*
145 HJails, 1922, F.280.
146 Behlmer, 1982, 220–2.
147 HJails, 1928, F16/IV/28.
148 ARRS Madras Presidency, 1934, 1936.
149 Bombay to GOI, 2 June 1876, HJ, June 1877, 303–17.
150 ARRS Madras Presidency, 1939.

4. Gendering the Reformatory

1 Chatterjee, in Sangari and Vaid (eds), 1990, 233–53.
2 Behlmer, 1998, 31–73; Rauchway, 2001, 155–78.
3 Braide, G F W, to Robert McNamara, 26 June 1896, LDPr, 1897. On the Female Penitentiary, see Sen, 2002a, 39:4, 417–38.
4 Mouat, F J, RJLPBP, 1867, HJPr, 1868.
5 Grewal, 1996, 23–56.
6 Gurdyal Singh Man to Punjab Chief Court, 26 June 1896, LDPr.
7 Greeven, R, to NWP&O, 18 June 1896, LDPr.
8 Lord Napier, President's Minute, 3 November 1867, HJ, 4 April 1868, 4D–4F.
9 John Woodburn, memo, 11 March 1897, LDPr.

10 Madras to GOI, 2 October 896, LDPr.
11 Bengal to GOI, 5 September 1896, LDPr.
12 Sen, 2002a, 39:4.
13 Drummond, J R, to Thorburn, S S, 27 June 1896, LDPr.
14 Ignatieff, 1978, 5–26.
15 Sarkar, 2001, 191–225.
16 Levine, 2003, 178–9. For Indian perspectives on prostitution, see Banerjee, 1998, 18–36.
17 Melville, P S, to Punjab, 3 May 1872, HJ, January 1875, 48–67.
18 Mackenzie, A, to Dampier, H L, 12 July 1872, HJ, January 1875, 48–67.
19 George Couper to Chief Commissioner of Oudh, 12 October 1865, HJ, January 1875, 48–67.
20 Trevor, G H, to Bayley, E C, 4 June 1872; Punjab to GOI, 19 June 1872, HJ, January 1875, 48–67.
21 Woodburn, J, 12 May 1896, LDPr.
22 Sen, in Chattejee (ed.), 2004, 261–91.
23 RCJJD, HJ, 23 June 1864, 47–51.
24 Phillips, H D, memo, 16 November 1867, HJ, 4 April 1868, 4D–4F.
25 *Ibid.*
26 Temple, Richard, memo, 11 March 1875, HJ, June 1875, 107–12.
27 Woodburn, J, 12 May 1896, LDPr.
28 Hooper, J, to NWP&O, 22 July 1896, LDPr.
29 Silcock, J G, to Chief Court of Punjab, June 1896, LDPr.
30 Foucault, 1979, 250–6; Freitag, in Yang, Anand (ed.), 1985, 141–5.
31 Sen, in Chattejee (ed.), 2004, 261–91.
32 Woodburn, J, memo, 11 March 1897, LDPr.
33 Duncan, D, to Madras, 1 June 1896, LDPr.
34 Narayan, 1997, 43–80; Singh, 1996, 79–119.
35 Section 31, RS Act, 1897.
36 ARRS Hazaribagh, 1897.
37 Man to Punjab Chief Court, 26 June 1896.
38 Even prostitution might be seen as a 'domestic' profession: a veiled and private transaction with the public world, with the brothel or *kothi* functioning as a parallel of the respectable home. Talwar Oldenburg, 1991, in Haynes, Douglas and Prakash, Gyan (eds), 23–61.
39 Sen, 2002b, 14:3, 53–79.
40 *Ibid.*
41 Forbes, 1996, 41–63, 70–91.
42 Rauchway, 2001, 1–31; Million, 2003, 139–52; Shiman, 1992, 151–70.
43 Garland, 2001, 27.
44 Burton, 1998, 110–51.
45 Burton, 2003, 71–2.
46 Burton, 1998; see also Sen, 2004b.
47 Burton, 2003, 66–100.
48 Cox, 2002, 153–7.
49 Cannadine, 2001, 10, 41–57.
50 Sorabji, Conrelia, to Bengal, 2 January 1926, 1928 precise date unclear, CS papers, Eur. MSS, OIOC.

51 See E C Bayley's remarks on Punjab government proposal for new legislation on 'bad characters', HJ Pr, December 1873 .
52 Sorabji, C, to Bengal, 1928, precise date unclear.
53 Sorabji, C, to Bengal, 26 June 1928.
54 Sorabji, C, to Bengal, 1928, precise date unclear.
55 *Ibid.*
56 *Ibid.*
57 Sorabji, C, to Bengal, 26 June 1928.
58 Dirks, 2001, 43–60.
59 Sorabji, C, to Bengal, 1928, precise date unclear.
60 Sorabji, C, to Bengal, 7 June 1929.
61 Sorabji, C, to Bengal, 1928, precise date unclear.
62 Grewal, 1996, 23–56.
63 Cox suggests that by the turn of the century, *zenana* visitors had moved from highlighting 'immorality' to emphasizing an 'inefficient' domesticity that obstructed the recruitment of girls for the professions, particularly medicine. Cox, 2002, 159.
64 Sorabji, C, to Bengal, 1928, precise date unclear.
65 Chandra, 1998, 5–6.
66 The incident narrated by Burton, in which Sorabji intervenes in the British doctor's coercive treatment of the Maharani of Bettial, might also be read in this light. Burton, 2003, 74.
67 She meant Bharatpur.
68 CS papers, 1928.
69 On the politics of minority administrations, see Ramusack, 2004, 110–1.
70 Sorabji, C, to Bengal, 2 January 1926.
71 *Ibid.*
72 Sen, 2002b.
73 Sorabji, C, to Bengal, 1928, precise date unclear.
74 Behlmer, 1998, 230–71.
75 Sorabji, C, to Bengal, 1927, precise date unclear.
76 Behlmer, 1982, 15–16.
77 *The Statesman*, Calcutta, 13 August 1929.
78 *Ibid.*
79 *Ibid.*
80 Greenfeld, 1992, 371–8.
81 Sen, 2004b, 146–62.
82 On the Sarda Bill, which sought to raise the age of consent for girls in reaction to the publication of Katherine Mayo's *Mother India*, see Forbes, 1996, 87–9.
83 Sorabji, C, to Bengal, 26 June 1928.
84 *Ibid.*
85 Burton, 2003, 67–8.
86 Sorabji, C, to Bengal, 7 September 1929.
87 On 7 June 1929, Croft asked the Home Department for information that would help him write a speech on 'women and children'. He wrote, 'Past Indian delegates have rather warned the humanitarian enthusiasts at Geneva against interference with the social and religious traditions of the East etc. But I need hardly say that *Mother India* has made them rather curious and sceptical, and it would probably be a good thing to give as good an account as possible of the changes which are more less sponta-

neously taking place, and particularly to adduce any evidence which shows that there is an increasing amount of unofficial initiative in social welfare work among the more enlightened members of the community, and particularly among the women themselves.' He specifically asked for a memo on the Madras Devadasi Act, the AIWC, the Age of Consent Bill, medical care for women and education. He added that some of this would be outdated and irrelevant, but that would not pose a problem at the League, where 'the members seem to like listening to accounts of what is taking place in other countries, especially the more remote ones'. He added, 'As likely as not the subject will fall to Kapurthala [the maharaja of Kapurthala was also a member of the Indian delegation in Geneva], and so it would not be a bad thing if something could be included about progress in these matters in the [princely] states.' In response, the Home Department sent Croft a detailed memo, including a legislative history of the ages of marriage and sexual consent. HJ, 1929.
88 HP, 1931.
89 Unlike their British predecessors and counterparts such as the SPCC, which had engineered themselves to address specifically 'juvenile' problems such as cruelty to children, colonial associations that concerned themselves with children spoke to a range of 'cultural'/gendered problems that directly afflicted native women, and only indirectly, children. On the SPCC, see Behlmer, 1982, 193–227.
90 Trial of Juveniles in Calcutta: Need of Reform, *The Statesman*, Calcutta, 21 April 1929.
91 *Ibid.*
92 Juvenile Offenders in Bengal: After Care, *The Statesman*, Calcutta, 16 March 1929.
93 On the 'mental science' of metropolitan child-saving, see Behlmer, 1998, 128–78. Behlmer argues that psychological expertise did not become hegemonic in English family life. While that is also generally true of India, it should be noted that experts like Sorabji addressed themselves to their peers and racial competitors, rather than to parents. In that sense, they sought to transform themselves, rather than the children they 'saved'.
94 Sorabji, C, memo to GOI, 1927, precise date unclear.
95 *The Statesman*, 13 August 1929.
96 Sorabji, C, to Bengal, 1928, precise date unclear. The reliance on 'philanthropies' may appear to be at odds with Sorabji's quasi-Progressive emphasis on state action, but these philanthropies sought to justify their activism and existence by working with the state.
97 Sorabji, C, to Bengal, 26 June 1928.
98 *Ibid.*
99 Carpenter, 1868, 54, 61.
100 Behlmer, 1982, 17.
101 Sorabji, C, memo to Age of Consent Committee, 1928.
102 *The Statesman*, 16 March 1929.
103 Cox, 2002, 153–7.
104 She was critical of Indian magistrates who seemed not to recognize the specialized nature of juvenile delinquency, but this was not necessarily an indictment of their gender. Sorabji, C, to Bengal, 7 September 1929.
105 Sorabji, C, to GOI, 7 September 1929.
106 Forbes, 1996, 78–83.
107 Sorabji, C, to Bengal, 26 June 1928.

108 Forbes, 1996, 134.
109 Sorabji, C, to Bengal, 7 September 1929.
110 Sorabji, C, to Bengal, 1928, precise date unclear.
111 Man to Punjab Chief Court, 26 June 1896.
112 ARRS Madras Presidency, 1935–39.
113 RCTJDB.

5. Masters and Servants: School, Home and Aristocratic Childhood

1 McLeod, 1999, 25–8; Ramusack, 2004, 124–31.
2 The Chiefs' College at Rajkot was commonly known as the 'Rajkumar College'. However, 'Rajkumar College' was also a generic label for any Chiefs' College. I use 'school' and 'college' interchangeably to refer to these institutions, following the contemporary convention. These were not centers of higher education. Most students were between the ages of ten and eighteen.
3 Lawrence, Walter, to Curzon, 31 August 1901, Curzon papers, MSS Eur F. 112/252-3.
4 On the ambivalence of colonial Utilitarianism, see Stokes, 1959, 47–80.
5 Mangan, 1986, 122–41.
6 Howard, E I, memoirs of tour of Rajputana, HE, 12 May 1863, 10–11B.
7 *Ibid.*
8 *Ibid.*
9 *Ibid.*
10 Cohn, 1997, 5–11.
11 Marriott, 2003, 110–25, 144–8.
12 Burton, 2003, 71.
13 Sen, 2002b, 14:3, 53–79.
14 W S Atkinson, Howard's counterpart in Bengal, wrote about his eastern territories, 'It is on every account so desirable that these rude and savage Tribes should be drawn within the pale of civilization that no arguments can be required to recommend the establishment of schools.' Atkinson, W S, to Bengal, 29 July 1962, HE, 11 October 1862, 11–3.
15 In his accommodation of native informants and assistants, Howard falls short of the authority of subsequent administrators of the ethnographic state. He bears a trace of an earlier generation of colonial surveyors, like Colin Mackenzie and Alexander Boileau, who readily borrowed indigenous resources, methods and agendas of observation. See Peabody, 2001, 831.
16 Howard, E I, memoirs.
17 *Ibid.*
18 Lelyveld, 1996, 131–4.
19 Sen, in Mills and Sen (eds), 2004b, 58–79.
20 Howard, E I, memoirs.
21 Arnold, 1993, 116–58.
22 Howard, E I, memoirs. With variations, Howard's peers and forebears shared his enthusiasm for extant cultural-pedagogical resources. W D Arnold, brother of Matthew Arnold and Director of Public Education in Punjab immediately before the Mutiny, had wanted to base Indian schooling on elite-native languages, specifically Urdu and Farsi. See Cox, 2002, 190.

23 'The Marwaree merchants in Bombay are celebrated for their keenness and success, it might be added for their unscrupulousness, but in this imputation they only suffer the fate of all usurers.' *Ibid.*
24 Bayley, E C, memo, 26 May 1873, FPolitical, June 1873, 108–112.
25 *Ibid.*
26 FG, July 1876, 4–5, July 1877, 133–141B.
27 Tucker, A P L, to Chief Commissioner of Ajmere-Merwara, 26 December 1902, RSAP.
28 Metcalf, 1995, 125–7; Chowdhury, 2001, 40–65.
29 Campbell, Eur. MSS.
30 Chowdhury-Sengupta, in Robb (ed.), 1995, 282–303.
31 Sen, 2004b, 178.
32 Curzon, 4 June 1900.
33 Lawrence, Walter, to Curzon, 31 August 1901.
34 Ballhatchet, 1980, 120.
35 Lelyveld, 1996, 298; Tyndale-Biscoe, 1930, 15–17.
36 Ramusack, 2004, 181.
37 Stone, 1977, 254.
38 Bryant, 1978, 13. The 'Gopal model' of child-rearing can be seen as representative of a normative leniency that was recognized across a broad spectrum of medieval northern India, but it need not be viewed as an exclusive source of inspiration for parents. Even within the pan-Indian 'grand tradition', the *Mahabharata* highlights a model of child-rearing that emphasizes obedience and discipline. While this model appealed to nationalists, and might be glimpsed in pedagogical regimes ranging from the Ramakrishna Mission to the RSS, its application cannot be separated from the colonial discourses that informed the Chiefs' Colleges and similar schools. See Beckerlegge, 2000, 52–78; Embree, in Marty and Appleby (eds), 1994, 625–8.
39 Goody, 1983, 26.
40 Stone, 1977, 263.
41 The British contempt for native maternal influence anticipates the Freudian disapproval of a parental indulgence that warps the child by damaging its self-sufficiency. See Freud, 1929, 408. Stone writes that while an anxiety about mothers 'spoiling' their children is detectable in England by the mid-eighteenth century, it was a subordinate discourse. Kakar has suggested that the metropolitan perception of a debilitating parental influence upon the native child is related to the Weberian view of Indian society as a structure that prevents the development of autonomous individuals. Kakar, 1981, 10.
42 Meade, R J, to Aitchison, C U, 22 August 1875, FPolitical, January 1876, 112–6.
43 Kakar, 1981, 79–87.
44 *Ibid.*
45 Annual Report of the Mayo College, 1876–77, FG, November 1877, 219–36.
46 See Chapter Six.
47 Rudolph, Rudolph and Kanota, 2001, 234–5, 261; Cannadine, 2001, 41–57.
48 Dawson, 1994, 11–52.
49 Col. Brooke to Board of Revenue, 13 September 1872, FG, June 1873, 114–37.
50 Daly, H D, to GOI, 25 November 1875, FPolitical, January 1876, 1–1A.
51 Daly, H D, to Aitchison, C U, 5 August 1870, FPolitical, December 1870, 608–9.
52 Aitchison, C U, memo, 23 August 1870, FPolitical, December 1870, 608–9.

NOTES

53 Daly, H D, to Aitchison, C U, 5 August 1870.
54 Pelly, Lewis, to Aitchison, C U, 28 July 1873, FG, June 1876, 1–6.
55 Cohn, 1997, 106–62. On shoes and colonialism, see Sen, 2004b, 179, 191.
56 Pelly, Lewis, to Aitchison, C U, 28 July 1873.
57 Howard, E L, memoirs.
58 Pelly, Lewis, to Aitchison, C U, 28 July 1873.
59 Mookerjee was an English-speaking bureaucrat and diplomat who successfully moderated Jaipur's relations with the paramount power, and modernized the organization of the durbar. Rudolph, Rudolph and Kanota, 1984, 96–106.
60 Haley, 1978, 141–4.
61 Pelly, Lewis, to Aitchison, C U, 28 July 1873.
62 *Ibid.*
63 Rudolph and Rudolph, 2001, 236; Goradia, 1993, 200–9.
64 Curzon, 4 June 1900, Curzon papers.
65 Bayley, S C, to Bengal, 2 January 1874, BPrC, 1874. S C Bayley was not closely related to E C Bayley.
66 Worsley, C F, to Bayley, S C, 28 July 1873, BPrC, 1874.
67 Metcalf, 1989, 77–81.
68 FG, June 1873, 114–37.
69 Col. Brooke to Political Agent, Marwar and Jaisalmer, 24 May 1873, FG, July 1873, 10–5.
70 Metcalf, 1989, 78; Ramusack, 2004, 111.
71 Minutes of Ajmere conference on reforming the Chiefs' Colleges, RSAP, 1902, 13.
72 Sarkar, 2002, 10–37.
73 Lawrence, Walter, to Curzon, 31 August 1901.
74 Pinhey, A F, to AGG Rajputana, 24 March 1903, RSAP, 1902, 1.
75 RSAP, 1902, 13.
76 Lawrence, Walter, to Curzon, 31 August 1901.
77 Annual Report of the Mayo College, 1876–77.
78 Lelyveld, 1996, 102–46; Minault, 1982, 117–9; Chatterjee1992, *passim.*
79 Howard, E I, memoirs. On the contested borders of the 'Rajput', see Sen, 2004b, 51–61.
80 Lawrence, Walter, to Curzon, 31 August 1901.
81 McLeod, 1999, 55.
82 This was the Nowgong College, which struggled to attract students until it was incorporated into the Daly College in 1898.
83 FPolitical, June 1873, 108–12.
84 Sen, 2004b, 21–2. For a hagiography, see Khan, 1904, 31–7.
85 FPolitical, April 1874, 2–5.
86 Meade, R J, to Aitchison, C U, 22 August 1875, FPolitical, January 1876, 112–6.
87 Lelyveld, 1996, 254–61.
88 On the tensions of this field, see Rudolph and Rudolph, 2001, 260, 273. See also McDevitt, 2003, 20:1, 1–27.
89 Pelly, Lewis, to Aitchison, C U, 28 July 1873.
90 Pelly also wrote, 'I would induce some of these youths to become unpaid Attaches to the AGG and to the Political Agents of Rajpootana, thus leading them on to full manhood in the society of English officers.' Nothing came of the plan. *Ibid.*
91 Meade, R J, to Aitchison, C U, 22 August 1875.
92 Lawrence, Walter, to Curzon, 31 August 1901.

93　*Ibid.*
94　*Ibid.*
95　*Ibid.*
96　Guha, 1997, *xii.*
97　McNabb, Rawdon, to McNabb, James, 21 December 1911, McNabb family papers, Eur. MSS.
98　*Ibid.*
99　McNabb, Rawdon, to McNabb, James, 18 September 1913.
100　Ramusack, 2004, 134—5.
101　McNabb, Rawdon, to McNabb, James, 12 November 1914.
102　*Ibid.*
103　McNabb, Rawdon, to McNabb, James, 18 November 1912.
104　McNabb, Rawdon, to McNabb, James, 9 March 1913.
105　McNabb, Rawdon, to McNabb, James, 20 April 1914.
106　On guardianship of Indians in England, see Lahiri, 2000, 131–3.
107　Daly, H D, to Aitchison, C U, 5 August 1870, FPolitical, December 1870, 608–9.
108　Guha, in Chatterjee (ed.), 2004, 75–6. By *fitna*, Wink refers to the pursuit of sovereignty by constantly creating and exploiting divisions among potential political rivals. Wink, 1983, 160–1.
109　Guha, in Chatterjee (ed.), 2003, 79.
110　Lawrence, Walter, to Curzon, 31 August 1901.
111　Ramusack, 2004, 133.
112　OBC St. John to Lyall, Arthur, June 1877, FG, November 1877, 219–36.
113　Procida, 2002, 87–97; Marriott, 2003, 82.
114　Khan, 1904, 4–5, 24–30.
115　Lawrence, Walter, to Curzon, 31 August 1901.
116　*Ibid.*
117　*Ibid.*
118　*Ibid.* The maharaja of Alwar had been the first student at Mayo College, and St. John's personal ward. His 'capture' by the college in 1875 had inspired much self-congratulation at various levels of the colonial government. Powlett, P W to Lyall, Arthur, 5 November 1875, FPolitical, January 1876, 184–7.
119　Pinhey, A F, to Lawrence, Walter 12 February 1901, Curzon papers.
120　Presumably this meant 'during the school term', and not 'in the classroom'. Fuller, A, to Lawrence, Walter. 20 January 1902, Curzon papers.
121　*Ibid.*
122　Ramusack, 2004, 165.
123　Lawrence, Walter, to Curzon, 31 August 1901.
124　Lord Curzon, 27 January 1902, RSAP, 1902, 1.
125　Curzon, 27 January 1902.
126　Lawrence, Walter, to Curzon, 31 August 1901.
127　Arnold, in Arnold and Hardiman (eds), 1994, 148–87; Mills, 2000, 108–28.
128　Gunion had included native teachers in his rant to Lawrence about 'blackguards'.
129　Lawrence, Walter, to Curzon, 31 August 1901.
130　Curzon to Hamilton, George, 16 July 1903, RSAP, 1902, 1.
131　*Ibid.*
132　Lawrence, Walter, to Curzon, 31 August 1901.

133 The expression 'Eton in India' was pioneered by C Walter, the political agent in Bharatpur, in 1868–69. (FPolitical, December 1870, 608–9.) It was from Walter, more directly than from Howard, that Lord Mayo acquired the idea of Chiefs' Colleges. (FG, May 1877, 37–8).
134 Pelly, Lewis, to Aitchison, C U, 28 July 1873.
135 'Eton flourishes under traditions and glories which cannot be called up in India; but much which it is in our power to do may be done,' Daly, H D, wrote to Aitchison, C U, 5 August 1870, FPolitical, December 1870, 608–9.
136 *Ibid.*
137 The Pioneer, 17 January 1902, Curzon papers.
138 RSAP, 1902, 1.
139 Campbell had been deeply interested in how the transplantation of races and institutions might shape intelligence and childhood. He had argued that scientific pedagogy and childhood itself could be used as counterweights against the damaging effects of the environment upon a dislocated race. *Address to the Anthropology Section of the British Association*, 1886, George Campbell papers, Eur. MSS.
140 RSAP, 1902, 1.
141 The American Presbyterians' version of 'Eton in India' was 'Princeton in Punjab'. Such references served to mark out the exclusionary boundaries of class, rather than replicate the metropolitan model in the colony. Not surprisingly, 'modeled' schools such as the Alexandra School of the CMS in Amritsar were plagued by the missionaries' misgivings about 'unsuitable' children and deracination. Cox, 2002, 201–6.
142 Metcalf, 1995, 28–65.
143 RSAP, Political, 1902, 1.
144 Howard, E I, memoirs.
145 Annual Report of Mayo College, 1876–77.
146 *Ibid.*
147 RSAP, 1902, 13.
148 Lawrence, Walter, to Curzon, 31 August 1901.
149 *Ibid.*
150 Rajkot seems to have been the exception. Macnaghten and Mayne were relatively kind to their students; Mayne reserved his ire for his native staff. RSAP, 1902, 13.
151 C W Waddington, the Principal of Mayo, wrote to the AGG Rajputana's office on 25 March 1903 that final exams and degrees were unnecessary in a school where eighteen year olds would either join the ICC or simply return to their homes. RSAP, 1902, 1.
152 On 13 August 1901, J B Hutchinson, Principal of Aitchison College, told the Foreign Department that the curriculum in Lahore had been changed to prepare boys for the ICC and careers in estate management, with courses in veterinary medicine, animal husbandry, land management and agriculture. In addition, there was English, mathematics and drawing. Hutchinson's innovations were not universally appreciated; Gunion, at Daly, wrote to the Foreign Department on 14 October 1901 that 'professional studies' were a waste of time, as were matriculation examinations. Curzon papers.
153 Cited by Cobb, H V, letter to Martindale, A H T, 21 March 1903, RSAP, 1902, 1.
154 *The Lahore Observer*, 22 January 1902, Curzon papers.

6. The Politics of Deracination

1. Bombay PD 515, 1913.
2. *Ibid.*
3. Lelyveld, 1996, 128–56, 265.
4. Minault, in Jones (ed.), 1992, 179–99; Forbes, 1996, 32–63.
5. Mukherjee, in Leach and Mukherjee (eds), 1970, 67–9.
6. Metcalf, 1982, 11–2.
7. McLeod, 1999, 35–48.
8. *Indian Social Reformer*, 26 October 1913, NNR, Bombay, 1913.
9. Sarkar, 1997, 228–9.
10. Khan, 1904, *v, vi*, 2, 6; Sen, 2004b, 26.
11. Rudolph, Rudolph, and Kanota, 2001, 13.
12. Tod, 1920; a good example of the latter is Kincaid, 1931, *passim*.
13. KPA, R/C 590, 1918.
14. Bombay, PD, 515, 1913.
15. Begum Asha Bibi to Lord Hardinge, 24 February 1913; R/2/681/75.
16. *The Parsi*, 16 October 1913; *Akbar-e-Saudagar*, 17 October 1913; *Bombay Gujarati*, 16 October 1913; NNR, Bombay, 1913.
17. *Praja Bandhu*, 16 Februrary 1913, NNR, Bombay, 1913.
18. *Kathiawar Vartaman*, 3 March 1913, NNR, Bombay, 1913.
19. *Jam-e-Jamshed*, 14 October 1913, NNR, Bombay, 1913.
20. Sukhdeo's memo was forwarded to the AGG Rajputana by Jennings, R H, Resident WRS, on 27 March 1903, RSAP, 1902, 1.
21. Sukhdeo Pershad to Jennings, R H, March 1903, RSAP, 1902, 1.
22. Sen, 2002b, 14:3, 53–79.
23. Dirks, 2001, 161–4. Dirks does not, perhaps, give due recognition to the dissident potential of such native representations.
24. Chatterjee, in Sangari and Vaid (eds), 1990, 233.
25. Sukhdeo Pershad to Jennings, R H, March 1903, RSAP, 1902, 1. On the contemporary politics of Rajput purity, see Sen, 2004b, 53–7.
26. Sukhdeo Pershad to Jennings, R H, March 1903.
27. *Ibid.*
28. *Ibid.*
29. On Hutchinson's quarrel with Gunion on the issue of professional training, see Chapter Five, n 152.
30. Sukhdeo Pershad to Jennings, R H, March 1903.
31. Chatterjee, 2002, 32–45.
32. *Indu Prakash*, 13 May 1914, NNR, Bombay, 1914.
33. *The Parsi*, 16 September 1914, NNR, Bombay, 1914.
34. *Kathiawadno Himayati*, 9 August 1896, NNR, Bombay, 1896.
35. *The Gujarati*, 13 December 1914, NNR, Bombay, 1914.
36. KPA R/C 590, 1918; R/2/747/342.
37. Sen, 2004b, 63.
38. Metcalf, 1995, 105–6.
39. Rudolph, Rudolph and Kanota, 2001, 268.
40. *Ibid*, 337.
41. *Ibid*, 442.
42. *Ibid*, 333.

43 The *Sahachar*, 24 June 1896, NNR, Bengal, 1896.
44 *Ibid*.
45 *Poona Observer*, 9 June 1914, NNR, Bombay, 1914.
46 Valette, 1931, 27–8.
47 KPA R/C 590, 1918.
48 Lawrence, Walter, to Curzon, 31 August 1901.
49 Bhagwan, 2003, 2.
50 *Ibid*, 3–8.
51 Lawrence, Walter, to Curzon, 31 August 1901.
52 *Ibid*.
53 Jodhpur durbar to Marwar Political Agency, 11 May 1873, FG, July 1873, 10–5.
54 Lawrence, Walter, to Curzon, 31 August 1901.
55 The 1904 conference in Ajmere included the rulers of Udaipur, Jaipur, Bikaner, Kota, Gwalior, Rewa, Orchha, Bahawalpur, Kutch, Gondal and Sailana. RSAP, 1903, 13.
56 Meade, R J, to GOI, October 1901, Curzon papers.
57 Marwar and Jaisalmer Political Agency to AGG, Rajputana, 23 May 1873, FG, July 1873, 10–5.
58 Gen. Black, 1892 report from Aitchison College, Curzon papers.
59 Lawrence, Walter, to Curzon, 31 August 1901.
60 *Ibid*.
61 Pinhey, A F, to AGG Rajputana, 24 March 1903, RSAP, 1902, 1.
62 *Ibid*.
63 Ramusack, 2004, 132; Sen, 2004b, 100–9; Price, 1996, 9–38.
64 FG, June 1873, 114–37.
65 Lawrence, Walter, to Curzon, 31 August 1901.
66 Civil and Military Gazette, Punjab, 1890, Curzon papers.
67 Meade, R J, to Foreign Dept, October 1901, Curzon papers.
68 Lawrence, Walter, to Curzon, 31 August 1901.
69 Middle-class parents in eighteenth-century England often saw schools as 'training grounds for vice' and preferred that their children be tutored at home. Stone writes that this facilitated the development of a less violent pedagogy. Stone, 1977, 273–4.
70 Lawrence, Walter, to Curzon, 31 August 1901.
71 *Ibid*.
72 *Ibid*.
73 Curzon to Hamilton, G, 16 July 1903, RSAP, 1902, 1.
74 *Ibid*.
75 Lawrence told Curzon that the Mairtia Rathor chief had begged to have his relatives admitted to the ICC, but refused to send them to Mayo because 'they don't learn any good there'. His son had been at Mayo, but had apparently been withdrawn. Lawrence, Walter, to Curzon, 31 August 1901.
76 Said, 1979, 73–92.
77 Sukhdeo Pershad to Jennings, R H, March 1903, RSAP, 1902, 1.
78 RSAP, 1902, 13.
79 *Ibid*.
80 Jones, 1992, 52; Lelyveld, 1996, 113.
81 RSAP, 1902, 13.
82 *Ibid*.
83 *Ibid*.

84 *Ibid.*
85 Fussel, 1975, 18–29.
86 In this context, see Mary Carpenter's frustration with Brahmos who praised Christ but criticized Christianity, scoffed at revealed miracles and refused to convert. Carpenter, 1868, vol. 1, 176–7.
87 Thakur of Gondal, Note of Dissent, 16 March 1904, RSAP, 1902, 13.
88 *Ibid.*
89 RSAP, 1902, 13.
90 Rev. Dr Macalister to Cobb, H V, forwarded to Martindale, A H T, AGG Rajputana, 21 March 1903, RSAP, 1902, 1.
91 Nandy, 1983, 27–9; Sarkar, 1997, 216–81.
92 Cox, 2002, 70–84, 193–201.
93 RSAP, 1902, 13.
94 Remarks of the Raja of Sailana, RSAP, 1902, 13.
95 *Ibid.*
96 Sen, 2004b, 178.
97 Lawrence, Walter, to Curzon, 31 August 1901.
98 Sen, 2004b, 147–9.
99 Thakur of Gondal, Note of Dissent, 16 March 1904, RSAP, 1902, 13.
100 Tucker, A P L, to Chief Commissioner, Ajmere-Merwara, 26 December 1902, RSAP, 1902, 1.
101 Remarks of Mayne, C, RSAP, 1902, 13.
102 Sen, in Mills and Sen (eds), 2004, 58–79.
103 Remarks of Waddington, C W, RSAP, 1902, 13.
104 Lelyveld, 1996, 262.
105 Sen, in Mills, and Satadru (eds), 2004.
106 FG, December 1871, 7; June 1873, 114–137; also see Metcalf, 1989, 69–71.
107 FG, June 1873, 114–137.
108 Meade, R J, to Aitchison, C U, 22 August 1875, FP, January 1876, 112–6.
109 *Ibid.*
110 McNabb, Rawdon, to McNabb, James, 18 November 1912.
111 *Ibid.*
112 *Bombay Chronicle*, 8 April 1920, NNR, Bombay, 1920.

Conclusion

1 Kaviraj, 2004.

BIBLIOGRAPHY

Selected Primary Sources

National Archives of India, New Delhi:
Home Department, Government of India (GOI)
    Judicial Branch proceedings (HJPr)
    Judicial Branch (HJ) records
    Public Branch (HP) records
    Political Branch (HPolitical) records
    Education Branch (HE) records
    Ecclesiastical Branch (HEcc) records
    Police Branch (HPolice) records
    Jails Branch (HJails) records
    Port Blair Branch (HPB) records
Foreign Department, Government of India (GOI)
    Political Branch (FPolitical) records
    General Branch (FG) records
Legislative Department Proceedings (LDPr)
Rajputana States Agency, political files (RSAP)
Proceedings of the legislative councils of Bengal, Madras, Central Provinces, Bombay, and Northwest Provinces & Oudh (NWP&O)
Proceedings of the Lieutenant-Governor of Punjab (PrLGP)
Reports on the Jails of Punjab (RJP)
Special Reports on the Jails of Punjab (SRJP)
Reports of the Inspector-General of Police, Punjab (RIPP)
Reports on the Jails of the Lower Provinces of the Bengal Presidency (RJLPBP)
Oriental and India Office Collections, British Library:
Western Rajputana States (WRS), Kathiawar Political Agency (KPA), Residency and Crown Representative Records (R1, R2 and R/C), Secret & Political Department (PD) files, Political & Judicial (L/PJ) records
Annual reports of reformatory school administration (ARRS)
Annual Report of the Bombay Probation & Aftercare Association (ARBPAA)
Native Newspaper Reports (NNR)
Personal Papers, European Manuscripts Series (Eur. Mss.)
Bengal Proceedings and Consultations (BPrC)
Reports on Jails and Jail Discipline in India (JJDI)
Report of Indian Jails Committee (RIJC), 1922
Report of the Committee appointed to consider the Treatment of Juvenile Delinquency in Burma (RCTJDB), 1928

Selected Secondary Sources

Anderson, Benedict, 1983, *Imagined Communities*, London, Verso.
Anderson, Clare, 2000, *Convicts in the Indian Ocean*, London, Macmillan.
Anderson, Clare, 2004, *Legible Bodies: Race, Criminality and Colonialism in South Asia* Oxford, Berg.
Anon., 1929, Juvenile Offenders in Bengal: After Care, *The Statesman*, Calcutta, 16 March 1929.
Anon., 1929, Trial of Juveniles in Calcutta: Need of Reform, *The Statesman*, Calcutta, 21 April.
Anon., 1929, *The Statesman*, 13 August.
Anon., 1932, Boy-Picketers to be Whipped, *The Hindustan Times*, 30 January.
Aries, Philippe, 1962, *Centuries of Childhood: A Social History of Family Life*, New York, Vintage.
Arnold, David, 1993, *Colonizing the Body: State Medicine and Epidemic Disease in Nineteenth-Century India*, Delhi, Oxford University Press.
Arnold, David and Hardiman, David (eds), *Selected Subaltern Studies VIII*, Delhi, Oxford University Press.
Ballhatchet, Kenneth, 1980, *Race, Sex and Class Under the Raj: Imperial Attitudes and Policies and Their Critics, 1793–1905*, London, Weidenfeld and Nicolson.
Bandyopadhyay, Sivaji, 1991, *Gopal-Rakhal Dwandwa Samash: Upanibeshbad o Bangla Shishusahitya*, Calcutta, Papyrus.
Banerjee, Sumanta, 1998, *Dangerous Outcast: The Prostitute in Nineteenth Century Bengal*, Calcutta, Seagull.
Barton, Patricia, 2004, Medical Murders: Safeguarding the Medicinal Market in British India, paper presented at the Annual Conference of South Asia Studies, University of Wisconsin, Madison, 15 October.
Beckerlegge, Gwilym, 2000, *The Ramkrishna Mission: The Making of a Modern Hindu Movement*, Delhi, Oxford University Press.
Behlmer, George, 1982, *Child Abuse and Moral Reform in England, 1870–1908*, Stanford, Stanford University Press.
Behlmer, George, 1998, *Friends of the Family: The English Home and its Guardians, 1850-1940*, Stanford, Stanford University Press.
Beisel, Nicola, 1997, *Imperiled Innocents: Anthony Comstock and Family Reproduction in Victorian America*, Princeton, Princeton University Press.
Bentham, Jeremy, 1995, *The Panopticon Writings*, London, Verso.
Beteille, Andre, 1992, *Society and Politics in India*, Delhi, Oxford.
Bhagwan, Manu, 2003, *Sovereign Spaces: Princes, Education and Empire in Colonial India*, Delhi, Oxford University Press.
Bose, Purnima, 2003, *Organizing Empire: Individualism, Collective Agency and India*, Durham, Duke University Press.
Breckenridge, Carol (ed.), *Consuming Modernity*, Delhi, Oxford University Press.
Breckenridge, Carol and van der Veer, Peter (eds), *Orientalism and the Postcolonial Predicament*, Philadelphia, University of Pennsylvania Press.
Bryant, Kenneth, 1978, *Poems to the Child-God: Structures and Strategies in the Poetry of Surdas*, Berkeley, University of California Press.
Burton, Antoinette, 1998, *At the Heart of the Empire: Indians and the Colonial Encounter in Late-Victorian Britain*, Berkeley, University of California Press.

Burton, Antoinette, 2003, *Dwelling in the Archive*, Delhi, Oxford University Press.
Campbell, George, On the Races of India as Traced in Existing Tribes and Castes, *George Campbell Papers*, Eur. MSS.
Cannadine, David, 2001, *Ornamentalism: How The British Saw Their Empire*, Oxford, Oxford University Press.
Carpenter, Mary, 1967, *Reformatory Prison Discipline*, Montclair, P. Smith.
Carpenter, Mary, 1868, *Six Months in India*, London, Longman and Green.
Chandra, Sudhir, 1998, *Enslaved Daughters: Colonialism, Law and Women's Rights*, Delhi, Oxford University Press.
Chatterjee, Bankim Chandra, 1992, *Anandamath*, Delhi, Orient Paperbacks.
Chatterjee, Gautam, 1995, *Child Criminals and the Raj*, Delhi, Akshaya Publications.
Chatterjee, Indrani (ed.), 2004, *Unfamiliar Relations: Family and History in South Asia*, Delhi, Permanent Black.
Chatterjee, Partha, 1986, *Nationalist Thought and the Colonial World: A Derivative Discourse?*, London, Zed.
Chatterjee, Partha, 1993, *The Nation and Its Fragments*, Princeton, Princeton University Press.
Chatterjee, Partha, 1997, *Wages of Freedom*, Delhi, Oxford University Press.
Chatterjee, Partha, 2002, *A Princely Imposter? The Kumar of Bhawal and the Secret History of Indian Nationalism*, Delhi, Permanent Black.
Chowdhury, Indira, 2001, *The Frail Hero and Virile History: Gender and the Politics of Culture in Colonial Bengal*, Delhi, Oxford University Press.
Cohen, S and Scull, A (eds), 1983, *Social Control and the State*, Oxford, M. Robertson.
Cohn, Bernard, 1997, *Colonialism and its Forms of Knowledge*, Delhi, Oxford University Press.
Coleborne, Catharine and Kirkby, Diane (eds), 2001, *Law, History, Colonialism: The Reach of Empire*, Manchester, Manchester University Press.
Collini, Stefan, 1985, The Idea of Character in Victorian Political Thought, *Transactions of the Royal Historical Society*, 5:35, London.
Cooper, Frederick and Stoler, Ann (eds), 1997, *Tensions of Empire: Colonial Cultures in a Bourgeois World*, Berkeley, University of California Press.
Copland, Ian, 1997, *The Princes of India in the Endgame of Empire, 1917–1947*, Cambridge, Cambridge University Press.
Cowlishaw, Gillian, 1988, *Black, White or Brindle: Race in Rural Australia*, Cambridge, Cambridge University Press.
Cox, Jeffrey, *Imperial Fault Lines: Christianity and Colonial Power in India, 1818–1940*, Stanford, Stanford University Press.
Cunningham, Hugh, 1995, *Children and Childhood in Western Society Since 1500*, London, Longman.
Dawson, Graham, 1994, *Soldier Heroes: British Adventure, Empire and the Imagining of Masculinities*, London, Routledge.
DeMause, Lloyd, 1974, *The History of Childhood*, New York, Psychohistory Press.
Dirks, Nicholas, 1987, *The Hollow Crown: Ethnohistory of an Indian Kingdom*, Cambridge, Cambridge University Press.
Dirks, Nicholas, 2001, *Castes of Mind: Colonialism and the Making of Modern India*, Princeton, Princeton University Press.
Donzelot, Jacques, 1979, *The Policing of Families*, New York, Pantheon.
DuBois, Ellen and Ruiz, Vicki (eds), 1990, *Unequal Sisters: A Multicultural Reader in US Women's History*, New York, Routledge.

Eisenstadt, S N, 2002, *Multiple Modernities*, New Brunswick, Transaction.
Elias, Norbert, 1978, *The Civilizing Process: The History of Manners*, New York, Pantheon.
Ernst, Waltraud, 1991, *Mad Tales From the Raj: The European Insane in British India, 1800-1858*, London, Routledge.
Forbes, Geraldine, 1996, *Women in Modern India*, Delhi, Cambridge University Press.
Foucault, Michel, 1979, *Discipline and Punish: The Birth of the Prison*, New York, Vintage.
Foucault, Michel, 1990, *The History of Sexuality*, New York, Vintage.
Fox, Lionel, 1952, *The English Prisons and Borstal Systems*, London, Routledge.
Freud, Sigmund, 1929, *Introductory Lectures in Psycho-analysis, no. 16*, London, Allen & Unwin.
Fussel, Paul, 1975, *The Great War and Modern Memory*, Oxford, Oxford University Press.
Garland, David, 1985, *Punishment and Welfare: A History of Penal Strategies*, Aldershot, Gower.
Garland, David, 2001, *The Culture of Control: Crime and Social Disorder in Contemporary Society*, Chicago, University of Chicago Press.
Ghose, Indira, 1998, *Women Travellers in Colonial India: The Power of the Female Gaze*, Delhi, Oxford University Press.
Gillis, John R, 1974, *Youth and History: Tradition and Change in European Age Relations 1770-Present*, New York, Academic Press.
Goody, Jack, 1983, *The Development of the Family and Marriage in Europe*, Cambridge, Cambridge University Press.
Goradia, Nayan, 1993, *Lord Curzon: Last of the British Moghuls*, Delhi, Oxford University Press.
Greenfeld, Liah, 1992, *Nationalism: Five Roads to Modernity*, Cambridge,,Harvard University Press.
Grewal, Inderpal, 1996, *Home and Harem: Nation, Gender, Empire, and Cultures of Travel*, Durham, Duke University Press.
Guha, Ranajit, 1997, *Dominance Without Hegemony: History and Power in Colonial India*, Cambridge, Harvard University Press.
Haley, Bruce, 1978, *The Healthy Body and Victorian Culture*, Cambridge, Harvard University Press.
Hall, G and Hall, Stanley, 1904, *Adolescence; Its Psychology and its Relations to Physiology, Anthropology, Sociology, Sex, Crime, Religion and Education*, New York, Appleton.
Harrison, Mark, 1999, *Climates and Constitutions: Health, Race, Environment and British Imperialism in India, 1600–1850*, Delhi, Oxford University Press.
Harrison, Mark and Pati, Biswamoy (eds), 2001, *Health, Medicine and Empire: Perspectives on Colonial India*, Delhi, Orient Longman.
Hartnack, Christiane, 2001, *Psychoanalysis in Colonial India*, Delhi, Oxford University Press.
Hasan, Mushirul, 2004, *From Pluralism to Separatism:* Qasbas *in colonial Awadh*, Delhi, Oxford University Press.
Horn, Pamela, 1997, *The Victorian Town Child*, Thrupp, Sutton Publishing.
Haynes, Douglas and Prakash, Gyan (eds), 1991, *Contesting Power*, Delhi, Oxford University Press.
Ignatieff, Michael, 1978, *A Just Measure of Pain: The Penitentiary in the Industrial Revolution, 1750–1850*, London, MacMillan.
Jones, Kenneth, 1992, *Religious Controversy in British India*, Albany, SUNY Press.
Joshi, Sanjay, 2001, *Fractured Modernity: Making of a Middle Class in Colonial North India*, Delhi, Oxford University Press.
Kakar, Sudhir, 1981, *The Inner World: A Psycho-analytic Study of Childhood and Society in India*, Delhi, Oxford University Press.

Kaviraj, Sudipta, 2004, The Politics of Subalternity, presented at Annual Conference on South Asia, University of Wisconsin, Madison, 16 October.
Khair, Tabish (ed.), 2003, *Amitav Ghosh: A Critical Companion*, Delhi, Permanent Black.
Khan, Nasrullah, 1904, *The Ruling Chiefs of Western India and the Rajkumar College*, Bombay, Claridge.
Kincaid, Charles, 1931, *The Land of Ranji and Duleep*, Edinburgh, Blackwood and Sons.
Kirby, Peter, 2003, *Child Labour in Britain, 1750-1870*, Houndmills, Palgrave.
Kumar, Nita, 2000, *Lessons From Schools: The History of Education in Banaras*, Delhi, Sage.
Lahiri, Shompa, 2000, *Indians in Britain: Anglo-Indian Encounters, Race and Identity, 1880-1930*, London, Frank Cass.
Leach, Edmund and Mukherjee, S N (eds), 1970, *Elites in South Asia*, Delhi, Cambridge University Press.
Lelyveld, David, 1996, *Aligarh's First Generation: Muslim Solidarity in British India*, Delhi, Oxford University Press.
Levine, Philippa, 1996, Rereading the 1890's: Venereal Disease as 'Constitutional Crisis' in Britain and British India, *Journal of Asian Studies*, 55:3.
Levine, Philippa, 2003, *Prostitution, Race and Politics: Policing Venereal Disease in the British Empire*, New York, Routledge.
Mangan, J A, 1986, *The Games Ethic and Imperialism*, New York, Viking Penguin.
Marriott, John, 2003, *The Other Empire: Metropolis, India and Progress in the Colonial Imagination*, Manchester, Manchester University Press.
Marty, Martin and Appleby, R S (eds), *Accounting For Fundamentalisms: The Dynamic Character of Movements*, Chicago, University of Chicago Press.
Maskiell, Michelle, 1984, *Women Between Cultures: The Lives of Kinnaird College Alumni in British India*, Syracuse, Maxwell School of Citizenship and Public Affairs.
McDevitt, Patrick, 2003, The King of Sports: Polo in Late Victorian and Edwardian India, *International Journal of the History of Sport*, 20:1.
McLane, John, 1977, *Indian Nationalism and the Early Congress*, Princeton, Princeton University Press.
McLeod, John, 1999, *Sovereignty, Power, Control: Politics in the State of Western India, 1916-1947*, Leiden, Brill.
Metcalf, Barbara, 1982, *Islamic Revival in British India: Deoband, 1860-1900*, Princeton, Princeton University Press.
Metcalf, Thomas, 1989, *An Imperial Vision: Indian Architecture and Britain's Raj*, Delhi, Oxford University Press.
Metcalf, Thomas, 1995, *Ideologies of the Raj*, Delhi, Cambridge University Press.
Middleton, Sue, 1998, *Disciplining Sexuality: Foucault, Life Histories, and Education*, New York, Teachers' College Press.
Mill, John Stuart, 1947, *On Liberty*, Arlington Heights, AHM Publishing.
Million, Joelle, 2003, *Woman's Voice, Woman's Place: Lucy Stone and the Birth of the Woman's Rights Movement*, London, Praeger.
Mills, James, 2000, *Madness, Cannabis and Colonialism*, London, Macmillan.
Mills, James and Sen, Satadru (eds), 2004, *Confronting the Body: The Politics of Physicality in Colonial and Postcolonial South Asia*, London, Anthem.
Minault, Gail, 1982, *The Khilafat Movement: Religious Symbolism and Political Mobilization in India*, New York, Columbia University Press.
Mukherjee, Rudrangshu, 1998, *Spectre of Violence: The 1857 Kanpur Massacres*, Delhi, Viking Penguin.

Nandy, Ashis, 1983, *The Intimate Enemy: Loss and Recovery of Self Under Colonialism*, Delhi, Oxford University Press.

Nandy, Ashis, 1992, *Tradition, Tyranny and Utopias: Essays in the Politics of Awareness*, Delhi, Oxford University Press.

Narayan, Uma, 1997, *Dislocating Cultures: Identities, Traditions and Third World Feminisms*, New York, Routledge.

Nasaw, David, 1979, *Schooled to Order: A Social History of Public Schooling in the United States*, New York, Oxford University Press.

Orwell, George, 1962, *Burmese Days*, New York, Harcourt, Brace and World.

Panikkar, K N, 2001, *Culture, Ideology, Hegemony: Intellectuals and Social Consciousness in Colonial India*, Delhi, Tulika.

Peabody, Norbert, 2001, Cents, Sense, Census: Human Inventories in Late Colonial and Early Colonial India, *Comparative Studies in Society and History*.

Prakash, Gyan, 1999, *Another Reason: Science and the Imagination of Modern India*, Princeton, Princeton University Press.

Price, Pamela, 1996, *Kingship and Political Practice in Colonial India*, Cambridge, Cambridge University Press.

Procida, Mary, 2002, *Married to the Empire: Gender, Politics and Imperialism in India, 1883–1947*, Manchester, Manchester University Press.

Radhakrishna, Meena, 2001, *Dishonoured by History: 'Criminal Tribes' and British Colonial Policy*, Hyderabad, Orient Longman, p. 831.

Ramusack, Barbara, 1978, *The Princes of India in the Twilight of Empire : Dissolution of a Patron-Client System, 1914–1939*, Columbus, University of Cincinnati Press.

Ramusack, Barbara, 2004, *The Indian Princes and their States*, Cambridge, Cambridge University Press.

Rauchway, Eric, 2001, *The Refuge of Affections: The Family and American Reform Politics, 1900–1920*, New York, Columbia University Press.

Redfield, Peter, *Space in the Tropics: From Convicts to Rockets in French Guiana*, Berkeley, University of California Press.

Robb, Peter (ed.), 1995, *The Concept of Race in South Asia*, Delhi, Oxford University Press.

Rosselli, John, The Self-Image of Effeteness: Physical Education and Nationalism in Nineteenth-Century Bengal, *Past and Present*, 86.

Rudolph, Lloyd, Rudolph, Susanne, Kanota, Mohan Singh, 1984, *Essays on Rajputana: Reflections on History, Culture and Administration*, Delhi, Concept.

Rudolph, Lloyd, Rudolph, Susanne, Kanota, Mohan Singh, 2001, *Reversing the Gaze*, Delhi, Oxford University Press.

Said, Edward, 1979, *Orientalism*, New York, Vintage.

Sandner, David, 1996, *The Fantastic Sublime: Romanticism and Transcendence in Nineteenth-Century Children's Fantasy Literature*, Westport, Greenwood Press.

Sangari, Kumkum and Vaid, Sudesh (eds), 1990, *Recasting Women: Essays in Indian Colonial History*, New Brunswick, Rutgers University Press.

Sargant, Norman, 1987, *Mary Carpenter in India*, Bristol, A.J. Sargant.

Sarkar, Sumit, 1973, *The Swadeshi Movement in Bengal, 1903–1908*, Delhi, People's Publishing House.

Sarkar, Sumit, 1997, *Writing Social History*, Delhi, Oxford University Press.

Sarkar, Sumit, 2002, *Beyond Nationalist Frames*, Bloomington, Indiana University Press.

Sarkar, Tanika, 2001, *Hindu Wife, Hindu Nation*, Bloomington, Indiana University Press.

Semple, Janet, 1993, *Bentham's Prison: A Study of the Panopticon Penitentiary*, Oxford, Clarendon Press.

Sen, Satadru, 1999, Rationing Sex: Female Convicts in the Andamans, *South Asia* 30:1.
Sen, Satadru, 2000, *Disciplining Punishment: Colonialism and Convict Society in the Andaman Islands*, Delhi, Oxford University Press.
Sen, Satadru, 2002a, The Female Jails of British India, *Indian Economic and Social History Review*, 39:4.
Sen, Satadru, 2002b, The Savage Family: Colonialism and Female Infanticide in Nineteenth-Century India, Journal of Women's History, 14:3.
Sen, Satadru, 2004a, A Juvenile Periphery: Geographies of Literary Childhood in Colonial Bengal, *Journal of Colonialism and Colonial History*, 5:2.
Sen, Satadru, 2004b, *Migrant Races: Empire, Identity and K.S. Ranjitsinhji*, Manchester, Manchester University Press.
Sen, Satadru, 2004c, *Journal of the American Academy of Religion*, 72:2, 566.
Shiman, Lilian, 1992, *Women and Leadership in Nineteenth-Century England*, New York, St. Martin's.
Singh, Jyotsna, 1996, *Colonial Narratives, Cultural Dialogues: 'Discoveries' of India in the Language of Colonialism*, New York, Routledge.
Singha, Radhika, 1998, *A Despotism of Law: Crime and Justice in Early Colonial India*, Delhi, Oxford University Press.
Sinha, Mrinalini, *Colonial Masculinity: The 'Manly Englishman' and 'Effeminate Bengali' in the Late Nineteenth Century*, 1995, Manchester, Manchester University Press.
Springhall, John, 1977, *Youth, Empire and Society: British Youth Movements, 1883–1940*, London, Croom Helm.
Stokes, Erik, 1959, *The English Utilitarians in India*, Oxford, Clarendon.
Stone, Lawrence, 1977, *The Family, Sex and Marriage in England 1500–1800*, New York, Harper Colophon.
Strobel, Margaret, 1991, *European Women and the Second British Empire*, Bloomington Indiana University Press.
Thapar, Romila, 1999, *Sakuntala: Texts, Readings, Histories*, Delhi, Kali For Women.
Tod, James, 1920, *Annals and Antiquities of Rajasthan, or The Central and Western Rajput States of India*, London, Oxford University Press.
Tolen, Rachel, 1991, Colonizing and Transforming the Criminal Tribesman: The Salvation Army in British India, *American Ethnologist*, 18:1.
Tyndale-Biscoe, E D, 1930, *Fifty Years Against the Stream*, Mysore, Wesleyan Missionary Press.
Valette, John de la, 1931, *An Atlas of the Progress in Nawanagar State*, London, East and West.
Viswanathan, Gauri, 1987, *Masks of Conquest: Literary Study and British Rule in India*, New York, Columbia University Press.
Walkowitz, Judith, 1992, *City of Dreadful Delight: Narratives of Sexual Danger in Late-Victorian London*, London, Virago.
Walvin, James, 1982, *A Child's World: A Social History of English Childhood 1800–1914*, Harmondsworth, Pelican.
Weitzberg, Keren, 2005, The Colonial Reform School in Senegal and Kenya, honors thesis, Washington University, unpublished.
Whitehead, Clive, 2003, Colonial Educators: *The British Indian and colonial Education Service 1858–1953*, London, I.B. Tauris.
Wiener, Myron, 1991, *The Child and the State in India* Delhi, Oxford University Press.
Wild, Roland, 1934, *The Biography of Colonel His Highness Shri Sir Ranjitsinhji*, London, Rich and Cowan.
Wink, Andre, 1983, *Land and Sovereignty in India*, Hyderabad, Orient Longman.
Woerkens, Martine van, 2002, *The Strangled Traveler: Colonial Imaginings and the Thugs of India*, Chicago, University of Chicago Press.

Wullschlager, Jackie, 1995, *Inventing Wonderland: The Lives and Fantasies of Lewis Carroll, Edward Lear, J.M. Barrie, Kenneth Grahame and A.A. Milne*, London, Methuen.
Yang, Anand (ed.), 1985, *Crime and Criminality in British India*, Tucson, University of Arizona Press.
Yegenoglu, Meyda, 1998, *Colonial Fantasies: Towards a Feminist Reading of Orientalism*, Cambridge, Cambridge University Press.
Zinoman, Peter, 2001, *The Colonial Bastille: A History of Imprisonment in Vietnam: 1862–1940*, Berkeley, University of California Press.

INDEX

adolescence 1, 3, 28–9, 32, 38, 51, 53, 72–7, 92, 100, 112, 167, 190, 225(104), 228(108)
African Asylum 35
Ahmedabad College 145
Ahmedabad Normal School 145
Ahmed, Nihal-ud-Din 25
Aikman, RS 38
Aitchison College 143, 151, 174–5, 178, 184, 198–9, 201, 237(152)
Aitchison, CU 149, 153, 155–8, 165–6, 172, 179–80, 237(152)
Aiyar, KR 24, 28
Ajmere College 146
Ajmere Conference on Chiefs' Colleges 163, 206
Ali, Muhammad 219(94)
Alipore Jail 61, 69, 99, 183
Alipore Reformatory 17, 22, 23, 65, 101, 109–111
Aligarh College 4, 148, 164, 166, 188, 201, 206
Alwar, Chief of 174, 236(118)
Amar Singh, 195–6
Andaman Islands penal colony 62, 93, 100, 121, 227(64)
Anderson, Clare 42
Arbuthnot, AR 106–7
architecture 11, 13, 15, 69, 110
  cellular institutions 97, 101
  Chiefs' Colleges 144, 161, 172, 198, 207, 216(11)
Aries, Philippe 7, 215(8)
Arnold, David 102, 176

Arnold, Matthew 233(22)
Arnold, Thomas 89, 158, 179
Arnold, WD 233(22)
Arya Samaj 200
Asha Bibi 187, 190, 196, 207–8
Atkinson, WS 233(14)
Australian (Aboriginal) children 57

Baden Powell, Eric 3
Bahadursinhji 194, 196
Bandyopadhyay, Shivaji 44
Baring, Evelyn 61
Barton, Patricia 9
Bates, Crispin 81
Bayley, EC 15, 17, 19, 36–8, 48, 57–8, 68, 89, 93, 101, 107–110, 121, 139, 149, 150, 218(65), 221(45)
Bayley, SC 160, 161
Behlmer, George 39, 134, 226(6), 232(93)
Beisel, Nicola 5
Bell, W 60, 111
Bengal Committee on Reformatory Schools (Heeley-Mackenzie-Lambert Committee) 9, 53, 70, 97–8
Bengal Presidency Council of Women (BPCW) 136–8
Bentham, Jeremy 89, 97
Bhagalpur Jail 110
Bhagwan, Manu 197
Bhugwat Singhjee 202–3, 205
Bicetre prison 100
Bird, HM 43–4

250 INDEX

Boer War 3
Bombay Aftercare Association 84
Bombay Chronicle, The 209
Bombay School of Industry 21
Borstal Schools (and Borstal Acts)
 28–33, 48, 53, 68, 73–5, 77, 80,
 81, 84, 113, 220(134), 225(104)
 Borstal Associations 30–1, 81
Bose, Bijoy Krishna 31, 32
Bose, Girindresekhar 84
Bose, Purnima 76
Brahmo Samaj 18, 21, 135, 202
Brand, F 19
Bryant, Kenneth 152, 234(38)
Bundelkhand Chiefs' College 155, 165
burkandaz teachers 96
Burma 17, 18, 28, 47, 48, 54, 60, 63,
 64, 66, 69, 76, 80, 103, 105, 141,
 220(110), 221(148), 228(108)
Burton, Antoinette 127, 132, 231(66)

Calcutta Vigilance Association 138
Campbell, George 150–1, 181, 237(139)
Cannadine, David 128
Canning (Lord) 36
Carpenter, Mary 3, 13, 15, 18–9,
 20–2, 25, 95, 103, 107, 110, 113,
 125, 127, 129, 133, 138, 223 (31),
 240 (86)
caste 19, 27, 42–4, 59–60, 69, 77, 82,
 95, 120, 123–4, 135, 148, 151, 157,
 192, 200–1, 218(76)
Chakravarti, Jogindra Chandra 32
Chandra, Sudhir 131
Chatterjee, Gautam 4
Chatterjee, Partha 4, 7, 12, 77 115
Chever's Medical Jurisprudence 120
Chief's Colleges 1, 6, 98, 143, 144,
 145, 148–151, 154–171, 173–182,
 184–186, 188, 190–193, 195, 197,
 198, 200–207, 212, 233(2), 234(38),
 237(133)
Child Protection (Amendment) Bill
 129–30

Children Acts
 Bengal 133–4
 Central Provinces 40–2, 72, 224(86)
 England 29, 112, 133, 219(81)
 Madras 112
Children's Employment Commission
 67
Chingleput Reformatory 24, 47, 54,
 59, 78, 81, 183
Christianity and Evangelical/missionary
 activity 15, 21, 25, 26, 35, 36, 37,
 41, 118, 124, 127, 132, 13, 201,
 202, 204, 218(65), 237(141)
 See also Mary Carpenter
Church Missionary Society 35,
 237(141)
Cohn, Bernard 11, 147
Comins, DWD 22, 23, 86
Committee on Jails and Jail Discipline
 (1864) 121, 217(48)
consent (age of) controversies 4, 68,
 119–20, 127–8, 135, 137–8
Contractor, SC 76, 83–5, 133, 137
Cornwallis (Lord) 155
corporal punishment 19–20, 89–90,
 103–14, 198, 206–7, 217(48),
 227(48), 228(119)
Costello, J 137
Couper, George 120
Court of Wards 75, 127
Cox, Jeffrey 128, 139, 182, 204,
 219(105), 231(63), 237(141)
Criminal Procedure Code 105
 Act XIX (1850) 65, 89, 217(43)
Criminal Tribes (Criminal Tribes Acts)
 15, 16, 35, 44, 47, 57, 58, 59, 71,
 78, 113, 147, 160, 222(134),
 249(28), 249(31)
Croft, WD 136, 231(87)
Crofton, Walter 13
Cunningham, Hugh 7, 215(8)
Curzon (Lord) 5, 144, 149–51, 154,
 159–60, 162, 172, 175–8, 180–3,
 186, 196–207, 237(152), 239(75)

INDEX

Dallas, AM 40, 92–6, 101, 103, 106–7
Daly College 143, 162–4, 167, 173, 176, 178, 183–4, 197–9, 201, 235(82)
Daly, HD 148, 155–7, 160, 171–2, 180, 188, 237(135)
Darbhanga, Raja of 23, 196
Dawson, Graham 3
delinquency 11–3, 15, 21–2, 32, 38, 42, 45, 47, 49, 52, 54–64, 73, 76–8, 80–2, 86, 91, 97, 101, 107, 109–10, 115–7, 119, 121, 139, 147, 232(104)
Demause, Lloyd 7, 215(8)
Demetz, Frederic-August 13, 17, 113
Deoband madrasa 188
Derozio, HV 188
Devadhar, CS 48
Dharwar Borstal School 48
diet and childhood 66, 126, 223(60)
  penal diet 111–2, 227(48)
Dirks, Nicholas 4, 81, 238(23)
Discharged Prisoners Aid Societies 30
Doctrine of Lapse 172
dormitories 171–8
Drummond, JR 118–9
Dumerge, JWF 104
Duncan, D 54, 78–80, 108, 124–5, 127, 137, 228(117)

Edgerton, FW 58
education 4–5
  and racial assimilation 84
  curricular debates in the Chiefs' Colleges 144–50, 155–7, 178–85, 189–96, 200–6
  in the reformatory 15, 24, 27, 41–2, 57, 83, 91–6, 99, 112, 117–8
Elias, Norbert 7, 34
Ellis, Havelock 219(94)
Ellis, RS 36, 37, 100, 221(145), 228(117)
Ernst, Waltraud 89
'Eton in India' 145, 160–1, 177–83, 196, 212, 237(133, 135, 141)

Eurasians 15, 36, 209
expertise 2, 6, 8, 9–20, 22–5, 28, 31–3, 37, 39, 42, 48, 54, 97, 124, 126, 128, 134–40, 151, 178, 201, 204, 212

Famine Relief Fund 35
Fawcus, S 99, 111, 69, 70
Female Penitentiary (Lahore) 116
Fitzpatrick, Peter 10
Forbes, Geraldine 126, 188
Forrester, J Campbell 31, 80–83, 132, 183
Foucault, Michel 8, 22, 89, 94, 96, 218(50)
Fox, CE 66
Freud, Sigmund 84, 152, 234(41)

Gandhi, Mohandas 135, 139
  see also Salt Satyagraha
Garbett, C 27
Garland, David 13, 59, 126, 215(8), 218(50)
Gidumal, Dayaram 26, 27, 28, 94
Giffard, GG 81–2, 112, 183
Godley, A 144, 184, 199
Gondal, Thakur of 202, 204
Gopal/Rakhal dichotomy 44, 152, 234(38)
Gordon, J 207
Gordon, JD 46, 59, 222(31)
Gray, P 43
Great India Peninsula Railway 22
Great War (First World War) 6, 82, 190, 206
Greeven, R 59, 117–8, 61–2
Grey, R 95–6
grihalakshmi 126
Guha, Sumit 6, 172
Gujranwala Jail 100
Gujarati, The 193
Gunion, M 164, 167, 184, 193, 197, 236(128), 237(152)
Gurdaspur Reformatory and Jail 92

habituality (and 'habitual offence')   17, 35, 39, 45, 52, 54, 56, 58–60, 69, 71–2, 76, 78, 80, 82–3, 86, 90, 98, 104, 108–10, 112–3, 121, 128–9, 151–2, 156, 157, 159, 166, 169–70, 174–5, 180, 182, 191, 200, 203, 205, 211
Hall, Stanley G   3, 72
Hamilton, George   200
Handley, FF   38–9, 101
Harrison, Mark   102
Hartnack, Christiane   84
Hasan, Mushirul   219(94)
Hathaway, Charles   89–94, 97, 100–2, 127
Hazaribagh Reformatory   27, 97, 109, 111, 229(125)
Hervey, C   78
Hill, J   109, 222(15)
Hindu College   188
Hooper, J   43–4, 122
Horn, Pamela   70
Howard, EI   145–50, 155, 157–8, 160, 164, 183–4, 189, 202, 233(15, 22)
Howell, Arthur   37, 38, 85, 98, 100, 107–8, 110
Hukam Singh   175
Hutchinson, JB   192, 196, 237(152)
Hyderabad Assigned Districts   28

Ignatieff, Michael   13, 89
Ilbert Bill   23
Imperial Cadet Corps (ICC)   143–44, 157, 159–60, 175, 180–1, 184, 195, 198, 201, 237(151, 152), 239(75)
incorrigibility   47, 56, 65, 72, 85–6, 91, 98, 104, 109, 225(104)
infanticide   126, 128, 132–3, 191
   Female Infanticide (Prevention of) Act   126, 133
Indian National Congress   23
Indian Penal Code   103, 223(50), 224(73)
Indian Social Reformer, The   189

individuality   6, 12, 42–3, 45, 49, 58, 76–7, 80, 83–4, 101, 104, 107, 138, 153, 176, 185, 209
Indu Prakash   193
inheritance (of property)   75

Jackson, FS   33
Jai Singh   146
jailors   9, 13
Jails Committee (1922)   55, 62–4, 67, 74–6, 80, 112, 217(42)
Jamia Millia   164
Johnston, RL   26
Joshi, Sanjay   31
Jumnabaee   208
juvenile courts   28, 40, 48, 64, 127, 129, 133–4, 136–9, 178

Kakar, Sudhir   4, 72, 84, 153, 234 (41)
Kathiawadno Himayati   193
Kathiawar Vartaman   191
Kaviraj, Sudipta   211
Kipling, Rudyard   1, 34, 36
   Kim   3
Kirschner, JG   17, 65, 72, 109–111
Krishna   152, 221(139)
James, S Harvey   54
Jewish community   21

labor   26–7, 35, 91–6, 99, 110–1, 218(65)
   apprenticeship   21–2, 65, 84, 217(43)
   see also education
Lahore Observer, The   186
Larymore, AD   23, 27, 38, 86
Lawrence Asylum   36
Lawrence (Lord)   14, 15, 93
Lawrence, Walter   162, 163, 164, 167, 168, 172–178, 184, 197, 199, 200, 220 236(128), 239(75)
League of Nations   136, 231(87)
Lelyveld, David   4, 166
Levine, Philippa   119

Loch, Col.   176–7
Lyall, Alfred   17, 47, 57, 61, 63, 236(178)
Lynch, S   16, 18, 61, 63, 78, 98–100, 11, 223(63)

Macaulay, TB   10, 27, 97, 144, 154–5, 157, 183, 185–6
Macalister, Rev. Dr.   185, 203–4
Mackintosh, JS   43–5
Mackenzie, JSF   102
Mackenzie, SC *see Bengal Committee on Reformatory Schools*
Macnaghten, Chester   98, 144, 165–6, 196, 237(150)
Maconochie, E   194
Madras Penitentiary   14, 24
Mahabharata   72, 234(38)
Majority Act   75
Man, Gurdayal Singh   117, 140–1
Mangles, RL   69
Maori children   84
Maratha children   6, 164
marginality (and peripherality)   1–3, 9, 12–3, 16, 34–5, 40, 44, 48–9, 52, 55–61, 83–4, 94, 110, 115, 121–4, 126, 129, 135, 139–40, 211
Marriott, John   11, 147, 173
'martial races'   150
Mary (Queen)   168–9
masculinity   4, 72, 101, 122–3, 125, 131, 138–9, 150–1, 153–6, 159, 166, 168, 170–1, 174, 179–80, 194, 205, 228(108)
Maskiell, Michelle   4, 215(17)
Mayne, C   178, 206, 237(150), 172
Mayo (Lord)   149, 161, 207, 237(133)
Mayo College   143–4, 146, 149, 153–4, 156, 158, 160–2, 166, 168, 172–4, 178–9, 184, 188, 191, 198–201, 207, 213, 236(118), 237(151), 239(75)
Mayo, Katherine (and *Mother India*)   135–6, 231(82, 87)

McLeod, John   143, 164
McNabb, James   168, 171
McNabb, Rawdon   168–71
Meade, RJ   153–4, 165–8, 170, 199, 208
medicine   12, 33, 77, 79–80, 111, 129, 133, 135, 137–9, 148, 227(48), 229(133), 231(63),
    Indian Medical Service (IMS)   76, 81, 111, 126, 221(152)
    psychology and psychiatry   67, 76, 133, 234(41)
Melville, PS   120
Metcalf, Barbara   188
Mettray reformatory   108, 113, 183, 212–3
Middleton, Sue   84
Midnapore School   34, 35
Miller, AE   54
minority   69
    minority administrations   132, 169, 231(69)
Mir Shahamut Khan   155
Mirabeau, Comte de   97
Mills, James   22
Minault, Gail   188
Mitter, Omrita Nath   22, 27
Mohabat Khan   187, 189–91, 196
Mohammed Raza Khan   24
Montague-Chelmsford reforms   28
Montgomery, R   100, 102, 106
Mookerjee, Kanti Chunder   158–9, 168, 235(59)
Mouat, FJ   16–20, 63, 73, 76, 85, 97, 100, 101, 113, 116, 117, 121, 127, 139, 145, 227(69)
Muir, William   69
Mukerji, Besveswar   27, 28, 94
Mukherjee, Rudrangshu   103

Naboo   109
Nailer, HAF   79, 80, 82, 84
Nandy, Ashis   4, 36, 70
Naoroji, Dadabhai   135

Napier (Lord) 13–17, 19, 20, 33–38, 63, 68, 76, 85, 89, 93, 110, 118, 121, 127, 139, 145, 149, 218(65)
Narayan, Kamakshi 189
Narsinghpur Jail 33
Nasaw, David 51, 217(43)
Nath, Pandit Bishumber 25
Nation, The 187
National Society for the Prevention of Cruelty to Children (NSPCC) 89
nature/nurture 3, 9, 12, 36, 45, 51, 55–6, 59–60, 62, 71, 85–7, 90, 99, 117, 140, 143, 145, 151–2, 155, 158, 162–3, 166–7, 177–9, 181–2, 185, 203–4, 208, 212
  inherited tendencies 51, 60, 77–85
Nowgong College 235(82)

Obbard, R 28
Orange, WH 192–3
orphans (and orphanages) 34–7, 41, 45–6, 49, 56, 65, 68, 118, 123, 125, 146, 199, 219(105), 220(110, 111), 222(15), 224(69), 226(10)
'orthodox' Hindus 11, 189, 203, 205
  and Cornelia Sorabji 127–36, 140, 147
Orwell, George 103

Panikkar, KN 27
Panna Singh 168–71
Pantulu Garu, MR 24
parents and parenting 3–6, 8–10, 12, 22, 28, 33–49, 56–8, 60, 64, 72, 78, 80, 82, 95, 97, 104, 107–8, 129–30, 133–4, 136–8, 157, 161, 176, 184, 187–8, 196–8, 200–3, 206, 221(143, 148, 155), 239(69)
  families 12, 93, 124, 170, 173, 190, 217(48), 218(65), 221(145)
  fathers 34, 75, 125, 144, 152–3, 165–6, 169, 171, 178, 186, 191, 196–7, 199, 206–7, 211–2

mothers 37, 41, 116, 126, 132–3, 152–3, 160, 170, 187–8, 190–2, 197, 207–8, 211–2, 234(41)
Parsis 21, 127, 132
Parsi, The 193
Paterson, A 17, 18
Pelly, Lewis 156–9, 166, 168, 179–81, 235(90)
Pentonville 89, 91, 97, 103
Permanent Settlement (1793) 155
Phillips, HD 121–2, 218(65)
Pinhey, AF 163–4, 174, 199
Pioneer, The 180–1
plasticity 1, 11, 19, 33, 51–2, 55, 60–2, 73–5, 77, 82, 85–6, 104, 153, 159, 171, 182–3, 185, 201, 212
play and recreation 26, 83, 99, 156, 160–1, 166, 169, 176, 181,
  athletics 26, 151, 165, 179, 194, 204–7, 219(108)
Praja Bandhu 190
Prakash, Gyan 6, 230(38)
precocity 1, 38, 51, 53, 65, 67, 69, 71, 73, 85–6, 100, 121, 151, 159–60, 219(108)
Presidency Jail 16, 20, 95, 97, 98, 100
Preston Jail 63
Prison Act (1894) 30, 32
Prisoner Act (1900) 30, 32
probation 28, 30, 43, 48, 53, 62–3, 90–1, 134–7, 197, 217(42), 221(155)
Procida, Mary 173
Progressive era 18, 116, 126, 232(96)
prostitution 41–2, 69, 71–2, 119–2, 124, 127, 129–30, 139, 174, 224(86), 230(16, 38)
policewomen 139
Poona Observer, The 196

Radhakrishna, Meena 78
Raipur College 174
Rajkumar College (Rajkot) 149, 160, 165, 167, 172–3, 191, 193, 233(2)

INDEX 255

Ramabai 131
Ramusack, Barbara 143, 173, 199
Rangnekar, S 48, 84, 85, 133
Rajendra Narain 195
Ranjitsinhji, KS 3, 135, 194, 196
Ravenshaw, RE 56
Ray, Kshaunish Chandra 30–32
Rebellion of 1857 ('Sepoy Mutiny') 3, 20, 23, 34, 103, 121, 143, 150, 160, 172, 185, 188, 233(22)
Redfield, Peter 102
Reformatory Schools Acts (Bills) 1, 14, 20, 22, 25, 26, 38, 40, 43, 46, 53–75, 91, 97, 98, 113–118, 122, 125, 126, 218(48), 223(50)
resistance by children 8, 10, 28, 66, 109–10, 114, 180, 211, 229(125)
Risley, HH 51, 80–1, 182
Robertson, L 190
Roman Catholic Order of Mercy 15
Romanticism 5, 7
Ross, TS 112
Roy, Ram Mohun 18
Rudolph, Lloyd and Susanne 158, 235(59)
Rukhmabai 131

Sahachar, 195–6
St. John, OBC 98, 153–4, 164, 173, 184, 236(114)
Sailana, Raja of 202–6
Saldanha, JA 29, 75
Salt Satyagraha 29
Salvation Army 137–8, 220(110), 222(18)
Sanskrit 157–8, 179, 202, 207
Sarda Bill 135, 231(82)
Sarkar, Sumit 189
Sassoon Reformatory 13, 21, 60, 121
sati 150
servants 153, 160–1, 171–4, 178, 181, 188, 191–2, 197
  musahibs 172–3, 178, 181, 191, 197

sex 3, 7, 54, 67, 71–2, 74, 96, 100, 115, 117, 119–21, 129–30, 139–40
  homosexuality 68–71, 92, 151, 191, 200
  venereal disease 174–5
Sheppard, Jack 81, 183
Sholapur Reformatory 48
Singh, Anrudh 62
Sinha, Bhupendra Narayan 31, 82, 83
Sirsa Jail 96
Sleeman, William Henry 34, 78, 174, 229(128)
social workers 9, 18, 137, 139
Society for the Protection of Children in India (SPCI) 137–8
solitary confinement 91, 96–103, 109, 114, 206
Sorabji, Cornelia 116, 147, 153, 231(66), 232(93), 232(96), 232(104)
  critique of native society and women 128–31
  critique of male agency and the colonial state 131–40
  professionalism in child-saving 137–40
  racial location 125–8
  see also probation and juvenile courts
Springhall, John 3
Sreenivasan, Ramya 6
Statesman, The 134, 137–8
Stone, Lawrence 100, 152, 234(41), 239(69)
Strachey, John 100, 121
Sukhdeo Pershad 191–3, 196, 201
Syajee Rao 153
Syed (Sayyid) Ahmed Khan 188, 206

Tanjore Borstal Association 30–1, 80
Taylor, W 23
teachers 19, 22, 96, 99, 136, 174, 188, 197
  racial significance of 6, 35, 94–6, 156–8, 160, 166–8, 198, 200, 236(128)

Temple, Richard   38, 61, 65, 70, 73, 97–8, 110, 122, 149–50, 218(48)
Thomas, WF   47, 59–60
Thompson, Rivers   35
Thug (Thuggee)   15, 34, 35, 78, 108, 110, 149–50, 174, 229(128)
time   162–4
Tod, James   5, 157–9, 189
Trethewy, AW   43–4

urbanity   1, 47, 56, 59–60, 79, 211, 225(121)
  rural visions   44, 47, 56, 59–60, 111, 147, 150, 205
Tucker, APL   150, 206

Vali Uddeen Khan   195
Vidya Shal   148
Vidyasagar, Ishwarchandra (Bandyopadhyay)   189, 204

Viswanathan, Gauri   4, 27
Vitoria, Francisco   10

Waddington, CW   200, 206, 237(151)
Walker, JP   100, 121
Walter, C   148, 237(133)
Waugh, Benjamin   89
Weitzberg, Keren   218(49)
Westmacott, EV   27, 58, 111
Whipping Act   90, 97, 104, 108
Wiener, Myron   27
Wink, Andre   172, 236(108)
Woodburn, J   121–2

YWCA   138

Zenana   4, 108, 116, 117, 127, 130–3, 152, 171–4, 176, 188, 231(63)
Zinoman, Peter   91

Printed in the United States
202993BV00007B/58-60/A